Executive Turned Consultant

Transitioning from Experienced Executive to Trusted Advisor in Healthcare

Scott A. Mason

HAP

ACHE Management Series

Library of Congress Cataloging-in-Publication Data
Names: Mason, Scott A. author. | American College of Healthcare Executives, issuing body.
Title: Executive turned consultant : transitioning from experienced executive to trusted advisor in healthcare / Scott A. Mason.
Other titles: Management series (Ann Arbor, Mich.)
Description: Chicago, IL : Health Administration Press, [2022] | Series: HAP/ACHE management series | Includes bibliographical references and index. | Summary: "This book provides a road map for executives contemplating a move into management consulting. It walks readers through key considerations and includes firsthand accounts of executives who have navigated the transition"— Provided by publisher.
Identifiers: LCCN 2021055778 (print) | LCCN 2021055779 (ebook) | ISBN 9781640553378 (paperback : alk. paper) | ISBN 9781640553347 (epub)
Subjects: MESH: Health Services Administration | Consultants | Vocational Guidance
Classification: LCC RA418 (print) | LCC RA418 (ebook) | NLM W 64 | DDC 362.1—dc23/ eng/20211124
LC record available at https://lccn.loc.gov/2021055778
LC ebook record available at https://lccn.loc.gov/2021055779

The paper used in this publication meets the minimum requirements of American National Standard for Information Sciences—Permanence of Paper for Printed Library Materials, ANSI Z39,48-1984.♾™

Acquisitions editor: Jennette McClain; Manuscript editor: DeAnna Burghart; Project manager: Andrew Baumann; Cover designer: James Slate; Layout: Integra

Found an error or a typo? We want to know! Please e-mail it to hapbooks@ache.org, mentioning the book's title and putting "Book Error" in the subject line.

For photocopying and copyright information, please contact Copyright Clearance Center at www. copyright.com or at (978) 750-8400.

Health Administration Press
A division of the Foundation of the American
    College of Healthcare Executives
300 S. Riverside Plaza, Suite 1900
Chicago, IL 60606-6698
(312) 424-2800

To my trusted advisors—
my wife, Melanie,
and my children, Kayla and Nicholas—
for their love and support.

Contents

List of Exhibits

Preface

MANY YEARS AGO, I was part of a group of healthcare consultants who gathered at an educational meeting in Scottsdale, Arizona, to discuss several topics of interest. Although I have forgotten most of the conversation, one thing that stuck in my mind was when we went off script and talked about how we would most like to spend our time if we were not consulting. It was obvious as we went around the group that some had not given it much thought. Gardening and travel were among the common answers, but by far the most popular was writing. I think part of this stemmed from the near universal belief that, as experienced professional consultants, we each felt we had something of value we needed to share with others. After all, that is effectively how we made our living, and we each were well compensated for our opinions and insights. Yet as I look back on this conversation, very few who took part have taken up the pen.

In contrast, writing and thought leadership have long been part of my consulting practice, especially as it relates to the future of healthcare and related strategies for success.[1] Things didn't start out this way. "Time is the currency of experience," as noted in the updated introduction to Pine and Gilmore's seminal book *The Experience Economy* (Boston: Harvard Business, 2019; ix). The thoughts I share in this book accumulated after over time after I first received formal training in the skills of management consulting, and they have

---

[1] I was honored in 2016 to receive the coveted Dean Conley Award for best article of the year for "Retail and Real Estate: The Changing Landscape of Care Delivery," published in *Frontiers of Health Services Management*.

been greatly informed by a myriad of client experiences when put into practice over the course of more than 40 years. Some of these experiences were unique, others perhaps more common, but all involved lessons if one was attentive to the details.

These experiences led me to share some of the tradecraft I learned in my career as a healthcare strategy consultant. Some of this tradecraft pertains to consulting in general, some is more specific to the changing healthcare industry. I must confess that I have used this platform to point out some of the shortcomings embedded in the current state of healthcare, and to suggest some issues that must be addressed by leaders in the coming years. These are not only opportunities for healthcare consultants, who often lead major change initiatives, but for executives and policymakers as well.

Another motivation for writing this book is my fervent belief that there is a material difference between a trained professional consultant and one who has not received formal education or training. Observing the best among us over the years, I am struck by the realization that they had at least one thing in common—experience in operations within a healthcare organization, or at least completion of an administrative residency or fellowship. And while there were exceptions, most of the talented consultants I worked with and observed also received formal training early in their consulting careers, often by working for a large global consulting firm heavily invested with internal training capacity.[2]

I also noticed that a few prominent healthcare leaders had decided to enter consulting later in their careers, even without this earlier consultant training. When I first started out as a career consultant, this change from executive to consultant was rare; it represented much more than just a job change. Those who went down this path were a bit of an anomaly and aroused curiosity among their peers, to the point that they often found themselves asked to share their experiences in panel discussions (healthcare sponsors a lot of

---

2 It should be noted that early in my career, not many medium or larger specialty healthcare consulting firms existed. Healthcare was just coming into its own in the 1970s, and global firms were just starting to incorporate healthcare as a legitimate vertical.

meetings). I found some of the comments at these meetings quite revealing.

As I recall, these executives turned consultants said they enjoyed what they were doing and liked working with a variety of clients, but some noted that they may have lacked a full appreciation of the risks involved. Whether my impression was right or wrong, there was a stark contrast when these leaders discussed their executive careers versus their newfound consulting; when it came to consulting too many of them appeared as "deer in the headlights." Mind you, these newly minted consultants had been highly accomplished leaders of healthcare organizations. A few were quite successful in their new role. Others essentially played out their two- to three-year severance package from their last CEO position and quietly faded into retirement.[3] Perhaps they did not appreciate that merely sharing their successful experiences is rarely enough to address a client's situation, which almost always involves some unique twists and turns. Further, the role of decider is materially different from that of advisor. Understanding this difference is critical in making this career change.

Please note, in discussing a career change I am not referring to the retiring CEO who sells time back to her company while shifting to a part-time role on the path to retirement. Nor am I referring to the hobbyist who does consulting on the side, or the executive who has cards printed up that say "Consultant" while waiting for the right executive job to come along. Finally, I am not referring to the retired CEO who is a part-time member of a CEO network offering counseling to new CEOs. Rather, I am referring to the person for hire who hangs out their shingle or joins an existing firm and goes full-on at-risk pursuing their consulting practice. This is where consulting skills, including sales skills, come into play.

Seeing these respected leaders stumble with this career change disturbed me. These were talented people on an important mission to share their judgment and lessons from their illustrious careers as

---

3   I believe these rather generous severance packages may be an anomaly of this unique period of consolidation that won't be sustained in the future.

healthcare executives, yet they seemed to be missing some of the basics of how best to monetize the experience that they had spent so much of their career accumulating.

When I began to address this executive turned consultant trend, it became immediately obvious to me that the unregulated term *consultant* is confusing and subject to many interpretations, some of which are misleading. On top of that, it became painfully clear to me that, contrary to popular belief, not everyone is cut out for consulting. To be blunt, the profession of consulting is poorly understood and underappreciated, including in healthcare. This requires some redress.

The notion of what it means to be a professional consultant in healthcare is the topic of my previous book published by Health Administration Press, *The Healthcare Consultant's Handbook: Career Opportunities and Best Practices*. That book is relevant to anyone contemplating a career in consulting, but it focuses on early careerists just setting out on their journey—recent college and business school graduates who are just entering the job market. *The Healthcare Consultant's Handbook* devotes considerable time to defining the profession of consulting (how to be a superior consultant; the essential skills of consulting), both in general and specifically for healthcare organizations. I believe that much of the skill set required to be a successful independent management consultant is generic, but some aspects of the healthcare industry are not intuitive and require some explanation. *The Healthcare Consultant's Handbook* also includes a discussion of the rich history of consulting to healthcare organizations going back to World War II, which helps draw attention to some of the dramatic changes taking place in US healthcare and related factors that make healthcare today so ripe for consulting.

In contrast, the target audience for this book is the midcareer or near-retirement healthcare executive. These people may have spent decades managing healthcare organizations and their component entities, and the bulk of their career may now be behind them. They have been fully exposed to the nuances of US healthcare. But while these executives possess significant operating knowledge, their consulting experience may be somewhat limited. In other words, this book assumes that most readers lack the skills training that career consultants receive as they start out. Being a successful career consultant is not easy. Changing careers to consulting is at least as hard as, if not harder than, beginning your career in consulting, since you must overcome many hurdles to parlay your time as an executive into a successful consulting career.

In considering a potential consulting career, it is not enough to understand the state of a particular industry today; one must have some insight into what is to come. So, in addition to the requirements of transitioning from a managerial role to a professional consulting role for healthcare organizations, this book discusses factors relevant to the evolving challenge of managing these complex organizations. While the focus is on healthcare, much of the discussion applies to any executive, from any industry, who is interested in transitioning into a consulting career.

These two volumes on consulting are intended to be complementary. And while noticeably different from those of early careerists, the interests of midcareer professionals and those who are close to retirement are not always identical. Accordingly, these two subgroups are treated as similar in most sections of this book, but the discussion is more specific to the unique interests of each subgroup in a few key places.

Obviously, I have drawn on my own experiences as I have approached this work. I am therefore obligated to provide some additional context in this regard. I have spent some time in line management of provider-based healthcare organizations both as an employee and on an interim basis (i.e., as an independent contractor). I am also a serial entrepreneur; I set out to establish my own consulting firm when I turned 30 and was asked to run two other start-up organizations along the way, as an investor and as CEO.[4] The memories of weaning myself from a regular employee paycheck

---

4 Both organizations were focused on developing strategic and operational information through digital technology in the perioperative and personal health record arenas.

and starting out as a solo consultant are as vivid today as they were 40 years ago. To be sure, certain memories stand out more than others. It is hard to forget attempting to run a start-up organization and keep people motivated when there is no money. No one ever said being an entrepreneur was easy.

My experience as a healthcare executive, an entrepreneur, and a consultant have all come into play in writing this book. Admittedly, my background and experiences as a strategy consultant show through in my writing. Not all consulting is strategy. Compared to strategy engagements, more specialized consulting involves fewer gray areas, with less process, and with clearer right and wrong answers.

I firmly believe that that for many people, the concept of consulting and the reality of consulting are vastly different. The consulting experience differs from the current executive experience—sometimes in dramatic ways. This book is meant to help executives prepare for their new context. Approaching a career change in a casual manner ignores the inherent risk. Insight and awareness are required to enable a professional to lean into their new calling if they are to be well received as a trusted advisor. It is for this purpose that this book has been written.

Acknowledgments

TIME AWAY FROM the day-to-day grind has allowed for completion of this second book on consulting in Health Administration Press's Management Series. I am indebted to the many people with whom I have collaborated over the years who have helped me hone my skills through specific consulting engagements I have been fortunate enough to pursue. Along the way this has included collaborating with people from other firms, as well as conscripting solo experts where their unique skills could be applied.

I gained a genuine appreciation for the experience that these experts brought to various assignments. I mostly focused on strategic planning, organization structure and culture, mergers and acquisitions, and clinical service lines, which could be characterized as functioning more in the role of a generalist, not a specialist. Others were added to these consulting teams with specific expertise in such areas as medical group management, clinical medicine, reimbursement, finance, data analytics, facilities design, real estate, and quality improvement, to name a few.

Since I made the commitment to consulting right out of graduate school (and my administrative residency), writing this book on career change required that I approach a few colleagues who first spent more time in operations to capture their experience of making a true career change by joining the consulting ranks. My thanks go to the people who allowed themselves to be profiled in this book, including Ken Ackerman, Reginald Ballantyne III, Nicole Denham, Fred Hobby, Kim King, Chris Morgan, and James A. Rice. I have attempted to summarize what they shared with me as part of this discussion. To a person, they have been generous with their time and candid with their observations about their careers. The written observations are mine, but they have each had an opportunity to review drafts and provide comments.

While not obvious at first, it became clear to me that there is an element of recruiting involved in making a career change. Many if not most senior executive positions in healthcare are filled by search consultants, and these searches sometimes involve executive coaches. This exposes such advisors not only to key executives who are looking for a similar position elsewhere, but also to some who have determined to make a career shift to consulting. For insights in this regard, I am indebted to Jack Schlosser (formerly Spencer Stuart; now Desert Vista Advisors), J. Larry Tyler (formerly of Tyler & Company; now Practical Governance Group), Carson Dye (formerly of WittKieffer; now Exceptional Leadership), and Michael Hein (MEDI Leadership)—a few of the best in the business.

Any consultant will admit to learning much from their clients. I doubt there is a client I have worked with who has not caused me to at least pause and reconsider something involved in the work I was doing with them, regardless of similarities with other client engagements. In those rare situations where we are lucky enough to become the *trusted advisor*, the lessons learned seem most enduring.[1] I have been blessed with more than my share of such clients and am compelled to pay tribute to the many professionals who were most instrumental in my personal development as their trusted strategy advisor. Respect for privacy and adherence to brevity requires that I not attempt to list all of these people. While some have since passed, most are still with us; suffice it to say that you know who you are. Please know that I cherished our time together and am forever grateful for the partnership that we shared and that you allowed me and my colleagues to share our counsel and advice. That our collective

---

[1] See chapters 12 and 13 in *The Healthcare Consultant's Handbook* for a more detailed explanation of what is required to become a trusted advisor.

work helped your organization succeed in competing and growing while improving your ability to deliver quality health services more efficiently in the many cities where you operate throughout the United States is a legacy that will stay with me always.

I am also indebted to Andrew Baumann, editorial production manager at Health Administration Press, for squiring me through the completion of both books in this series—his steady hand has been much appreciated—and to Jennette McClain, acquisitions editor, who advised me regarding both volumes. I am particularly indebted to DeAnna Burghart for her professional editing support.

Introduction

THIS BOOK FOCUSES on making a career change from executive to consultant, which appears to be of interest to a growing number of experienced healthcare executives. For some, this will become their new career. Others may end up moving in and out of consulting over a few cycles. After all, career goals can change just as the healthcare industry is changing—through dynamic disruption. A career can take many paths.

Historically, consulting has been a road less traveled for people who are trained to manage healthcare organizations, but this is changing. When we begin selecting college courses and choosing between possible careers, we begin a journey that decides how we will spend a substantial part of our adult lives. The choice of a career is consequential. A career change is no less consequential, and can be stressful, yet since the 1990s it has become common to change careers at least once. As part of that historic shift, experienced executives are increasingly likely to consider a career change to full-time consulting.

It should be noted that *consulting* as used in this book refers to *management consulting*, which can include administrative, technical, and clinical interests in the context of management. Consulting is sometimes confused with outsourcing (e.g., IT or other technical operational services), which is not our focus. For our purposes, consultants make themselves available as independent contractors to complete discrete engagements for individual clients who hire them for advice that is both unbiased and cost-effective. Pure *clinical* consulting focused on individual patient care I leave to the clinicians.

> **Consultants make themselves available as independent contractors to complete discrete engagements for individual clients who hire them for advice that is both unbiased and cost-effective.**

At the core of this discussion is the recognition that consulting does not come naturally to everyone. Conventional wisdom might be characterized as, "Anyone can be a consultant." This is simply not true. Experience shows that consulting may fit better with certain personality traits, but even then, there is no guarantee of success.[1]

For those who start out in consulting, acquiring the relevant skills becomes natural, especially when they work for one of the global or larger specialty consulting firms that have significant resources invested in their internal leadership development programs. As training and experience accumulate over the years, these consulting-specific skills become muscle memory.[2] The skill set of the midcareer or senior executive is generally different from what is required in consulting. There is some possible overlap, to be sure, but the roles are materially different. This role transition will represent a serious hurdle for some. It may even require some executives to do some unlearning.

For purposes of this discussion, this book assumes that the midcareer or senior executive has not previously been a consultant, though they may have hired and worked with many consultants. If

---

1   See chapter 5 in *The Healthcare Consultant's Handbook* for a deeper discussion of this.

2   Muscle memory is an important concept covered in chapter 13 of *The Healthcare Consultant's Handbook*.

your background includes consulting, then some of what is in this book (and in my previous book), while helpful, will be review for you.

At this juncture, one might question whether the reverse is true—whether professionals who start out as consultants can apply consulting skills in executive positions. Clearly they can, and there are many examples, reinforcing the value of experience gained as a consultant working with many different clients. Consulting is a great way to start a professional career, in healthcare and in other industries. The transferability of consulting skills was reinforced in a 2020 campaign by one of the well-known healthcare consulting firms, the Chartis Group, to celebrate their 20-year anniversary. The campaign web page (https://info.chartis.com/chartis-20) includes an Alumni Spotlight video featuring former consultants who had moved on to key executive positions in different healthcare organizations.

ORGANIZATION OF THIS BOOK

Regardless of the motivating factor for a career change, the thesis of this book is that it helps to make the change in an organized manner. As a strategist, I have used a technique I call Strategic Building Blocks to organize this pursuit. This simple but profound construct can be applied to virtually any issue that involves strategic content. Used with skill and experience, its sequential framework improves the discipline of the analysis and increases the likelihood of a sound decision on the back end. Simply stated, the sequence builds content by starting with why and progressing through what, how, when, and who.

It is essential to understand that there is a proper sequence to the Strategic Building Blocks approach. One does not attempt to address the how until the why is fully baked. If the why is not fully considered, the purpose of the inquiry tends to get lost. The more granular the analysis, given this flaw, the more likely it will suffer from *goal displacement*, where a starting goal is ignored in favor of a new one. Goal displacement can be diagnosed wherever the common refrain is, now why are we doing this again? When considering a career change, skipping the why and the what can easily result in a false conclusion that a career change is necessary, when all that may be required is to change positions or employers. This is a tragic error when it occurs, and I fear that it occurs often.

We can tell the why has been fully considered when many *what* options arise. Rarely is there just one option (what) in a strategic inquiry. Typically, each option has multiple alternatives (how). A thorough process requires that you identify and sort options to determine which ones surface as priorities for further consideration. Something important can usually be learned from considering each option, even if the lesson falls into the category of "what not to do." Each option usually has certain favorable or unfavorable aspects; considering the whole group helps you determine which options stand out. Sometimes, the solution ends up being some combination of options. Further, it is imperative that the option selected is not only the best conceptually, but is also one that can reasonably be implemented (i.e., in terms of capacity, access to resources, competencies)—another fatal flaw in many strategic studies.

The Strategic Building Blocks approach becomes even more powerful when combined with *key questions*, which is how I have organized this book. Developing key questions is an important technique that I picked up when I first trained as a consultant with Booz Allen Hamilton (hereafter Booz Allen). It has stayed with me over the years and served me well, as has their unique writing style that translates easily into a cogent analytical construct. These skills provide an efficient and effective basis for approaching virtually any problem or challenge. The theory of key questions, like the 80/20 rule (also known as the Pareto principle), holds that spending more time up front on determining which of the many related questions are *core* to a given issue can save significant time and effort later by avoiding rabbit holes that are tangential or of no consequence.

Combining these two techniques sets up the Career Change Decision Framework, shown in exhibit 0.1. Icons from this framework

Exhibit 0.1. The Career Change Decision Framework

Strategic Building Blocks	Key Questions	Chapters
Why **?**	Why would a career change be warranted?	1. Why Consider a Career Change? 2. Making a Midcareer Assessment 3. The Mounting Challenges of Executive Roles
What	If a career change is warranted, what options do I have?	4. Identifying the Options 5. What Others Have Experienced 6. The Road Less Traveled
How	How does consulting compare, so I can determine whether it is the right option for me?	7. Executive Management Versus Consulting 8. A Closer Look at Consulting 9. CEOs Face Some Unique Challenges
When	When will I know that consulting is the appropriate option so I can finish preparing to launch this change?	10. Avoiding Common Mistakes 11. Making the Transition with a Firm 12. Starting a Solo Practice
Who	Who do I need to involve in this process to provide assurance and guidance along the way?	13. If Things Don't Work Out 14. Let the Journey Begin

are included at the top of each page to indicate the Strategic Building Block corresponding to that part of the book, to help you navigate. As previously mentioned, the process is sequential, so I encourage you to read the book from front to back.

How do we begin to answer these key questions? There are many potential sources of information on making a career change, not least of which is learning from others who have experienced this transition firsthand. It was tough enough to identify and pursue a career the first time. (My son suggests this has not gotten any easier.) Pursuing your chosen career might have involved taking certain courses in college or trade school and completing one or more internships. It might have involved reading different works over an extended period. It may have involved a progression of jobs providing valuable experience that has brought you to this point. Now you want to change all that?

Taking a systematic approach to considering a career change allows us to examine each step in an organized, disciplined way. Pursuing a regimented process with a clear sequence can instill confidence that you have examined the issue at several levels. Responding to key questions requires research, which in turn creates knowledge and can place you in a better position to make an informed decision with eyes wide open to both the opportunities and the risks.

A realistic attitude about risk recognizes that it can never be fully eliminated. The intent is to moderate some of the anxiety (fear of the unknown) with knowledge that creates confidence, to the point that big surprises become less likely. That way, any surprises that occur along this path (as they always do) should tend to be minor in the scheme of things. Of course, there are never any guarantees. The key here is to manage expectations, basing them on reality and not unrestrained idealism.

Again, I have approached consulting in both of these books from the perspective of *experiences*. However, I was not an executive who became a consultant. I went straight into consulting from graduate school and then shifted briefly into executive positions before launching my own consulting firm. I have relied on clients and others over the years to provide insights to their experiences starting out as executives, as you will see from numerous case studies.

INCLUSIVENESS IN HEALTHCARE CONSULTING

Although consulting is not for everyone, it can be an exciting career choice for anyone attracted to the mental, physical, and emotional highs and lows it entails. While part of the motivation for writing this book is to help people ask the right questions before they make a possible mistake by unnecessarily changing careers, another key motivation is to help open doors for people who may have been excluded or otherwise discouraged from following this path. In conducting research to share examples from people who have forged this path, it is notable how few examples have surfaced of people from racial and ethnic minority communities.

Credibility in consulting requires knowledge and experience that, when present with other key attributes, creates a trust relationship with the client. Knowledge is a core element of the Consultant Value Chain (see chapter 8), and forms the exclusive domain of the expert when combined with experience. Not everyone is or can be an expert. It takes time and experience. There is no getting around this. There is also no doubt that such expertise exists among people of all racial and ethnic backgrounds. Yet, as in most other professions, racial and ethnic minorities are underrepresented among the ranks of consultants. One could conclude that not all consulting firms have been as inviting to everyone as they could have been. My observations suggest this is less the case today, but this may not be widely known.

Diane L. Dixon, EdD, has published some important research on the executive path for racial and ethnic minorities in *Diversity on the Executive Path: Wisdom and Insights for Navigating to the Highest Levels of Healthcare Leadership*. Her research involved interviews of racially and ethnically diverse hospital and health system CEOs. Dr. Dixon captures the experiences and learnings from these leaders that helped with their advancement to CEO. Many of the insights from her research would apply to making a career change as well.

A FORMAL DISCERNMENT PROCESS

Finally, we must acknowledge that a career change is more than a job change. A job change can be stressful and involve considerable risk, but a career change is an even greater risk. I fear that many people who make a career change may find in retrospect that their real need was to make a job change; the difference is huge. If your current job is too stressful, a career change certainly might help. But how do you know if you need a job change or a career change? The theme of this book is that careful preparation can help you consider the right issues and make the right decision. Approached the right way, the change from executive to consultant is not only possible, it could become one of your best experiences as a healthcare professional.

Consideration of a career change takes place in the context of many other factors that must be carefully weighed from both a conceptual and a timing perspective. Ideally, a career change is chosen only after a period of careful reflection. The word that comes to mind is *discernment*, which *Merriam-Webster's Collegiate Dictionary* defines as "the quality of being able to grasp and comprehend what is obscure." Along my consulting journey, I was exposed to the concept of discernment in considerable depth during several merger discussions involving Catholic hospitals. Specifically, several religious women with whom I was privileged to work invoked the spiritual nature of discernment that was an integral part of their decision-making. According to them, spiritual discernment (sometimes called Christian discernment) results in understanding where God is leading you, understanding your individual calling.

Fundamentally, discernment is "the process of making judgments based on what you are learning and blending those judgments with your own experience" (Dixon 2020, 151). It involves taking steps to help us better understand something before we act. In the end, a career change is a matter of judgment. The final result of discernment is taking action, or not.[3] It is in this spirit that we will

---

3   Not taking action, commonly known as "the status quo," is always the default option.

examine the possibility of a career change for the midlevel or senior healthcare executive.

REFERENCE

Dixon, D. L. 2020. *Diversity on the Executive Path: Wisdom and Insights for Navigating to the Highest Levels of Healthcare Leadership.* Chicago: Health Administration Press.

PART I

WHY?

Why would a career change be warranted?

A CAREER CHANGE is not something to be taken lightly. As someone who has been in healthcare for some time now, you have been subjected to an enormous amount of change—change that, while exciting, is not all good. And it does not seem to be letting up. Of course, this can be said about much of society these days.

Something has compelled you to enter this thought process. The mere act of buying this book tells you that there is something intriguing about a career change. Is this a passing fancy or should you take it seriously? Best to find out now before investing much more time and treasure.

Bear in mind, I am not a human resources specialist, nor do I claim any expertise in talent acquisition. My observations are those of a strategy consultant looking closely at the situation through that lens. Too often, our thought process seems reactionary—it pushes us to the nearest comfort zone, where success may also be fleeting. We need to take the long view, the holistic view; this is where strategy resides. Certain options might address certain issues while falling well short on others. How can we ensure that we cover the bases and get beyond the emotional or reactionary response, taking a rational approach that considers the implications in both the short and long run?

Failure to fully consider the *why* question can have adverse consequences. Understanding the specific motivations for a change helps define success in the long run. The more clarity on this point, the better this process is likely to go. That is why we begin this process of discernment with a careful examination of the need for change. You are not alone in this regard. A lively dialogue within your network can be an indispensable component of this discernment process.

That more people would be open to career changes was not a surprise to some. Rice and Perry (2012, 1) set out some years ago to explore the concept of "a career of impact." They interviewed 21 respected hospital and healthcare leaders and predicted that "the decade from 2011 to 2020 will see thousands of hospital and health system leaders transition into retirement or make career changes." This turned out to be prophetic. Not all the motivations for change were obvious in 2013, but an aging leadership group is one factor that was hard to ignore.

This first step in the process, focused on the why, is truly foundational. Failure to give it proper attention can be catastrophic. People often make key decisions about their future and then succumb to doubts and second guessing. Proper preparation is the antidote to this tendency. In preparing, we will ideally go no further with this analysis until we have answered the why question. The chapters in part I will help you put this in the proper perspective and start down the right path.

Chapter 1. Why Consider a Career Change?
Chapter 2. Making a Midcareer Assessment
Chapter 3. The Mounting Challenges of Executive Roles

REFERENCE

Rice, J. A., and F. Perry. 2012. *Healthcare Leadership Excellence: Creating a Career of Impact*. Chicago: Health Administration Press.

Why Consider a Career Change?

Too often, people consider leaving behind an entire industry before they've fully explored other routes. And it doesn't make sense to throw away years of experience or leave a field you actually love or excel in because of something that's fixable.
—Wendi Weiner (2016)

WE DO NOT tend to think of things this way, but coming to work each day involves choices. Options always exist, though we rarely take note of them. If we routinely thought about these options, there would be little time for work, but a key event can cause these thoughts to surface. Perhaps the event is a family or other life change. Perhaps it is work related.

We usually suppress this matter of choices until it becomes relevant. We prefer the security of a daily routine and constantly seek places where we feel we belong. But at times we wonder why we continue to pursue a daily routine that is no longer interesting or increasingly leaves us dissatisfied. In that vein, I came across this wise observation by Mark Hyman, MD, of the Institute for Functional Medicine:

If we're stuck in a rut with our foot on the gas, we just keep going on the same path. But life is not static, as humans we need to be able to learn from our experiences, grow, and change. It's completely *okay to realize your current path is not making you happy and change directions—give yourself permission! (Hyman 2018)*

Suffice it to say that a typical professional will reconsider their current position and/or career at least a few times. This can occur for many reasons, as we will study in more detail. When faced with this concern, we must consider our options and evaluate them compared to the status quo. How do we do that?

TWO GENERAL APPROACHES

There are two general approaches to career change. The one most people favor when asked is to plan for such a transition, at least to some extent. The other, which is also common and perhaps equally important, is to be opportunistic—either by necessity or by choice.

Changing jobs in healthcare is not rare. A seasoned healthcare executive usually holds a slew of jobs before assuming the role of CEO. Obviously, not every healthcare executive becomes a CEO. And even CEO jobs are less than stable, especially in times of rapid change. According to data tracked by American College of Healthcare Executives (ACHE 2021), hospital CEO turnover increased to 20 percent in 2013, before declining to only 16 percent during the pandemic in 2020 (the latest data available from ACHE). In fact, as we came out of the pandemic in 2022, CEOs turned over at the accelerated rate of one every 72 hours in the first quarter (Ellison 2022). However, these job changes do not always occur by choice. Imagine pursuing a career where you run the risk of having to uproot your family the equivalent of every 5.5 years and move them to a new market to be CEO of a different healthcare organization. Not only are these jobs challenging, they are risky as well.

"Good people get fired at least once," says Christine Mackey-Ross, then a senior vice president with WittKieffer, although she notes that CEOs often use softer words to describe the event, such as saying they decided to pursue other interests (Gamble 2014).

Some experts have even suggested that with all the change occurring in healthcare today, anyone who gets through a healthcare career without being terminated at least once is not doing much.

Being terminated from a position can awaken emotions that are both scary and exhilarating. Not only might you be surprised by your former employer's action ("I didn't see that coming!"), you may be surprised that others around you did see it coming. Like many an executive, I have experienced this personally, and it is quite something to feel the flood of emotions that occurs at such a time. Kübler-Ross's Five Stages of Grief model is invariably invoked as the road map for such occasions, with great variation in individual experience as to how long each stage lasts (anger tended to linger a bit for me). And while you navigate that vulnerable time with help from your family, friends, and professional network, some comments begin to get through the mist of separation. For example, someone may ask, "Have you ever considered consulting?" The question may come as a surprise if you have never given any serious thought to the possibility of pursuing a consulting career.

ADVICE ABOUNDS

A simple literature search on the topic of career change will turn up a litany of advice intended to help you through your journey. Some is helpful, while some seems a bit puffy. Dorie Clark, of the Fuqua School at Duke University, has written extensively about the topic and has a few gems that I will refer to throughout this book. As quoted in an article by Allison Pohle in the *Wall Street Journal* ("How to Change Careers: Find What to Pursue Next," February 4, 2021), Clark advises, "Your skill set is probably very broad. . . . Other people aren't going to expend the time or the effort to think broadly on your behalf about what you can do." In the same article, Ebony Joyce, a career coach with Next Level Career Services, emphasizes the importance of knowing what you do not want to do, as well as what you do. Pohle also advises readers to think about changing their online presence. Clearly, you do not have to look far for some sound advice.

But beware: Thinking about a career change can also be a trap, according to Forbes career coach Wendi Weiner. Writing for career website The Muse, she suggests that three of the most common reasons people consider a change—a bad boss, poor compensation, or boredom—are often misleading, and recommends caution:

While changing careers can feel like a rebirth, jumping ship is not always the right answer. Do your homework, think things through, put together a plan, and consider the reasons why you want to change careers before you take the ultimate plunge headfirst. That way, you can avoid being several months down the road and wishing you'd never made the leap. (Weiner 2016)

We have tried to tailor the advice in this book specifically to those who are experiencing the dramatic changes taking place in healthcare. In some ways, the level and pace of change in healthcare is unique, particularly in relation to the COVID-19 pandemic. While some frontline providers were getting burned out from overutilization, other providers were on the sidelines, victims of the "elective procedures" label. By late April in 2020, one in five doctors had been furloughed or taken a pay cut as health systems looked for ways to reduce costs during the first wave of the pandemic (Rapier 2020). The impact has been dramatic, with some providers considering a career change out of medicine altogether.

As burnout has become a more prominent concern, especially for healthcare providers (Harvard School of Public Health 2019), it is worth noting that a career change can be either a serious source of stress or a serious stress reliever. I am reminded of the words of Quint Studer (2021): "Have a job and a place of work that you enjoy. If you are passionate about what you do, you're less likely to burn out." Sometimes just changing the place of work is all that is required to restore balance. Other times, you may find that you no longer enjoy the work. Clearly, the latter finding is more serious.

A CAREER CHANGE IS A LIFE STRESS EVENT

Few things are more stressful than a career change. To create their famous Social Readjustment Rating Scale, Holmes and Rahe (1967) reviewed over 5,000 medical records and developed a stress scale of 43 life events (exhibit 1.1). "Death of a spouse" ranked highest at 100, and other key events were indexed against this. "Dismissal from work" was ranked eighth, with a score of 47 (i.e., less than half as stressful as loss of a spouse). "Retirement" is only two ranks behind this, at number 10, with a score of 45 (tied with "marital reconciliation"). "Change to a different line of work" is ranked eighteenth

Exhibit 1.1. Partial List of Stress Scores

Live event	Life change units
Death of a spouse	100
Divorce	73
Marital separation	65
Death of a close family member	63
Imprisonment	63
Personal injury or illness	53
Marriage	50
Dismissal from work	47
Marital reconciliation	45
Retirement	45
Change in health of family member	44
Pregnancy	40
Business readjustment	39
Gain a new family member	39
Sexual difficulties	39
Change in financial state	38

Source: Adapted from Holmes and Rahe (1967).

with a score of 36. Importantly, these scores are designed to reflect the level of emotional stress induced by these life-changing events; that stress may be positive or negative, depending on circumstances.

Assigning a value to each of these life events individually is only one part of the Holmes and Rahe tool. Because many of these events seem to be a natural part of life at some point or another, I was more interested in the cumulative effect of these stress factors. In other words, what combination of these might cause a tilt in one's psychological makeup? Clearly, one must take care not to let too many stressors affect you at any one time. More on this later.

PUSH AND PULL SCENARIOS

A career change may be motivated by a push or a pull scenario. While both may be present, it is useful to determine which of the two dominates. Under the push scenario, what is the source of dissatisfaction (or failure) with the current situation? If we have been terminated, it is relatively easy to identify this as a push scenario. However, what are the underlying causes of this termination? Under the pull scenario, it is important to understand the attraction to consulting as an option. Reading my previous book, *The Healthcare Consultant's Handbook* (Mason 2021), can help test the attraction to consulting and add substance to your understanding of the experience of consulting. Is the pull based on myth or reality? It is important to get more granular about these scenarios.

To foster greater insight, it is imperative to understand the central motivation for a career change. Applying a clinical model, this is the diagnostic portion of the process. As any clinician will tell you, if the diagnosis is wrong, it will likely be followed by a bad or ineffective set of treatments. Better to get the diagnosis correct. Staying with the clinical model for the moment, it is also important to understand the underlying disease. All too often in medicine, treatments resolve symptoms but do not affect the cause. Although symptoms are important and may also need to be treated, it is better to address the underlying illness where possible. In a potential career change, this plays out through correct diagnosis of the problem. The push and pull scenarios are covered in more detail here.

The pull scenario can apply to a deliberate and systematic exploration of the general concept of consulting or to a specific opportunity that requires a quick decision. If circumstances are such that you must make a decision under severe time constraints, there is a greater risk that you will come to a wrong conclusion. But regardless of time constraints, the process should begin with finding the correct answer to the *why* question. If the question is urgent you must complete the process more quickly, but you must still understand the why of the pull scenario, lest you make a bad decision based on a false premise. Reducing the risk of making a bad decision is a key aim of this initial discernment process.

Under a push scenario, dissatisfiers in your current position are frequently the main motivation for a change. Understanding these dissatisfiers in depth can place guardrails on your journey and lead to a higher probability of a successful transition. The danger of the push scenario is the impulse to take a reactionary stance, characterized as, "I'll show you." The temptation is great, especially when you have been terminated, to prove that the decision was wrongheaded. Beware the potential of covering up how you might have contributed in some way to what has happened. Were there aspects of the position for which you were ill prepared? Did you make any fatal mistakes that can be avoided in the future? What part, if any, did you play in this outcome? Were there deficiencies that can and should be corrected? Are your current feelings merely a reaction to being hurt by this move, or were there more deep-seated considerations?

I'm not sure I fully appreciated this proverb when I first heard it: "Revenge is a dish best served cold." It cautions us to avoid the quick emotional or knee-jerk reaction of seeking vengeance, but rather to take time to cool off and be deliberate in "delivering justice." An emotional reaction can take several forms. One form is to quickly land the same job with another organization and perform admirably, thus raising questions regarding your previous employer's decision.

A more dramatic approach is to make a career change so you can better showcase your skills from a more relevant platform. Either can be the wrong response, depending on the underlying nature of the event. The key is to correctly identify what caused this termination, and/or your feelings about it. Did you somehow fail to meet the job requirements, or was it a reflection of a poor relationship with your boss (somewhat common, according to the literature)?

A correct diagnosis here should help you determine whether a change of venue is all you require. If you come to a precipitous conclusion, you may fail to address key dissatisfiers. For example, if a key dissatisfier is debilitating bureaucracy, then you are not likely to cure it by taking a line management position in another healthcare organization that turns out to be even more bureaucratic. You will have a new employer, but you will not change the fundamental source of your frustration. If you change careers to consulting but end up with a firm that has significant bureaucracy, you may end up dealing with the same dissatisfiers. In either case, you likely have not improved your job satisfaction. Beware the reactive response that ignores the underlying causes.

CAREER GOALS

Another tool to help you rise above the moment is to consider a broader aim—your career goals. Career goals can be tricky things. They tend to fall into two categories: long term and short term. Generally, you should start with long-term goals and then focus on the short term (Simpson 2019). But career goals also change.

Nothing in healthcare today remains the same; the only constant is change. Healthcare organizations are asked to put the patient in the center of their mission ("patient-centered care"). Some of us argue that even a focus on "patients" is losing potency and that a "customer orientation" must emerge if we are to make the transition from illness care to true *health* care. Just as the organizations that serve people's healthcare needs are undergoing radical change, so too are changes required of the executives who lead or consult to such organizations.

Managing change is the alpha and omega of this transition. The integrating theory is that change is all about us. Change requires knowledge and leadership; leadership must be enlightened to lead change well. Outside expertise can be essential to successfully addressing a change agenda within an organization. Ubiquitous change is an enabler for consulting services, which clearly have a strong future in healthcare.

> **Ubiquitous change is an enabler for consulting services, which clearly have a strong future in healthcare.**

As healthcare is changing, your career is clearly subject to change as well. Less clear, perhaps, is the realization that your *career goals* may change too. The story of the boiling frog comes to mind here; the need to change career goals may not be immediately obvious. Like many goal-oriented people, I have found it extremely hard to move away from an established goal. We tend to be fixated on it for so long that it becomes hard to displace. Not recognizing that our goals may have changed can lead to tragic consequences and poor career choices. It can also be unrealistic. "You need to evaluate your current *knowledge, skills*, and *experience* so that you can compare them with what will be required" (Malvey and Sapp 2020, 8; emphasis added). The authors go on to invoke SMART goals (specific, measurable, achievable, relevant, and time-bound) as a good place to start. But there is more to it than that.

Life brings many changes—some expected, some not. Ideally, goals are refined over time. What tends to remain constant (or should) is *values*. Goals need to be linked to consequences. Often, a career change is prompted by an event such as a job loss or change in family circumstances. It can also be preceded by a loss of interest in your current employment. Sure, some tinkering with the current job might correct the situation (e.g., a reset of responsibilities), but it may run deeper than that. If you are intensely dissatisfied with your current job, and especially with what is required of you and how it makes you feel, it is natural to re-examine not only your job choice but perhaps your career goals.

What specifically caused you to start looking in the direction of a career change? To understand this thoroughly, it helps to try to remember your career goals when you first started. This requires introspection and can involve many personal considerations—family, friends, a desire to avoid relocating, the need to continuously learn, to be creative, to have some control. You might find yourself revisiting some of the core idealism of your youth before you were hit by the two-by-four of the work world:

- To make a difference
- To have job security
- To be challenged
- To enjoy the journey

Because idealism tends to dissipate with time, let's examine each of these briefly; doing so might put you back in touch with some important *feelings* that were more present at the outset of your career journey. By idealism, I am not necessarily referring to "save the whales" or some starry-eyed vision from our youth, but rather the things that we found motivating at the time. To be fair, this can differ substantially from one generation to another. Accordingly, it is helpful to offer some context as to how each generation may embrace some of these.

To Make a Difference

More than a few studies suggest generational differences regarding this goal (Paychex 2019; Weeks 2017; West Midland Family Center 2019). In other words, you may be influenced by where you stand in the generational calendar. The Greatest Generation is often credited with having achieved this goal. Children of the Depression era, they grew up watching their parents struggle to make a living, went to school, got jobs, and then fought World War II. Once they survived the travails of the war, raising their family and holding down a job was gravy.[1] They survived the war after all.

Then came the children of the Greatest Generation—the baby boomers. Unlike their parents, who felt blessed to be out of the war successfully and to be left alone to pursue family goals, baby boomers rebelled from day one. Nothing was as it should be. They questioned everything and tried to change all that they touched. Boomers were disruptors before there were disruptors. While their parents were relatively quiet and sought anonymity, boomers were loud and attracted attention. This made for some interesting interactions at the dinner table.

The generations since the boomers seem somewhat more subtle in contrast—until the millennials, that is. But many of the supposed differences captured in internet memes and generational insults may simply come down to the differences in motivation and perspective that come with age. Millennials (born between 1981 and 1996) behave more like boomers—questioning everything yet again, but with a bit more attitude about the establishment. Ryan Jenkins (2019) suggests that the reason millennials are different comes down to one word—*access*. "As far back as they can remember, Millennials have had access to the world's information curated into a blank search box in the palm of their hand."

Millennials grew up watching their parents suffer through the Great Recession of 2008 and the emerging politics of division. The culture wars were at the center of their universe. And while they did not necessarily have a point of view to start, they were forced to pick sides over time. Generally, they did not like much of what they saw. They were presented with a binary world, and they were either on one side or the other; nothing remained in the middle.

---

1 It is interesting to note the impact of life events such as the Great Depression and World War II. It begs the question of how the coronavirus pandemic will affect the career outlook of future generations, notably the schoolchildren who have been subjected to remote learning.

Their response, in Jenkins's words, was to use their access to reform the world they were given:

Access is holding every company accountable to be better.

Access leads us away from average. If there are better employers, superior services, or improved products out there, they will be found.

Access has made it easy for disengaged employees to find a better company culture, move to a different location, and learn the new skill required to start a new job.

Access has made it easy for dissatisfied customers to search for an improved solution, watch testimonials, cost compare, and buy it at the lowest price.

While it initially appears that boomers and millennials have little in common, one value that seemed to stick out for both is the desire to make a difference—each in their own way.

Because disruptions have different implications for different generations, I must discuss the impact of COVID-19, albeit preliminarily. According to McKinsey & Company,

For millennials and members of Generation Z—those born between 1980 and 2012—this crisis represents the biggest disruption they have faced. Their attitudes may be changed profoundly and in ways that are hard to predict. The tourism, travel, and hospitality sectors may see their businesses subject to long-term changes in business and individual travel preferences. Concern over the possibility of other "black swan" events could change how consumers approach financial security—saving more and spending less. The list of questions about how consumers will behave after COVID-19 is long, and uncertainty is high. As a result, this is the subject of much research by McKinsey and others. (Sneader and Singhal 2020)

To Have Job Security

The importance of job security can vary by generation as well. It is more important to some than to others, possibly correlated with their risk tolerance. For some, the security of employment (executive) is more important than the relative instability of contracting (consulting). Millennials watched their parents lose their jobs after being with the same firm for decades. They saw the resurgence of patriotism, but with much controversy also in evidence. They saw their parents challenged by new technology that they found intuitive. Many of the key technology disruptions—personal computers, cell phones, sensors, genetic testing—had occurred before they were born. Then the disruptors became more challenging.

They watched as their neighbors were forced to sell their house at a steep discount while the housing market collapsed. They watched older people bagging groceries because they were unable to afford retirement without supplementing their income. They saw their distracted parents consumed with uncertainty, and often working two jobs to try to make ends meet. They experienced the growing anxiety around climate change and the need to shift away from fossil fuels. They experienced the pandemic. This was all alarming; they wanted more predictability in their lives.

Advanced schooling is no longer a guarantee of a fulfilling career. Artificial intelligence is one of the newest threats to job security, as vast segments of the workforce (e.g., truck drivers) may be displaced by new technologies. Legions of displaced workers will have to be absorbed somehow into the new economy (e.g., energy workers from the fossil fuel industry). For millennials, the "gig economy" has begun displacing traditional employment as a career choice, favoring entrepreneurs able to sell their services as independent contractors. While this has afforded millennials greater freedom, it can seem much riskier than the experience of previous generations. Contract work is less steady, requiring constant sales and new client generation. There is also the liability to provide benefits (relatively easy for corporations) that is now shifted to the gig worker (far more challenging). The trap for executives is the security of a paycheck and benefits to which they have been tethered as employees. It may be hard to break these bonds.

To Be Challenged

It may seem like an oxymoron to be both secure and challenged, yet these are common career goals for many aspiring executives. After a long hiatus, technical schools are expanding dramatically along with the realization that not everyone requires a liberal arts education and some people are surely content to do piecework in the tradition of the trades (e.g., carpenters, plumbers, electricians, mechanics). In fact, the trades are beginning to look attractive again, given the turnover of traditional employment and scarcity of labor to fill these gaps. Have you tried to find a good mechanic lately? Thankfully, trades are becoming a more viable employment avenue than ever.

But for others, the trades represent repetition and are not intellectually challenging. It was not that they necessarily need more, rather they need different. The idea of going to work each day to repeat the experience of previous days is not compelling.[2] Line management has its challenges as well. Personnel issues can become overwhelming, replacing other tasks that were more rewarding. Responsibility is often out of alignment with authority. Frustrations can build over time. Those who succeed in leading teams enjoy some freedom to exercise their values, but not every executive is able to reach this level of self-actualization. Consulting, in contrast, can offer a constant array of new challenges, not least of which is new clients in new settings.

---

2   Sadly, this accounts somewhat for the relatively high suicide rate among dentists (CBS News/AP 2016).

To Enjoy the Journey

At first, building a career was stimulating and enjoyable. The joy of being exposed to new things, learning, and succeeding brings back fond memories. Peer recognition and the stimulation of trial and error were once your North Star. Promotions led to greater responsibility. Greater responsibility brings greater income and the ability to enjoy a better lifestyle and nicer vacations.

Yet, the career experience is not always what it is cracked up to be. Virtually any career includes ebbs and flows. The adrenaline rush wears off over time. Some people are content with this and settle into a comfortable routine. For others, new priorities take over, such as family, hobbies, and health. What replaces the excitement that was evident in the beginning when the learning curve was steep? Do they still get the thrill of new pursuits and advancement, or does routine begin to take overtake stimulating tasks? Perhaps the days become repetitive, at least to some degree. Time to enjoy life begins to take on more importance, and the desk, the job, and the job routine no longer hold the same joy. Trying to stay current, while certainly a challenge, may begin to feel overwhelming, or rank high on the boredom scale, and the executive may begin to look and feel like Bill Murray in the movie *Groundhog Day*. When the heart tilts more in this direction is when the idea of a career change comes into focus as an opportunity to possibly recapture the fun of new experiences.

MANAGE RISK

To the extent that our current situation falls short regarding career goals, where does consulting fit? I bring up consulting at this point because I have seen the "grass is greener" phenomenon play out many times. When people experience what might be a brief setback, it is natural to migrate to a safe place. Fantasizing that consulting might be a better alternative can bring temporary relief, but it is a mirage, at least at this stage. It is imperative that we not fall into this trap. Therefore, I emphasize up front the need to define the current situation more precisely, as well as to have an accurate picture of other opportunities that might exist and what the related risks are.

> **To the extent that our current situation falls short regarding career goals, where does consulting fit?**

To move from employment to consulting you will have to overcome many barriers. The odds are stacked against you in a number of ways. I have witnessed this difficult transition and its effects on others who found that consulting was not their path to success. The purpose of this book is to improve your odds of success in such a move. Understanding some of these barriers becomes even more important because this career move is increasingly popular. But it has been hard for people who harbor such thoughts to gain insights into what is required to be successful with such a radical change. I hope to provide a foundation based on experience, including the experiences of others who are familiar with this transition. Doing so at this critical time in the transformation of healthcare will surely help consulting continue to play an important role in improving the performance of healthcare organizations to better meet the growing needs of a fickle and demanding consumer.

Perfection is the enemy of good, they say. Rather than allow consulting to be raised on a pedestal, let us consider the realities. The risks inherent to consulting cannot be ignored. Of course, risk is not exclusive to consulting. Traditional employment also holds the risk of losing a good job or landing in a bad one. Everything involves some element of risk.

The risks inherent in consulting occupy significant space in my previous book, a snippet of which is repeated here:

That consulting comes with its fair share of risk should surprise no one. In my experience, however, many new or prospective consultants fail to fully appreciate the risk that are taking. If you are in consulting long enough, you are sure to experience disappointment or even outright failure sooner or later. Is that something you can bounce back from, or will it haunt you going forward? Dealing with disappointment and loss is never easy. But it comes with the territory. (Mason 2021, 17)

A career change always involves some risk. We may not always be aware of it, but the status quo involves risk as well. Sometimes, that risk is unclear until a key event occurs, such as being terminated because of a merger. As boxer Mike Tyson famously pointed out, everybody has a plan until they get punched in the face. An unplanned career change can feel like a punch in the face. I hope that this book can ease the pain and help you deal with the risk.

An important consideration in managing the risk of a career change is to recognize your options. The more informed you are, the better you are positioned. The risk you face can never be fully extinguished, but it can be minimized. The following five steps can help:

1. *Manage your expectations.* Depending on what you are leaving, this may be a big change or a small one. The key is to set your expectations realistically. Do not underestimate the learning curve. Different triggers and levers are involved in being a consultant. These may come naturally to some people, but not everyone.

2. *Have a clear understanding of the status quo.* Often, a key to making such a decision is the recognition that the status quo represents the higher risk. If things were working out, you might not be considering this option. A clear understanding of the risk of *not* making a change is important.

3. *Do your homework.* Learn everything you can about your potential new surroundings. Some things cannot be learned ahead of time, but much can. Do not be afraid to ask questions, especially of people with whom you will be working.

4. *Recognize there will be surprises.* You cannot anticipate everything. With help, I hope you will not miss much, but you will miss some things. May they be little things. To find out more about the rigors of consulting, please refer to chapter 10, which includes a checklist of common mistakes—avoiding these will help you minimize risk.

5. *Consider the timing.* Timing will be discussed in more detail in chapters 11 and 12, but you should understand that it is natural to become impatient to move, especially if a specific opportunity awaits you or you are made to feel like a lame duck in your current position. Best not to rush into something if you can avoid it. (Obviously, this cannot always be avoided.) Avoiding a rushed decision minimizes the possibility that your doubts will morph into a feeling that you acted precipitously.

Timing is one of the most important factors to consider here. With any entrepreneurial activity, the most common failure is not giving it enough time to be successful. If you follow a clear path faithfully and diligently, you should not feel you have rushed into something. Then you must be prepared to give this new path a chance to succeed. There will be discomfort; anything new tends to bring some discomfort. Comparisons to your previous situation are natural; that is why it is so important to have a clear understanding of the discomfort that exists in the status quo.

Clearly, some life situations are better for this type of decision than others. Before you enter into this process, have you cleared the deck of other stress-inducing events? Ideally, you will not pile a career change on top of expecting a new child, going through a divorce, or some other major life event.

Have you decided a minimum amount of time that you will give this new job before you sit back and evaluate the situation? Do you have at least six months of salary set aside to fall back on in the event this does not work out? (Some experts suggest a year.) These considerations are discussed in more detail in chapters 11 and 12, but it is worth raising these questions early.

Finally, do you have a clear definition of success? Feeling good about things is a clear indicator, but it may not be the most important one in the long run. Short run considerations are also important. What makes you happy? What are you not happy about? What three things do you most want to happen in the first 90 days? The first six months? Later, you can ask, Did these three things happen? Why? Why not? How to you feel about things overall? Are you able to manage this situation so that more happy things happen, and you can neutralize the unhappy? You get the idea.

These five questions can give you comfort from a timing perspective:

1. Have you carefully explored your other options?
2. Are you clear that you have negotiated the best deal you can for this change?
3. Have you identified and answered all important questions?
4. Do you have a client lined up for your first assignment, and are you comfortable with it?
5. Is there anything else you can or should do before you jump ship?

RECOMMENDATIONS

1. Understand, in specific terms, your motivation for change. Is it a push scenario or a pull scenario?

2. Do not underestimate the stresses that occur in life's journey, and recognize that a career change adds substantially to this stress, even under the best of circumstances.

3. Take the time to reconnect with past career goals and determine if they have changed.

4. If your career goals have not changed but other things have changed (e.g., dissatisfiers), determine whether these other things can be fixed.

5. Determining that change is required is not the final answer; understanding what kind of change you need (e.g., do more of and do less of) and when (e.g., soon or after more reflection) is equally important.

REFERENCES

American College of Healthcare Executives (ACHE). 2021. "Hospital CEO Turnover Rate Shows Small Decrease." Published June 28. www.ache.org/about-ache/news-and-awards/news-releases/hospital-ceo-turnover-2021.

CBS News/AP. 2016. "These Jobs Have the Highest Rate of Suicide." Published June 30. www.cbsnews.com/news/these-jobs-have-the-highest-rate-of-suicide/.

Ellison, A. 2022. "Hospital CEO Exits Nearly Double This Year." *Becker's Hospital Review*, April 28. www.beckershospitalreview.com/hospital-management-administration/hospital-ceo-exits-nearly-double-this-year.html.

Gamble, M. 2014. "The CEO's Guide to Getting Fired." *Becker's Hospital Review*, May 9. www.beckershospitalreview.com/hospital-management-administration/the-ceo-s-guide-to-getting-fired.html.

Harvard School of Public Health. 2019. "Leading Health Care Organizations Declare Physician Burnout as 'Public Health Crisis'" (news release). Published January 17. www.hsph.harvard.edu/news/press-releases/leading-health-care-organizations-declare-physician-burnout-as-public-health-crisis/.

Holmes T. H., and R. H. Rahe. 1967. "The Social Readjustment Rating Scale." *Journal of Psychosomatic Research* 11 (2): 213–18. https://doi.org/10.1016/0022-3999(67)90010-4.

Hyman, M. 2018. "Tips to Nourish Your Spirit." Dr. Hyman (blog). Published April 12. https://drhyman.com/blog/2018/04/12/tips-to-nourish-your-spirit/.

Jenkins, R. 2019. "This Is What Caused Millennials to Be So Different." Technology (blog), *Inc.* Published January 23. www.inc.com/ryan-jenkins/this-is-what-caused-millennials-to-be-so-different.html.

Malvey, D., and J. L. Sapp. 2020. *Your Healthcare Job Hunt: How Your Digital Presence Can Make or Break Your Career.* Chicago: Health Administration Press.

Mason, S. A. 2021. *The Healthcare Consultant's Handbook: Career Opportunities and Best Practices.* Chicago: Health Administration Press.

Paychex. 2019. "How to Manage the 5 Generations in the Workplace." Paychex Worx. Last updated July 26. www.paychex.com/articles/human-resources/how-to-manage-multiple-generations-in-the-workplace.

Rapier, G. 2020. "1 in 5 Doctors Has Been Furloughed or Taken a Pay Cut as the Coronavirus Pandemic Hits Hospitals. Some Say They're Considering New Jobs." Business Insider, April 25. www.businessinsider.com/doctors-see-furloughs-pay-cuts-coronavirus-hospitals-survey-2020-4.

Simpson, M. 2019. "What Are Your Career Goals? (+ Answers)." TheInterviewGuys.com (blog). Published February 26. https://theinterviewguys.com/what-are-your-career-goals/.

Sneader, K., and S. Singhal. 2020. "The Future Is Not What It Used to Be: Thoughts on the Shape of the Next Normal." *McKinsey & Company* digital article. Published April 14. www.mckinsey.com/featured-insights/leadership/the-future-is-not-what-it-used-to-be-thoughts-on-the-shape-of-the-next-normal.

Studer, Q. 2021. "Healing Leader Burnout." The Busy Leader's Handbook (website). Published January 18. https://thebusyleadershandbook.com/healing-leader-burnout-a-few-quick-tips/.

Weeks, K. P. 2017. "Every Generation Wants Meaningful Work— But Thinks Other Age Groups Are in It for the Money." *Harvard Business Review* digital article. Published July 31. https://hbr.org/2017/07/every-generation-wants-meaningful-work-but-thinks-other-age-groups-are-in-it-for-the-money.

West Midland Family Center. 2019. Generational Differences Chart. www.wmfc.org/uploads/GenerationalDifferencesChartUpdated2019.pdf.

Weiner, W. 2016. "Three Common Reasons People Change Careers (That They Later Regret)." Advice (blog), The Muse. Published September 1. www.themuse.com/advice/3-common-reasons-people-change-careers-that-they-later-regret.

CHAPTER 2

Making a Midcareer Assessment

*What we hear over and over again is that [people] fell into their line
of work, and 10 years later, they don't know why they're still there.*
—Natasha Stanley (2016)

PEOPLE OFTEN BEGIN a career change by focusing on how they
want to spend their remaining time in a profession. While perhaps
hesitant to make a dramatic change, they may be more open to
evaluating options. In the previous chapter, I discussed the motivation for change as being driven by a push or pull scenario; you
could also view these as two sides of a coin: On one side is the
attraction of consulting, on the other is the status of your current
executive experience.

The allure of consulting should be acknowledged. Is the promise
real? To some extent, but some myths exist as well. Perhaps you have
had satisfying and enjoyable interactions with consultants and left
these encounters with some envy that people had the time to consider
such things and to earn a living doing so. Some of this might be a
grass is greener mentality, but that should not detract from your
intellectual curiosity. *The Healthcare Consultant's Handbook* further
illuminates some of the realities of the consulting experience.

The other side of the coin is where you are now—your thoughts
about your current trajectory and the satisfaction that you derive (or
not) from your position. Might you find greater satisfaction doing
something different? For those who are later in their careers, there

is also a natural tendency to consider your legacy and the impression you want to leave as you move toward retirement. Rice and Perry (2012) have written eloquently about *impactful leadership*, and as you will see in the profiles in chapter 5, people have made a career change to consulting because they believed they could have a greater impact than they could as an executive. Others are simply seeking a soft landing as they near retirement. Some are motivated by "doing what I really want to do." All these factors, and others, can prompt someone to reconsider their present career trajectory.

You have some decisions to make, after you complete some analysis. But before we discuss the mechanics of a midcareer assessment, we must distinguish between the reality of consulting and the concept of consulting. Have you experienced consulting from the consultant's side? Some discussion from my previous book is summarized here:

- Even experienced executives who have worked with consultants may be ill-informed about the rigors of consulting.
- There are many misleading myths about consulting.
- Knowledge and experience, while essential, are insufficient. Someone must be willing to pay you for your knowledge and experience. Consulting, at its core, is an exchange.
- Often, a consulting engagement will require skills you do not possess. Can you easily call on others to augment what you bring to the table?
- Are you clear about what you must do to attract clients long term? Are you also clear that these future clients are not likely to be current friends and colleagues? In my experience, friends do not buy from friends.
- Whether you are considering work as a solo consultant or as part of a firm, are you clear on the *business* of consulting? This is separate from the *profession* of consulting. To be successful as a consultant, you must

master both. If you join a firm, you can rely on others for the business portion, at least to some extent, but as a solo consultant you'd better have a holistic view.

ESTABLISH A BASELINE

You can find a plethora of online self-assessment tools designed to measure preferences, personality type, and aptitude for certain occupations, from the relatively simple to the more complex Myers–Briggs Type Indicator sometimes used to guide personality types toward certain careers (Conlan 2021). These tools can be useful, as can working with a professional who specializes in this area—an executive coach can be extremely helpful, as recommended throughout this book.

The assessment contemplated here is more basic. Effectively, it starts by comparing what you like about what you are currently doing with what you find dissatisfying. Often, I find this sheds light on your skill set as well. People tend to be attracted to work they do well, though there are exceptions.[1]

In any kind of comparison we must ask, compared to what? Many books and articles are devoted to the reality that in most considerations of change the status quo wins (i.e., change fails). In part, this is because the status quo is familiar and takes the least amount of effort. It has become routine. It is comfortable—until it is not.

> **The status quo is familiar and takes the least amount of effort. It has become routine. It is comfortable—until it is not.**

---

1 For example, I decided to take more science courses in college because I felt I had a deficiency in this area. Science was not necessarily something I did well, nor did I enjoy it the most (my grades proved this). It did not become my life's work, but I did succeed in closing my knowledge gap.

Our comfort with the status quo is often due in large part to not knowing what the options are. Ignorance is bliss. Considering other options is, by definition, disruptive—it disrupts the status quo. Disruption can be energizing when it helps us to look at things in a different way; we must be willing to accept disruption in order to fully consider options. We must be willing to raise issues that we have ignored or have not previously considered. I am convinced that some people are stuck in their current jobs because they are unwilling to risk considering alternatives that make them realize just how miserable they are.

This is where dreams and vision come into play. Said differently, ignorance can also take the form of naivete. Friends and family can play a key role here by pointing out things that we may have overlooked. The key is to establish a baseline before getting into any depth regarding alternative career paths. We must have a clear and accurate assessment of the current situation as a basis for comparison with other options.

A *situation assessment* is a classic tool of the strategist. The following suggestions are derived from my personal experiences, as well as the experiences of others who have made this career change:

Focus first on the current experience. How do certain activities make you feel? What brings you satisfaction? What do you find frustrating? Set up a table of likes and dislikes. Does one side clearly outnumber the other from day-to-day (constant imbalance), or do things vary considerably (e.g., with seasons or budget cycles)? Which things are harder to get over than others? Emotional intelligence is a factor here: Are you exhibiting self-awareness in this assessment or are others making clear to you that they see some important things you might be missing (Dye and Lee 2016)?

Don't rely only on your personal perceptions. What do others say about you? What have your job reviews suggested? Is there consensus between what you perceive and what others observe? If a gap exists, where is it? How big is the gap?

What are the best moments from your current job? Looking back, what are you most proud of? What are the main accomplishments that you would list on a resume? How does this list make you feel? Do you expect more of these moments, or fewer?

What tend to be the worst moments from your current job? Are they unavoidable dissatisfiers that come with the territory or circumstances that might be corrected (e.g., a difficult boss)? The difference is important. Sometimes fixing one thing—for example, changing bosses—can change the picture entirely.

What would you most like to change about your current situation, if you could? You have probably thought about this question already, but it can be a game changer. If you could change one thing, what would it be? Would this change solve the current problem? How likely is it that you can make this change?

Of your desired changes, which, if any, are under your control? Are they worth pursuing or is the likelihood of success just too remote? Which things are beyond your control, and how important are those things? Who controls those things? Do you feel trapped?

What are the prospects for change? Do you believe that things can improve, or is your dissatisfaction growing? How do you feel about the future, given current prospects (e.g., promotion)? Is change just a matter of time or is it unlikely?

Is this mostly a personnel issue? The literature makes clear that people tend to quit their supervisors, not their employers. Is this the main issue you face, or are you unhappy with many of your coworkers? Do you otherwise enjoy your job? If you enjoy the work but not the people, a change of venue might be the cure.

Could most current issues be addressed by doing the same job for some other organization? This is an important question. If you are simply in the wrong setting, perhaps a change of employer is the easier course of action. While challenging, a job change is far less stressful than a career change.

I can't stress enough the importance of talking with others during this period of self-assessment. How do their observations compare with yours? Do they see your situation the same way you do? Are their comments reinforcing your impressions or raising new questions that you have not fully considered?

IDENTIFY DISSATISFIERS

You must protect against the age-old grass is greener fantasy. As previously noted, a critical analysis of your current situation should identify key dissatisfiers—negative factors that come with the territory in your current career. You can manage these, but they are not likely to disappear. It is the nature of the beast.

Every profession has its dissatisfiers. By using consulting as an example, we can also address a few myths. Following are some of the major dissatisfiers that consultants experience (Mason 2021, 51):

- *Long workdays.* There are still only 24 hours in a day, despite efforts to increase this number (perhaps space travel will change this). Too often, there is insufficient time to do a project as well and as thoroughly as you would like. It can get frustrating.

- *Bad clients.* While bad clients are rare in my experience, having a bad client is tough. Usually, the selection process addresses client chemistry well; the consultant becomes aware of a poor fit, or the client/prospect lets you know by not selecting you in a competitive situation. Still, the occasional bad situation will slip through the cracks of a vetting process. When this happens, resiliency comes into play. Your creative side shifts into gear and you try to morph it into a rewarding situation for both you and the client. I can attest that it can be done!

- *Bad engagements.* Even with a good client relationship, you can end up in a bad engagement—one that is poorly planned or poorly executed, or that involves unsavory or unappealing issues (e.g., personnel problems). It could involve work that is uninteresting or outside your area of expertise. The engagement may start off in your sweet spot but migrate out. Scope creep may set in. Whatever the circumstances, try to complete or hand off bad engagements as quickly as possible so you can move on.

- *Inadequate budgets.* Most budgets are adequate. They are rarely excessive. Some are simply inadequate. Scope of work becomes important here. It is a worthy goal to attempt to match an adequate budget to all consulting work—not just for you but for the team and the client. Budget frustrations can damage even strong client relationships. When this happens, you have two choices: You can finish the work and take the budget hit, or you can negotiate adjustments to the project scope or budget. In my experience, necessary adjustments are easily negotiated with a trusting client.
- *Lack of work–life balance.* While listed last, this may be the most common concern. Everyone learns how to manage this challenge in a way that works for them. If things become chronically out of balance, it may be time to consider getting out of consulting.

We are in remarkable times globally, which makes it more difficult to distinguish between the mundane inconveniences and the profound. Virtually all jobs have dissatisfiers, especially during times of upheaval. The COVID-19 pandemic created stress for everyone in healthcare—particularly for providers, but we should not underestimate the stress for administrative staff. But dissatisfiers exist even in the best of times. Exhibit 2.1 lists some common dissatisfiers, based on research and interviews with a wide variety of healthcare executives. As a healthcare executive yourself, you are familiar with many of these dissatisfiers, but it can be easy to underestimate their impact.

Exhibit 2.1. Key Dissatisfiers for Healthcare Executives

Dissatisfier	Definition	Implications
Politics	Relates to team interactions both generally and specifically. More tolerable to the extent that you can influence this. Can be a serious issue when it involves the board.	Can reduce the importance of merit; can become the "invisible hand" in key decisions over which you have no control.
Slow advancement	No clear path to advance or opportunity to grow; lack of access to formal training.	Job becomes less satisfying over time; hard to set future goals.
Supervisory interference	"Hands-on" oversight is oppressive and limits ability to function.	Loss of interest or motivation.
Misalignment of authority and responsibility	Too much is expected of you and/or you lack authority to gain support from others.	Burnout; inability to support your people adequately.
Boredom	Tasks become routine and no longer feel rewarding.	Erodes commitment.
Lack of recognition or appreciation	Leadership plays favorites and you are not among them; accomplishments are not acknowledged.	Stifles innovation and saps energy.
Poor compensation and/or benefits	Compensation is rarely a satisfier; at best, this is neutral, as long as you are keeping up with the Joneses.	Saps motivation if you know you can make more with better benefits doing the same job elsewhere.

SEEK OUTSIDE HELP

When an executive determines that they have a high level of dissatisfaction, what help is available? Some career coaches specialize in this challenge; several are quoted throughout this book. Executive coaching is a popular choice; senior executives increasingly seek access to such professionals as part of their benefits package. Seeking an executive coach is not a casual undertaking. It requires a commitment of time and money. Perhaps the key benefit relates to things you might be missing: A coach can help you see a more complete picture and understand where and when a change may be indicated.

Executive coaching is now taught in some graduate schools and by the private sector, and certifications are available. It has also begun to permeate other forms of consulting. One friend who was a search consultant has shifted his practice toward executive coaching as he nears retirement, which he suggests is a natural transition from the way he has approached searches in the past.

Contrary to what might be assumed, those most adept at this kind of coaching are taught to "lead from behind," according to Michael Hein, an executive coach with MEDI Leadership who also happens to be a physician.[2] Executive coaches must recognize at the outset that the interaction is not about the coach; it is about the executive. These coaches are taught to see things through the executive's eyes and take themselves out of the picture. How the coach may feel about something is irrelevant. What matters is how an event makes the executive feel—and, perhaps, those around the executive. Better yet, the key focus relates to how the executive makes sense of what is happening. Ultimately, some coaching is involved in these engagements, but the interaction is driven entirely by what the executive is trying to achieve and what is preventing that.

As in athletics, the coach cannot play the game for the executive, but the coach can help the executive develop insights and tools, raise awareness, and adopt the right attitude in pursuit of their goal. In

---

2   Michael Hein, MD (executive coach with MEDI Leadership), in discussions with the author on January 24 and February 24, 2021.

our conversations, Hein spoke of the importance of his experience as a swimming coach; when he was at his best in that context, he was encouraging but didn't have to offer much direction; the athlete knew what to do to excel. Likewise, executive coaches make gains when they hear the feedback from their clients. They come to new understandings and new ways of looking at things.

People are used to telling others what to do. Executives certainly are. A coach resists this propensity to give advice. Instead, coaches steer the conversation to make the executive the object of discussion, not the subject. The coach and the executive partner then look at the object together. An executive who is the subject of the conversation tends to become defensive, which reduces the potential for learning. Coaches learn to identify teachable moments, when a question or suggestion can lead the client in a new direction of self-discovery. Fundamental to the interaction is understanding the executive's mindset first, and then the context in which the executive is operating. After that, it is all about fit: Does the executive fit into their idealized construct, or is that not possible in the current context (which can be a basis for frustration)? Simplistically, an executive may be in the wrong position or the wrong organization, or there may be some personal deficiencies that need to be addressed or new skills to be assimilated.

Many people would consider executive coaching a form of consulting. Executive coaches resemble a sports coach, in that they are trying to bring out the best in someone. This involves trying to enhance the executive's ability to examine the current situation, evaluate the source of their dissatisfaction, and consider what opportunities might be open to them that could fit their skills and interest. It is not coincidental that Quint Studer (2020, 3) begins his interesting book *The Busy Leader's Handbook* with the key skill, "Strive to be self-aware and coachable."

A solid executive coaching experience should leave something with the client. Ideally, they become more aware of their strengths and weaknesses and have a clearer understanding of what functions appeal to them most and where they might best fit professionally. You may find an executive coach helpful in completing your midcareer assessment.

VALIDATE THE NEED FOR CHANGE

Forbes online contributors have published several interesting articles on employment experiences over the years. At the core of this series is the famous Gallup employee survey statistics indicating that nearly two-thirds of US employees are disengaged (Adkins 2016; Harter 2018; Harter 2021). When I first read the observations, I was shocked. The series is so enlightening that key findings from several of these articles are shared here.

In one pre-pandemic article, Sturt and Nordstrom (2018) compiled the following statistics from a variety of sources:

- Fifty-eight percent of managers said they received no management training, according to CareerBuilder.com.
- Eighty-nine percent of bosses believe employees quit because they want more money, according to *The 7 Hidden Reasons Employees Leave*, by Leigh Branham—in reality, only 12 percent do.
- Fifty-eight percent of people say they trust strangers more than their own boss, according to a *Harvard Business Review* survey.
- Seventy-nine percent of those who quit their jobs do so because of "lack of appreciation," according to Global Studies. "People don't leave companies," say Sturt and Nordstrom. "They leave bosses."

A 2020 article by contributor Dawn Graham advised readers to use the disruption created by the pandemic and its hardships to address some of these dissatisfiers: "If you love what you do, then focus on how to continuously reinvent your skills to morph with the changing market. But, if you've been dreaming of making a major career change, now may be the perfect time."

Writing almost a year later, contributor Jack Kelly (2021), founder and CEO of the Compliance Work Group, acknowledged the impact of the pandemic on workplace satisfaction:

There's been a mood shift and change in the zeitgeist. We've learned firsthand how fragile life is. Many people have reexamined their lives. They realize they have a limited time here in this world. This has caused a bit of an existential moment. People have started thinking about what they've been doing and whether they want to continue on in the same job or career for the next five to 25 years. The results of this introspection clearly show that they want to make a move.

As you consider the issues raised in this chapter, think about which circumstances are under your control and which are not. I have long believed that if you are motivated by the true mission of helping others (e.g., servant leadership), it is almost impossible not to be inspired as part of a healthcare organization. Where a lack of inspiration exists, something else must be present: a need for change.

"Trust but verify," as President Reagan famously said. Some people who think they need a career change will find on further reflection that things can be reconciled in their current situation. This is not a grass is greener situation; it is more of a rush to judgment. A more positive frame is to suggest that the situation assessment becomes an *opportunity assessment*—testing the theory that there must be something better than what you are experiencing now.

RECOMMENDATIONS

1. A key part of making a midcareer assessment is determining the extent to which you are moving away from something (e.g., an executive position) or moving toward something (e.g., consulting); consulting has a certain allure.

2. Assessment should start with what you like and dislike about your current situation, and whether some of

these factors are under your control and can be changed (fixed).

3.   Another consideration is the changes in the marketplace that are beyond your control. How have job losses and furloughs influenced your current outlook?

4.   Be careful to not rely just on your judgment. Seek input from others, especially from people who know you and/ or are familiar with your situation.

5.   All professions have dissatisfiers that must be managed if one is to thrive. Verify that your current situation demands consideration of a career change.

REFERENCES

Adkins, A. 2016. "Employee Engagement in U.S. Stagnant in 2015." News, Gallup. Published January 13. https://news.gallup.com/ poll/188144/employee-engagement-stagnant-2015.aspx.

Conlan, C. 2021. "Career Tests: Our Top 10." Career Advice (blog), Monster. www.monster.com/career-advice/article/best-free-career-assessment-tools.

Dye, C. F., and B. D. Lee. 2016. *The Healthcare Leader's Guide to Actions, Awareness, and Perception*, 3rd ed. Chicago: Health Administration Press.

Graham, D. 2020. "Why This Is the Perfect Time to Make a Career Switch." Careers (blog), *Forbes*. Published June 13. www. forbes.com/sites/dawngraham/2020/06/13/why-this-is-a-perfect-time-to-make-a-career-switch/.

Harter, J. 2018. "Employee Engagement on the Rise in the U.S." News, Gallup. Published August 26. https://news.gallup. com/poll/241649/employee-engagement-rise.aspx.

————. 2021. "U.S. Employee Engagement Rises Following Wild 2020." Workplace, Gallup. Published February 26. www.gallup.com/workplace/330017/employee-engagement-rises-following-wild-2020.aspx.

Kelly, J. 2021. "Workers Are Quitting Their Jobs in Record Numbers, as the US Experiences a Booming Job Market." Careers (blog), *Forbes*. Published June 14. www.forbes.com/sites/jackkelly/2021/06/14/workers-are-quitting-their-jobs-in-record-numbers-as-the-us-experiences-a-booming-job-market/.

Mason, S. A. 2021. *The Healthcare Consultant's Handbook: Career Opportunities and Best Practices*. Chicago: Health Administration Press.

Rice, J. A., and F. Perry. 2012. *Healthcare Leadership Excellence: Creating a Career of Impact*. Chicago: Health Administration Press.

Stanley, N. 2016. Quoted in S. Rapacon, "Career Change Is the New Normal of Working." CNBC, April 29. www.cnbc.com/2016/04/26/career-change-is-the-new-normal-of-working.html. Brackets in original.

Studer, Q. 2020. *The Busy Leader's Handbook: How to Lead People and Places That Thrive*. Hoboken, NJ: John Wiley.

Sturt, D., and T. Nordstrom. 2018. "10 Shocking Workplace Stats You Need to Know." Careers (blog), *Forbes*. Published March 8. www.forbes.com/sites/davidsturt/2018/03/08/10-shocking-workplace-stats-you-need-to-know/#27b99d7ef3af.

CHAPTER 3

The Mounting Challenges
of Executive Roles

Many of us, especially in a beleaguered industry like healthcare,
reach a point where our job is no longer challenging, it has been too
challenging, or it is no longer appealing. Or maybe we have more
compelling things we would like to do.
—James Rice and Frankie Perry (2012)

THE PREVIOUS CHAPTER offered some techniques to help you complete a midcareer assessment. Taking stock of the current situation involves getting in touch with your current feelings. The second key component of a typical situation assessment—the marketplace— will influence those feelings.

As Yogi Berra once said, "The future ain't what it used to be." I have consulted with almost 500 healthcare organizations over more than 40 years—rural, suburban, and urban organizations of all sizes in 40 states. In that time, it has become clear to me that healthcare executives are experiencing significant stress. Management in general is being refocused on such things as diversity and inclusion, compliance, physician engagement, increased rigor related to measurable accountability and quality controls, and disparities related to social determinants of health, just to name a few. Some of these changes are occurring in virtually all industries; others are unique to healthcare. It is hard to keep up and know where to set priorities.

Some of the frustration of executives is clearly a symptom of loss of or lack of control. All the world's a stage, and one of the attractions of consulting is the opportunity to run your own show. Leaders have a natural tendency to seek some level of control as they guide a team or organization toward a better future. Yet, some things are simply beyond anyone's control. You must identify the source of your discomfort in the midcareer assessment, to the extent possible. Accordingly, let's pause to take stock of some of the market forces that affect the daily lives of healthcare executives. Many of these forces seem conflicting, resulting in intractable issues that are truly vexing. That the single largest user of healthcare services (the US government, through Medicare and Medicaid) pays hospitals less than the cost of providing services is a simple illustration of how irrational some elements of the system are (American Hospital Association 2021a).

MARKET FORCES ARE BEYOND YOUR CONTROL

A critical consideration in any assessment is to acknowledge at the outset that you cannot control the market. The previous chapter focused more on introspection—how things make you feel. You often cannot change the circumstances, but you can control your reactions. This is where emotional intelligence comes into play. In this chapter, I will discuss some of the more important factors causing dramatic changes in healthcare today. Some of these factors are subtle; some less so. As you review, see what resonates with you. If your level of frustration has been growing, this review sets up a test (How has this change affected me?) and prompts the realization that you can choose your reaction to these changes (Do I continue to do what I am doing?). Market changes can have a significant influence over our perception of the situation, often in ways that are not obvious. By shining a light on several of the more influential ones, I hope to help you see some of these stressors less as dissatisfiers and more as opportunities to influence change in the capacity of a consultant (i.e., change agent).

Many of these changes may be welcome, and some people are energized by them. At the same time, this never-ending cascade of change can sometimes overwhelm us, becoming a source of dissatisfaction. So many moving pieces are in the market that it behooves us to step back occasionally and try to bring some clarity to what often feels like a murky future. Although some elements of the future are quite clear, if unsettling, when it comes to management of healthcare organizations.

This discussion is complicated to say the least, and some sensitivity is required. I have long admired healthcare leaders who exhibit the patience required to effect change in large, complicated organizations over extended periods of time. Jack Welsh famously said that he managed to successfully implement only three key strategies during his long reign at General Electric. I have spent a lot of time cheerleading executive teams to create energy around a critical strategic initiative, so I know the resolve required to effect such change.

The last thing I want to do is to convince someone that things are not working out in healthcare. I consider this fatalistic; I have never felt this way, nor do I feel this way today. I have always approached work with executive teams in an optimistic fashion. Still, it's true that maintaining this kind of sustained effort is not easy. It's ironic when you think about it: If everything were great, there would be no need for consultants.

A key source of frustration for many executives is the relatively slow pace of change in healthcare. My consultant clock simply runs faster than a typical healthcare organization can change. This made several of the executive positions I held in healthcare organizations rather uncomfortable at times. That feeling of discomfort was often clearer than the precise source of the discomfort.

Few of us relish the idea of living in a fishbowl, but being a healthcare executive often feels like that. Everyone has an opinion about healthcare, and many of them are not positive, often because of a bad personal experience. I harbor no need to convince you that healthcare has challenges; instead I want to help you wrestle with your inner self so you can determine more precisely what may be contributing to your discomfort. Perhaps one key tenet that most of us in healthcare share is the desire to make a difference—to foster needed change. Attempting to do as an executive may not be as effective as it once appeared. This may lead to a more serious exploration of other career options.

KEY MARKET CHANGES IN HEALTHCARE

It is easy to get lost discussing key market factors. The shift toward value-based care is often presented as a consensus vision, but this consensus has not yet translated into any level of proven changes (e.g., materially lower costs) that will achieve the desired outcome (i.e., there is no clear cause and effect relationship). Since the pandemic, change seems ubiquitous in society, yet the transformation taking place in healthcare remains unique in its scope and scale. As Rice and Perry (2012, 26) wrote in *Healthcare Leadership Excellence*, "While healthcare can be considered a microcosm of society in some ways, the level of complexity in healthcare management is disproportionately high compared to that of the corporate world in general."

When I am forced to be concise about key market changes, these three issues rise to the top: the slow pace of change, the redefinition of healthcare, and the unique nature of healthcare in the market. See which one resonates most with you.

Healthcare Is Slow to Change

Clearly, responding to the chaotic and at times contradictory issues confronting healthcare today represents a serious challenge. Attempts are being made to alter the fundamental economics of healthcare. The problem seems clear enough: Too many Americans are unable to afford healthcare in its current form. Healthcare in the US costs much more than it should and has yet to achieve high reliability in the quality of services delivered. It is the solution that remains elusive. The private health insurance market (versus employer-based insurance) remains unstable and expensive. Artificially low insurance premiums, limited or subsidized through the Affordable Care Act (ACA), are eclipsed by skyrocketing copayments and deductibles. Policymakers successfully increased coverage by extending Medicaid to more people,[1] but an objective review of the data verifies that healthcare today is no more affordable than it was before the ACA. It is understandable that executives are increasingly uncomfortable when the industry that employs them is the target of so much discontent and controversy.

> **Healthcare in the US costs much more than it should and has yet to achieve high reliability in the quality of services delivered.**

Healthcare and Medicine Are Being Redefined

While it can be hard to digest for many people who have devoted their careers to the healthcare industry, much of what is done in hospitals today has little to do with health and more to do with illness. This has resulted in wholesale introspection regarding the merits of continuing to operate this way. Study of social determinants of health has shown that significant disparities remain in the delivery of services, and more must be done if we are to truly improve the health of our citizens.[2] Some segments of our society undeniably suffer poor health because of illiteracy, poverty, the breakdown of the nuclear family, and lack of access to critical resources.

---

1 In hindsight, it is incredible that policymakers chose Medicaid as the core of the ACA, given that Medicaid is often branded as insurance for "poor people." Many of the people who now qualify for a subsidy under the ACA have incomes well above the poverty level, and likely resent being so connected.

2 See chapter 15 in *The Healthcare Consultant's Handbook* for a more detailed discussion of social determinants of health.

The result of this newfound enlightenment is the requirement to restructure the system more around key factors that influence health—to reduce the incidence of disease by reaching upstream and focusing more attention on housing, food supply, and other environmental influences. According to an important study by Fraze and colleagues (2019), only 24 percent of hospitals and 16 percent of physician practices reported screening for food insecurity, housing instability, utility needs, transportation needs, and interpersonal violence. Our ability to intervene in this regard is severely limited by this lack of screening. The study's conclusion is important enough to repeat in its entirety from the abstract:

This study's findings suggest that few US physician practices and hospitals screen patients for all 5 key social needs associated with health outcomes. Practices that serve disadvantaged patients report higher screening rates. The role of physicians and hospitals in meeting patients' social needs is likely to increase as more take on accountability for cost under payment reform. Physicians and hospitals may need additional resources to screen for or address patients' social needs.

A system built on the appearance of symptoms is not the way to promote health.

Healthcare's Unique Nature Makes It an Easy Target

Have you ever seen a person from general industry come into an executive role within a healthcare organization? This once-rare transition is becoming more common as the transformation of healthcare is pushed along and the industry embraces novel approaches. How often has a board member of a nonprofit hospital been attracted to the relatively high salary of a hospital CEO and thrust themselves politically into that leadership position when it comes open, only to fail miserably and put the organization through significant turmoil? As Peter Drucker is credited with first saying, culture eats strategy for lunch. These new executives from other industries usually meet with one of two fates, and swiftly: (1) they require major coaching once they realize their previous experience is not enough and the demands of a healthcare organization are quite different, or (2) they simply flame out and their leadership is rejected at all levels.

HEALTHCARE MANAGEMENT IS BEING DISRUPTED

Now that we have covered the three key market changes that have undeniably added complexity and made it more challenging to be successful as a healthcare executive, we need to examine some deeper issues influencing healthcare executives—disruptors affecting the status of healthcare management. As I have considered the plight of leaders of the future, several critical market factors stand out to me as subtle but substantive changes that are having a dramatic impact on the industry. Taken together, these factors have displaced some executives and made others less satisfied with their work. There are several of these factors, and each merits some discussion.

Industry Consolidation

Perhaps the most obvious change in the healthcare industry is the dramatic reduction in the number of independent acute care hospitals in the United States. There is a certain "chicken and egg" factor here—what came first, utility regulation or consolidation? Each seems to contribute to the other. When I first started in the 1970s, there were over 7,000 mostly independent hospitals in the United States. As of 2021, there are around 5,500, with the majority now consolidated into a few hundred large and growing regional health systems (American

Hospital Association 2021b). The coronavirus pandemic has created even greater vulnerability, especially among small rural hospitals.

The central concern arising from this decades-long trend is a feeling of loss of control. The freedom that an executive enjoys in leading a healthcare organization is being significantly curtailed. Further, the consolidation of hospitals into regional and multi-regional systems now includes physician consolidation and payer consolidation, and integrated regional systems are now attempting to integrate all these components.

The strategic challenge for every hospital during this disruptive period is that their previous core business (inpatient services) is declining rapidly (i.e., fewer admissions) while their new core business (community-based ambulatory care) is greatly expanding and has far more competition because there are fewer barriers to entry. The pandemic may have temporarily hidden this decline in hospitals' core business behind high hospitalization rates and high utilization of critical care beds, but I believe the financial losses experienced by the industry will eventually come into focus as a result of this overall decline.

To explain the impact of this transformational process, one must deal with difficult trade-offs for different stakeholders. Every dollar dedicated to off-campus ambulatory care is a dollar diverted from the critical ongoing capital needs of the traditional core business. Those providers whose income is dependent on traditional inpatient services have faced a dual threat—the decline in payments for inpatient services (notably for government patients) and the increased investment required to have a reasonable footprint in ambulatory care.

The Primacy of Demographics

Changing utilization has made community hospitals more dependent on local demographics and created vulnerability, especially where population trends are stagnant or decreasing. The result has been even more mergers and consolidations. This trend is similar to the disappearance of local banks in many rural areas. The demographic dependency is reinforced by Melody Goodman's shocking observation in 2014 that zip code is more important than genetics in determining longevity. "If you put my demographic information into a social epidemiology model," she told the symposium for the Department of Biostatistics Summer Program in Quantitative Sciences, "I am more likely to be a teen mom than a Harvard grad" (Healthbox 2019; Roeder 2014).

This statement gets to the essence of social determinants of health. Each community faces different demographic factors, whose management will have a significant impact on the overall health of residents. The challenge is figuring out how these factors present in each community and structuring the local health system properly to affect these key factors. Talk about a strategic challenge for future healthcare organizations!

Public Utility Regulation

Rates for a public utility (e.g., water service, gas and electric service) are fixed and set by others outside the organization. Utilities also face regulations that govern much of their daily activities. Sound familiar? This new world of regulated healthcare has greatly reduced some of the freedoms that executives enjoy in the private sector. Medicare (which is to say, the US government) is now the market maker for prices in healthcare.

In most US industries, private enterprises set prices according to how they intend to position their products or services, largely according to competitive factors. Under a utility model, the enterprise essentially trades in this right to charge different rates under a one-size-fits-all approach. In return, the utility is granted a monopoly or oligopoly license to serve a defined market. Some managers are attracted to the challenges and autonomy of running their own business; free to succeed and free to fail, but with a lot of flexibility regarding the direction that you take. A public utility manager does not have this freedom.

This change is not unique to healthcare; more and more economic sectors in the United States are moving toward utility-style regulation.[3] Have you had an experience lately with any of the emerging utilities: cable and phone companies/carriers? In most cases, one or maybe two utilities dominate a market for each of these growing services. Because competition is limited, their future business is both stable and predictable. In the case of healthcare, this utility orientation may not have arisen by intent. Rather, it evolved out of a realization that healthcare costs too much and we have otherwise been unable to curb annual increases in excess of the consumer price index. However, one should beware of the deceit of lowering prices while having virtually no effect on costs. No business entity can survive this for long.

The sophisticated buyer is the enemy of a public utility. Buyers require choices so they can compare the performance of one provider to another based on their needs and preferences. By definition, a utility orientation limits choice dramatically and is effectively a one-size-fits-all strategy that typically applies a pay-as-you-go orientation.

Importantly, quality of service offered by utilities is often abysmal; they have long been "plagued by bad customer service" (Nisen 2013). This is not a coincidence. Absent competition, they have no incentive to get better; the customer has no realistic options that might threaten the utility. These utilities effectively have monopoly power. While the ACA ("Obamacare") was supposed to expand competition, the exact opposite has occurred—health insurance companies left most small markets, leaving many counties with only one carrier that dominates. In other words, over time, in the absence of competition through a utility model, choice will erode and the quality of services offered will decline; the utility simply has no incentive to upgrade the service (i.e., threat of competition) because

---

3   It has long been the strategist's challenge to help businesses avoid becoming commodities and thus ruled by price alone over other potential features (e.g., user interface, service experience, appearance, interoperability).

there can be no return on this investment through growth—they already "own" the market. The typical utility is solely focused on keeping costs low through standardization and automation; they have no incentive to customize their services in ways that connect positively for the consumer.

A critical shortcoming of public utilities is their inability or unwillingness to address problems; what retailers refer to as *service recovery*. You know people who have had such experiences, because they go out of their way to share these negative experiences with others. It is no coincidence that this discussion of public utility regulation fits how critics currently refer to healthcare.

Drive for Greater Standardization in Performance

In 2018, the reform-minded CEOs of Amazon, Berkshire Hathaway, and JPMorgan Chase announced that they were uniting to form Haven Health. In 2021, after Haven Health failed to materialize anything meaningful, the venture ended in ignominy and they went their separate ways. One of the architects of the failure, none other than the Wizard of Omaha, Warren Buffett, characterized it as follows: "We were fighting a tapeworm in the American economy, and the tapeworm won" (Haefner 2021).

The battle lines for reform were drawn with the publication of *To Err Is Human* (Institute of Medicine 2000), which suggested that an estimated 98,000 people die each year from avoidable clinical errors. In other words, there is unacceptable and preventable variation in performance among providers and other healthcare organizations (e.g., hospitals). The desire to reduce unnecessary cost drives greater standardization and increased automation of repetitive functions; one example is robotic surgery. However, some of these efficiency gains can have a negative impact on hospital culture and the people affected. Managers in such situations may experience loss of control. This is significant where managers never felt like they had a lot of control in the first place, because providers are offering the services, not managers.

Impact of Consumerism

Each patient presents with a unique set of needs and challenges, not to mention aspirations and preferences, so providers increasingly try to offer customized care. The introduction of consumerism is slowly bringing healthcare closer to the retail and hospitality industries. Ultimately this will mean a far greater role for the individual consumer, giving them the ability to actively seek customized approaches to health. Failure to acknowledge the vital role of the consumer in transforming healthcare would be consequential. As noted by Donohue and Klasko (2020, 61), "the reality still comes down to flesh-and-blood providers stepping up and respecting the consumer's point of view, and the idea that consumers do in fact have some choice in where they go for healthcare services. Without this respect, it is hard to imagine any healthcare provider's offerings truly connecting with consumers."

The unique training and orientation of medical professionals (i.e., scientists) matched with the growing sophistication of management systems and structures (e.g., matrix management) makes for a unique brew that is ever-changing. Introduce the dynamic of the experience-seeking consumer (previously referred to as "patients") and you have a remarkable formula for change. Complexity is inversely correlated with predictability, adding increasing uncertainty to the mix. It is thus understandable that some executives develop a growing feeling of futility when it comes to improving healthcare in measurable ways. Burnout is a common result of tilting at windmills, as *Don Quixote* made clear.

Changing Management Structures

Management of healthcare organizations is undergoing dramatic structural changes. Before consolidation, the CEO of the freestanding hospital handled everything—regulatory changes, community relations, fundraising, recruiting physicians and other staff, managing a culture of safety, reducing costs, and reallocating capital to grow the enterprise. These were prized positions that were sought after by highly educated, bright, energetic executives.

Within a large, integrated regional system, much of this work is now provided through corporate resources, reducing the responsibilities (and burdens) that remain local. This consolidation of functions is true not only of the CEO position but also of functional leadership in the other C-suite areas, such as marketing and communications, finance, information services, planning, and patient care services. Mind you, consolidation of these functions represents important efficiency gains.

Most of these regional systems now have a dual-reporting structure: a direct link to corporate along with a dotted-line relationship to the local chief administrative officer (no longer CEO). Through this assimilation process, which is integral to the evolution of regional healthcare systems, the local chief administrative officer functions more as a manager responsible for performance and less as a leader responsible for vision and execution. This is a clear diminution of responsibilities at the local level. When these changes occur post-merger, I have often seen people leave for a position in another independent hospital that will restore some of the roles and responsibilities they previously enjoyed.

DYAD MANAGEMENT IS BECOMING PERVASIVE

One key management change deserves more discussion: the dyad structure in hospital management. According to Alan Belasen (2019, 7), "with the increase in size and complexity of health systems, it becomes more challenging for a single leader to possess the skills, knowledge, or perspectives necessary for optimal decisions." Many years ago, Peter Drucker (1988, 52) wrote that hospitals were the most complex organizations ever created, describing hospital management as a "two-headed monster." As he explained it, this complexity is born of the reality that there are two different professional aspects of this sector: medical and nonmedical.

If someone as knowledgeable about management as Peter Drucker draws a distinction between managing a healthcare enterprise and another commercial business, there must be something to it. Healthcare boasts the most educated workforce of any human enterprise. The unique elements in the culture of a healthcare organization are not lost on those of us who have spent any time in healthcare management. The consensus decision-making structure is but one example of what tends to make healthcare challenging and cumbersome at times. These traditional hierarchical structures may no longer be effective for the complexity that seems to be increasing as a result of continuing consolidation.

Belasen has done a detailed assessment of the dyad structure and its implications for clinical integration, synthesizing the expertise of academics and practitioners with organizational theory to help explain the approach. He proposes a dyad leadership framework with a focus on the roles and responsibilities of dyad leaders. Belasen's main thesis is that evolving regional health systems should be viewed as a complex adaptive system (CAS), which is distinct from the more common view of a healthcare system as merely "complicated." More accurately, health systems today involve multiple entities striving to become more interdependent, thus meeting the definition of a CAS. The CAS label best represents the challenge of offering clinically integrative care.

Done right, successful integration strikes the right balance of exploiting existing resources (e.g., core competencies) and exploring new resources and capabilities. Such a perspective describes complexity as involving "diverse, interdependent and semi-autonomous actors" that have the "capacity to self-organize" while functioning in an integrative fashion (Belasen 2019, 21). But our task here is less to understand CAS and more to understand the implications of dyad management for healthcare executives.

I have long been an advocate of dyad structures, notably for clinical service lines. Dye and Lee (2016) and Belasen (2019) each suggest that this model should be extended throughout the enterprise. In my experience, relatively few organizations have extended this model that thoroughly, though this may change. A few pioneers that have done so with some success include Swedish Medical Center in Seattle and ChristianaCare in Newark, Delaware. But fully implementing a dyad approach remains a difficult and expensive undertaking.

The rub is not only that relatively few physicians have been educated for or are inclined to pursue such management positions, but also that "not every physician or executive is well suited for coleadership" (Belasen 2019, 8). I suggest that dyad leadership is a form of what is more commonly known as matrix management. Matrix management violates one long-held tenet of organizational behavior: unity of command, where an employee only has one boss. There are legitimate concerns about how effective management can be if an individual reports to more than one person. How do we resolve conflicts? Are we just setting up this person to fail? Not everyone is cut out for this role; indeed, many employees require more hands-on supervision than is comfortable for two bosses to share. Which half of the responsibilities (clinical or administrative) wins out when?

Simply put, some executives have not and will not embrace this approach, which resistance may correlate with how long those managers have functioned in the more traditional structure. The tug-of-war between things clinical and things administrative will forever be a challenge in healthcare.

UNSETTLING IMPLICATIONS

As a consequence of these dramatic changes, some healthcare executives have begun to question their comfort going forward. Consolidation has resulted in fewer CEO positions with a traditional scope of responsibility. For some executives, the path to a CEO position has become less clear, if it is even possible. Larger regional systems are increasingly driven by centralized policies, leaving local managers to become more operational and less strategic in their duties.

New careerists may not see any difference, because everything is relatively new to them. But to the seasoned executive who has pursued the straight path to greater responsibilities and who has had a taste of autonomy while leading a freestanding, independent enterprise, these changes are disruptive. Thus, more midcareer and senior executives are likely to seek alternative ways to foster change in healthcare.

WE ARE AT AN INFLECTION POINT

We find ourselves at what strategists typically call an *inflection point*. Perhaps much of this discussion comes across as a criticism of key trends in healthcare today. That was not my intent. There may be some longing for the pioneer days of the past, but I believe these factors will be positive for the industry once things settle down a bit. The problem is one of balance and pace, not to mention finding ways to avoid losing sight of the impact of the social determinants of health and the individual consumer on the future delivery of healthcare services. Times have changed.

Any attempt to summarize the discussion in this chapter will fall short. But one conclusion seems painfully clear—healthcare executives of the future will need help navigating the enormous changes coming their way. This is an open invitation to consultants to forge partnerships with key clients in order to effect timely changes that will be necessary to better connect with the needs of society, customized to better meet the unique needs of individual consumers (patients).

> This is an open invitation to consultants to forge partnerships with key clients in order to effect timely changes that will be necessary to better connect with the needs of society, customized to better meet the unique needs of individual consumers (patients).

If one feels increasingly powerless to effect needed change from an executive platform, how then does it follow that consultants can make a difference? As it happens, the same things that are the source of dissatisfaction for executives are often at the heart of the value proposition that consultants exploit for clients that are trying to make sense of it all. As you will see in some of the interviews in chapter 5, many executives who made the career change felt they were able to have a greater impact using a consulting platform than they could as an executive. They were able to influence more change among more people, and to do it faster and better.

Yes, consultants have a tremendous opportunity to foster real change. Consulting firms play an important role when focused on accelerated cost reductions and operational improvements, in addition to the creative application of new technologies such as artificial intelligence, virtual health, and related innovations. The critical success factors common to retail and hospitality industries are slowly being integrated into healthcare boardrooms and executive suites. At some level, these innovations, which have been at the core of many consulting practices focused on other industries, bode well for midcareer and senior executives who are looking to leverage their experience to integrate new concepts into the cultures of these emerging regional health systems.

RECOMMENDATIONS

1. Rapid changes in healthcare have left executives feeling more vulnerable and powerless to lead critical changes.

2. There is some dissatisfaction with the ways healthcare is changing and the implications of these changes. Conflicting policies and regulations are making healthcare more of a target and generating increasing frustration. At the same time, this presents opportunities for consultants to intervene.

3.   There is also dissatisfaction with the reality that many if not most of these transformational changes are beyond the control of executives and will likely take a long time to play out.

4.   While the level and pace of change are disruptive to an executive, they also represent key opportunities for consultants. Consumerism, virtual health, and social determinants of health represent new horizons for thought leadership.

5.   Changing management structures, including dyad management, demand significant changes in how these organizations are managed. There is a role for consultants in helping management teams make this transformation.

REFERENCES

American Hospital Association. 2021a. "Fact Sheet: Underpayment by Medicare and Medicaid." Published January 7. www.aha.org/fact-sheets/2020-01-07-fact-sheet-underpayment-medicare-and-medicaid.

————. 2021b. "Fast Facts on U.S. Hospitals, 2021." www.aha.org/statistics/fast-facts-us-hospitals.

Belasen, A. T. 2019. *Dyad Leadership and Clinical Integration: Driving Change, Aligning Strategies*. Chicago: Health Administration Press.

Donohue, R., and S. K. Klasko. 2020. *Patient No Longer: Why Healthcare Must Deliver the Care Experience That Consumers Want and Expect*. Chicago: Health Administration Press.

Drucker, P. F. 1988. "The Coming of the New Organization." *Harvard Business Review* 66 (1): 45–53. https://hbr.org/1988/01/the-coming-of-the-new-organization.

Dye, C. F., and B. D. Lee. 2016. *The Healthcare Leader's Guide to Actions, Awareness, and Perception*, 3rd ed. Chicago: Health Administration Press.

Fraze, T. K., A. L. Brewster, V. A. Lewis, L. B. Beidler, G. F. Murray, and C. H. Colla. 2019. "Prevalence of Screening for Food Insecurity, Housing Instability, Utility Needs, Transportation Needs, and Interpersonal Violence by US Physician Practices and Hospitals." *JAMA Network Open* 2 (9): e1911514. https://doi.org/10.1001/jamanetworkopen.2019.11514.

Haefner, M. 2021. "Buffett on Failed Haven Venture: The 'Tapeworm Won'." *Becker's Hospital Review*, May 3. www.beckershospitalreview.com/hospital-management-administration/buffett-on-failed-haven-venture-the-tapeworm-won.html.

Healthbox. 2019. "Root Causes of Health." www.healthbox.com/insights/root-causes-of-health/.

Institute of Medicine. 2000. *To Err Is Human: Building a Safer Health System*. Washington, DC: National Academies Press.

Nisen, M. 2013. "The 15 Worst Companies for Customer Service." Business Insider, January 8. www.businessinsider.com/15-worst-companies-for-customer-service-2013-1.

Rice J. A., and F. Perry. 2012. *Healthcare Leadership Excellence: Creating a Career of Impact*. Chicago: Health Administration Press.

Roeder, A. 2014. "Zip Code Better Predictor of Health than Genetic Code." News, Harvard School of Public Health. Published July 24. www.hsph.harvard.edu/news/features/zip-code-better-predictor-of-health-than-genetic-code/.

PART II

WHAT?

If a career change is warranted, what options do I have?

DEPENDING ON WHAT you have determined thus far, you may be concerned about your current situation and the prospects for improvement, or you may be more excited about the opportunities for a career change. Either way, a change is in order. The question, then, is what kind of change.

Rather than jump immediately to consulting, you should consider other worthy options. You don't have to choose yet; at this point in the Career Change Decision Framework, you only have to recognize the disruption that a career change would entail; a simple job change would be less stressful, if applicable.

Do you only need a change "in place," implying that the current situation can be fixed and you can remain where you are? Or do you need a change of venue (to a different employer, a different geographic location, or both)? The profiles in these three chapters (supplemented by the full stories in the appendixes) provide examples of why people make career changes and describe some of the many possibilities that exist.

Career changes can come in many forms. Part II also addresses some of the challenges executives may experience in a career change, whatever form it takes.

Chapter 4. Identifying the Options
Chapter 5. What Others Have Experienced
Chapter 6. The Road Less Traveled

Identifying the Options

The pandemic has created both challenges and opportunities for Americans, leading many to consider the future of their personal and professional lives and, in some instances, a change in employment.
—Morneau Shepell (2020)

You ARE NOT alone in considering a possible career change. The quote at the beginning of this chapter appears in a news release from Morneau Shepell, now LifeWorks ("One in Four Americans Consider a Career Change as Pandemic Upends Professional Future," December 9, 2020). At the time, the firm's Mental Health Index was on a months-long downward "trend below the pre-pandemic benchmark, led by significant anxiety and depression." According to that survey,

Overall, 24 percent of respondents indicated that the pandemic has led them to consider a job or career change. Thirty-seven percent of respondents under the age of 40 said they are considering a job/career change, compared to only 13 percent of respondents over the age of 50 who indicated the same. Additionally, 19 percent said they are undecided, suggesting a greater proportion of workers may be at risk of turnover.

At the same time, consulting is becoming a more popular option. For new graduates, consulting offers "career capital," which is considered "highly transferable" (Todd 2019). In other words, the consulting experience is recognized as an asset regardless of what comes after. The story may be somewhat different for people who are halfway through their career, but consulting is growing more attractive to experienced executives as well.

CAREER PHASES

Options should be considered in the context of your entire career. James Citrin (2015) has provided a discussion of career phases that offers a helpful perspective in his book *The Career Playbook*, published when he was the leader of Spencer Stuart's CEO search practice and a member of its worldwide board of directors. Written mostly for young

Exhibit 4.1. The Six Phases of Your Career

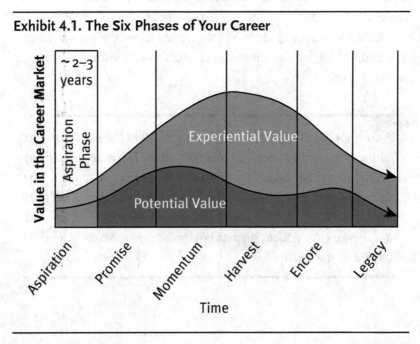

Source: Reprinted from Citrin (2015).

professionals just setting out, *The Career Playbook* is about getting a job and turning it into a rewarding career. Citrin's six-phase model (exhibit 4.1) is accompanied by sound advice related to each phase.

The phases are self-explanatory, but the depiction provides additional insights. The first three stages—aspiration, promise, and momentum—clearly relate to the early years of a career, when the value proposition might best be described as translating promise into achievements. Note that the experiential value curve is steep during these early phases. The reliance on potential value becomes less important as experience increases. Another way of describing this is that an initial focus on management is eventually displaced by a focus on leadership. This shift is discussed in some depth later.[1]

As an example of how these phases play out, Citrin attaches some timeframes to each. He describes the Momentum Phase as tending to "run from your early thirties through your early or mid-forties, when you establish your track record and reputation in the marketplace. . . . The Momentum Phase is when the value of your experience will overtake your potential value as you increase your professional standing by capitalizing on your experience, stature, skills, and expertise" (Citrin 2015, 24–5).

Because his book is more focused on early careerists, Citrin discusses the first three phases in some detail and relegates the last three phases—harvest, encore, and legacy (exhibit 4.2)—to an appendix. For our purposes, with a focus on the midcareerist, these last three phases are most applicable. Quoting Citrin (28), "The key principle in the latter parts of your career is to find ways to redefine your experiences and apply them in new and hopefully valuable contexts." As you move further away from the early phases of a career, "you will inevitably yearn for all the uncertainty, the drama, and the sheer sense of possibility that you felt when you were an aspiring young professional." You will find that a few people who were interviewed for this book said something very similar about their transition to consulting.

---

1   See "Collaborative Leadership" in chapter 9.

Exhibit 4.2. The Latter Three Phases of Your Career

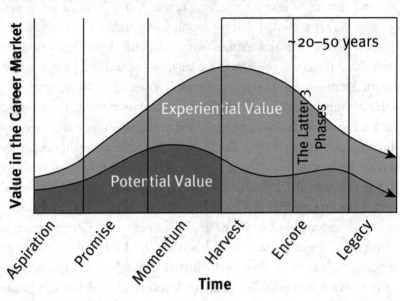

Source: Reprinted from Citrin (2015).

For many people, career progress starts to slow in the latter three phases. Rather than measuring progress against the more rapid advancement in earlier phases of your career, "the key to continuing to advance through your Harvest Phase is to keep learning and find ways to convert all of your experiences into new situations" (Citrin 2015, 206). This is where consulting may come into play for certain executives. As these three phases may last 20–50 years, you still have significant time to provide valued service in your career, and consulting is undeniably one of the best ways to do so.

Here I want to introduce you to another relevant book: Jonathan Dison's *The Consulting Economy* (2017). Dison takes the somewhat novel point of view that consulting is a great opportunity anytime in one's career, which supports the concept of the gig economy (Mason 2021). This makes some sense when you consider his take on why consultants are hired: "Companies have realized that it makes more sense to outsource the bulk of their work to an external workforce of consultants and contractors who they pay on a project-by-project basis, as opposed to hiring full time, salaried employees for every project" (Dison 2017, 26). Like Citrin, Dison identifies different periods of one's career, but he suggests consulting can work in any of them:

- *Early Career: Get Paid to Learn*
- *Midcareer: Make Your Job Support the Busiest Time of Your Life*
- *Late Career: Monetize Your Experience and Relationships*
- *Semiretirement: Work on Your Terms and Never Stress About Money*

"When you hear the term 'consultant,' you most likely conjure up images of suits instructing high-level management on strategy," he notes in the cover copy. "But the trade of consulting is so much more—and so much bigger—than you might imagine." He stated at the time that the $425 billion consulting industry was on pace to double, meaning most professionals will one day be consultants instead of employees.

NON-CONSULTING CAREER OPTIONS

Consistent with the Career Change Decision Framework, we will now review potential career choices. As previously noted, the strategic question in any form of disciplined analysis is to compare consulting to other options. The baseline for this comparison is what you have been doing until this point, but why limit the comparison to consulting or the status quo? What about the other options that might be available besides consulting?

Too many strategic plans in too many healthcare organizations articulate a clear strategy without discussing the alternatives that were also considered. If you select consulting for your next step, you should be clear that you are choosing it over other opportunities. Much may be learned from considering these other opportunities. Perhaps you would consider becoming an advisor in an IT firm. What could you learn from rejecting this option? For example, "I don't want to be an IT advisor" is a valuable lesson.

This chapter will not attempt to compare the skill sets required of these other opportunities to those of consulting. That exercise is left to the reader. Involving your network is essential as you investigate that. Discuss your options with the people who know you best and have worked with you. Your network will influence which options might be most attractive and a best fit.

The non-consulting options for an experienced healthcare executive generally fall into five categories: interim management, work in medical products or medical supplies, going back to school, joining a private equity firm or a start-up, or joining an association or advocacy group. While some of these options share skills in common with consulting, they also differ in some important ways, as you will see from the discussion that follows.

Interim Management

Interim management is discussed in detail in *The Healthcare Consultant's Handbook*. A summary of that discussion is offered here. Interim management can be considered similar to consulting, but the differences are important.[2]

There are many temporary staffing firms, some of which are quite successful. A few focus exclusively on interim management, while others might rather characterize themselves as professional search

---

2   This use of *interim management* does not include cases where someone is waiting to be vetted for a permanent position and temporarily carries the title of "Interim." Rather, this is the more formal interim structure, where an outsider comes in for a specified period to achieve a specific goal and then leaves.

firms (operating under contingency or retained search contracts[3]) that also offer interim personnel. Not all search firms offer temporary staffing, and most consulting firms do not offer interim management, other than on an exception basis (e.g., for existing clients).

When the arrangement is properly structured, the value of interim management is that the incumbent is not attempting to hold the job; rather, they are there for a specific, short period to make needed changes that are otherwise difficult—changes not likely to be made by someone focused on keeping the job. Some churches use this as a form of succession planning, often with great success, when a pastor retires after a long and successful run leading their congregation. (Many churches are small and not able to retain a successor on staff.)

There is a danger in confusing consulting with interim management. Consultants have no authority to make changes; they are advisors. The advice of consultants may be accepted or rejected. In this advisory role, the consultant must create some space between the advice and the person acting on the advice. Shifting from *advisor* to *actor* risks a loss of perspective. It is hard enough to remain detached from a situation in order to offer dispassionate advice. Allowing yourself to get so close to the situation that you lose perspective runs the risk of you losing objectivity, both in your eyes and in the eyes of the client.

Medical Products or Supplies

A clear understanding of the medical–industrial complex[4] encompasses the broad array of companies that support the supply chain so

---

3 Contingency search is where there is no obligation to pay the recruiter unless they come up with the candidate who is selected by the client—a candidate who may be competing with candidates from other firms. In contrast, retained search is exclusive with the client for a specified period depending on the difficulty of the search.

4 The phrase *medical–industrial complex* gained popularity following an October 23, 1980, editorial in the *New England Journal of Medicine* (https://doi.org/10.1056/NEJM198010233031703).

essential to the delivery of healthcare services. This includes pharmaceutical firms, medical device manufacturers, and related suppliers, as well as their elaborate distribution networks. A key function common to all these supporting organizations is sales. These companies tend to have elaborate sales training programs, and their salespeople (or *reps*), come from different backgrounds in healthcare. Nursing is a favorite, as is administration.

The crucial consideration here is that sales involves a compensation approach based on commissions; something most healthcare managers have never experienced. It is one thing to be a salaried internal consultant to the sales team (recommended), another to be a commissioned member of the sales team (which I strongly do not recommend unless the commission is treated as a bonus on top of a base salary). I know a few seasoned, competitive executives who thought this transition would not be a big deal. They all found out differently.

I have some personal experience with this as well. The position was structured as a national representative and was incorrectly set up under a commission-based model. Because my territory overlapped with all existing salespeople (I was to be "added" to their team), any commissions I earned would be shared with others. In other words, people had to give up or share income in order to bring me in on deals. The results were predicable. Regrettably, lack of familiarity with this approach and my trusting nature made for an uncomfortable run in this position.

Selling products is different from selling services. Some service-based consulting firms also sell products (e.g., HR benefits such as life insurance or pension plans), often on a subscription basis (e.g., software licenses, membership in an affinity group). Each product has a different price point and customized sales approach.

Back to School

Another option, especially popular during an economic downturn, is to return to school for another degree, such as an MBA or PhD.

Before the COVID-19 pandemic, the relative value of an MBA was a matter of some debate, and enrollments were declining. But with the impact of the virus and the related economic slowdown, this once again became an attractive option. Furthermore, it is increasingly possible to complete a graduate degree remotely, as schools have retooled their program offerings to provide many or all of their classes online. Another notable trend is the ability to complete an MBA at some of the highest rated schools in the country in three semesters instead of four.

It will take the economy some time to return to full health following the pandemic. Completing additional education during the interim could make a lot of sense, especially if a firm is willing to help foot the bill in return for a future commitment.

Private Equity or Start-Up Firm

Healthcare has long been a favorite target of angel investors and private equity firms. Many well-known healthcare firms started out with funds from private equity firms attempting to exploit a niche in the market. Pharmaceutical companies are well known for letting small entrepreneurial firms come up with new drugs that they then purchase and bring to market. As the largest single segment of the US economy, healthcare thrives on new technologies and represents significant scale opportunities for the inventor who comes up with a new idea (e.g., magnetic resonance imaging, electronic health records, telemedicine, wearable technologies).

Private equity firms thrive by marrying risk-based funding to new ideas such as these, and often get involved in the sale and acquisition of existing entities. Some groups specialize in providing hands-on advisory services to start-up firms, helping them grow and eventually be sold or rolled into something larger. Some of these start-up firms end up going public. Private equity is a vast field, and firms can be highly specialized on such things as energy, supplies, drugs, equipment, consulting services, and health-related assets. Some groups even partner with consulting firms, providing vital capital to fund growth and expansion.

Private equity survives by accruing significant returns on invested capital. Return targets can be aggressive, with equally aggressive timelines. It does no good for these firms to sit on the sidelines. They place moneys with fast-growth firms with the understanding that some will fail and the hope that a few will be highfliers able to provide significant returns, to even out the overall return to investors. To say the least, these are high-stress jobs with lots of pressure to perform.

This discussion would be less than complete without acknowledging private equity's less attractive aspects. Movies and books such as *Wall Street*, *The Bonfire of the Vanities*, and *The Big Short* have highlighted the seedy side of this segment of the economy. Mitt Romney, when he was running for president, was criticized in the media for his founding of Bain Capital, which has a reputation for buying firms and then making money by selling the pieces as separate businesses. The criticism is that, while this disassembly makes lots of money for the bankers, it tends to displace many workers and it is questionable whether any real value is created through such actions. As someone who was displaced at one point in my career by just such an acquisition, I confess some sympathy for this point of view. Yet I also know several people who shifted from executive management in healthcare to being either advisors or investors in private equity firms and have made good on this option.

The ability to build your own business—either by boosting start-ups with private equity or by building your own start-up, possibly with private equity backing—is clearly attractive to some people. Suffice it to say that all the rules of starting any new business apply to healthcare. Entrepreneurship has been the backbone of the US economy for decades now, but it is not for the faint of heart. Getting others involved and going after investors is beyond the scope of this book; I am simply raising the option for consideration.

Associations or Advocacy Groups

I spent part of my early career at the American Hospital Association. This experience offered insights into the field and exposed me to the many facets of association work and advocacy. I spent several years focused on the effects of government relations on the healthcare industry.[5] As a member of the strategic planning committee, I was also exposed to the nuances of association planning. Most of the senior executives at the time had previous operating experience. I came to realize that the healthcare industry is made of up many networks (e.g., affinity groups), and that those who participate actively in these networks can have an enormous number of contacts.

Healthcare boasts many associations, and advocacy is a key function of many of these groups, at both the state and national levels. Some are focused on quality, others on accreditation, still others on specialties such as academic medical centers, rural health, primary care, or safety net hospitals with a high dependency on government payers. Association executives even have their own association, which is also an accrediting body for people in this line of work. Clearly, association work is a potential landing area for executives who enjoy policy and working with peers to advocate for health-related causes.

It is worth noting that associations are supported by "soft money." Hospital associations tend to have two major sources of revenue: member dues and diversified services. Most hospitals in the United States pay dues annually to a national hospital association and to state and/or metropolitan associations. They may also sponsor a variety of activities with these associations, including educational programs, group purchasing, and some specialized consulting and training programs.

---

5   My first book, *Multihospital Arrangements: Public Policy Implications*, was an edited collection of papers for an important conference that I organized as part of the AHA's Center for Multihospital Systems (now Health Systems).

A move to association and advocacy work has become a common career change among hospital administrators with very strong networking skills.

Retirement

I have been remiss in not discussing retirement up to this point. Obviously, it is always an option, depending on your personal goals and opportunities. I confess that many of my baby boomer colleagues ask openly, "What is the point in retirement anyway?" At the same time, there is no question that some of the changes in healthcare have resulted in some people retiring before they were ready. Improvements in compensation and benefits have made retirement more manageable for many executives, and it is an option to consider—but one beyond the scope of this book.[6]

RECOMMENDATIONS

1. There are several common non-consulting options open to healthcare executives seeking a career change. By comparison to non-consulting options, independent management consulting may be the most different of possible options, making it the most challenging transition.

2. The state of the economy often plays a role in selecting an option; for instance, returning to school is more popular during economic downturns.

3. Often, your network will influence which options might be the best fit and most attractive.

---

6   See for example Pau, W. D. 2021. *The Retirement Guidebook.* Vienna, VA: Retirement Researcher Media.

4. Each option has pros and cons that must be considered. The relevance of executive skills varies by option. No career change option should be considered easy.

5. Retirement may be the ultimate default option, although it is not discussed in this book.

REFERENCES

Citrin, J. M. 2015. *The Career Playbook: Essential Advice for Today's Aspiring Young Professional.* New York: Crown Books.

Dison, J. 2017. *The Consulting Economy: How to Manage Your Career in the Coming Workforce Revolution.* Carson City, NV: Lioncrest Publishing.

Mason, S. A. 2021. *The Healthcare Consultant's Handbook: Career Opportunities and Best Practices.* Chicago: Health Administration Press.

Todd, B. 2019. "Before Committing to Management Consulting, Consider Directly Entering Priority Paths, Policy, Startups and Other Options." Key Articles, 80,000 Hours. Published November. https://80000hours.org/articles/alternatives-to-consulting.

What Others Have Experienced

*I am always ready to learn, although I do not
always like being taught.*
—Winston Churchill

Now THAT WE have identified options, we are prepared to give
consulting full consideration. A vital input to this process is the path
forged by others who have made such a career change. From the
outset, I was convinced there were people who had accomplished
this transition and I was eager to have them share their stories.
When I first began writing this book, I planned to put these profiles
toward the back. But as these interviews unfolded, I realized that
much of this career change discussion is built around the stories
and experiences of others.

What are the possibilities? Why did others decide to change?
Concepts, while helpful, tend to be less compelling than experiences.
Consulting is all about experiences. Pine and Gilmore (2019, 17)
were right that "experiences are inherently personal," existing only in
the mind of an "individual who has been engaged on an emotional,
physical, intellectual or even spiritual level." From the experiences
of others, we may learn things that open our eyes in unanticipated
ways. We may even track back to the *why* of our current situation.
So, we moved this chapter toward the front.

When I first conceived of this book many years ago, there were
relatively few examples of people who had made this journey. That

has changed rather dramatically, in part as a result of the coronavirus pandemic, with people more willing to consider a career transition such as this than ever before.

I originally set out in search of basic skill requirements, but ended up enthralled by the creativity and resilience exhibited by the people profiled here. No longer just a search for basic enablers, these profiles became a testament to what is possible. These remarkable stories deserve to be told in detail. Accordingly, the profiles in this chapter focus on baseline information, and the complete summary interviews, stories, and observations are included in the appendixes.

In conducting these structured interviews I surveyed three distinct groups: search consultants/executive coaches (the talent people), and former executives who have transitioned to consulting, divided into two separate groups—*early pioneers* and *contemporaries*. As the name implies, most of the early pioneers made the transition to consulting well before it became popular, some toward the end of their careers. In contrast, the contemporaries are younger and made that shift after being an executive for at least five years; at the time of these interviews, all had spent at least one year as a consultant. In interviewing these executives, I sought to determine what specifically attracted them to consulting and to describe their career paths. I found no "typical" path for this career change in my research; the experiences varied widely. Most of the people I interviewed have consulted to the provider side of healthcare (versus pharmaceutical companies or payers), which mimics my personal experience.

There is nothing scientific about this survey. Most participants were found by word of mouth. Undoubtedly, many people who have made this change did not come to my attention. The sample is likely also skewed toward those who founded their own firms, especially among the contemporaries, as they probably achieved greater recognition than those who joined an existing firm.

SURVEY OF SEARCH CONSULTANTS AND EXECUTIVE COACHES

Consultants have become full partners in the transformation taking place in healthcare. This was inevitable, as healthcare remains a highly specialized area of management. While tracking down executives who have shifted full-time to consulting has certainly been a fruitful pursuit, as you will see shortly, I realized during that work that search consultants and executive coaches—the talent people—were another key source for insights to a career change.

Executives contemplating a transition to consulting often work closely with executive search consultants or an executive coach, and sometimes both. Often, such relationships arise because a search consultant stays in touch after placing the executive in a specific position. A search consultant can develop an extensive executive network this way. This naturally puts them in a position to find out when one of these executives becomes disenchanted with their role or curious about consulting. Virtually every search consultant interviewed for this chapter shared such experiences.

Whether a search consultant provides advice to a disenchanted executive can vary, especially if the executive mentions an interest in consulting.[1] All the search consultants I interviewed had interacted with executives before and after a career change to consulting, giving them a unique vantage point to watch such transitions.

Executive coaching is a similarly rich resource. In fact, some search consultants have even morphed into executive coaches. Executive coaching was initially better known for offering "outplacement services" than for its more positive interventions around performance improvement and career counseling. Like consultants, coaches

---

1   When a search consultant places an executive in a position, the executive must stay in that position for at least a year or two for the search consultant to retain the commission. It is also notable that most of the medium and bigger firms have in-house recruiting capabilities.

were relatively unregulated at first, but business and academia have expanded into formal training and certification for these professionals, and executive coaching has become more prominent since about 2010. Executive coaches focus on advising their clients about existing or future career performance and options, so they become a likely source of important information to anyone considering a career change—something that was not immediately obvious to me when I first set out to write this book.

As a result, I sought out a few prominent search consultants and executive coaches to the healthcare industry. Some of these interviewees have actively coached executives navigating the transition to consulting, while others reflected more on their own transition to consulting.

Carson F. Dye, FACHE

Carson Dye stresses that he has always thought of himself as a hospital administrator. Without this background, he does not believe he would have ever become a search consultant. His practice is focused primarily on physician executives.

Carson has known at least a dozen executives who have shifted to consulting; about half were running toward consulting, and the other half were running away from their prior position. About half succeeded in the transition and the rest went back to executive management or clinical practice.

The successful transitions Carson has observed included both setting up a solo practice and joining consulting firms. Among the solo consultants, the most successful individuals seemed to connect as independent contractors with other firms in a dyad arrangement. All were surprised by a variety of things they experienced. Carson recalls one person saying, "I know you travel a lot, but I had no idea. This is awful, horrible. Some places I go to don't even have an airport." Carson was taught early to recognize who the client is, using the name that is on the check received for such services—an organization, not an individual (i.e., the client sponsor).

While he observes that it is rare to work for a friend, Carson began consulting "on the side" by helping a few people with human resources issues that he was dealing with in his full-time job as an employee of a health system. This made the transition to full-time search consulting almost seamless.

Michael S. Hein, MD, FACP

One of Dr. Michael Hein's important cautions is that coaching requires you to suppress personal likes and dislikes in favor of the executive. Sublimating personal views and preferences is not easy for some people.

Having been a primary care physician and a healthcare executive, Michael sees the common trait in these roles as the desire to help people. Of course, there are differences too. Some coaching is involved in primary care to be sure, but executive coaching is more organized and less stressful—you have more control over your hours and are not subjected to late night calls to come to an emergency room. In patient care, you may give advice and rarely see improvement or key lifestyle changes based on it. In contrast, executive coaching is not about giving advice, and focuses less on life and death issues and more on helping the client develop the skills needed to achieve tangible successes with a shorter turnaround time.

Specific training and study of psychology and executive coaching skills have been especially important to Michael, but he values his prior sports coaching experiences as well.

Jack Schlosser, FACHE

Jack Schlosser has the distinction of being first a consultant and then a search consultant for most of his career. When he retired from search consulting, he got additional training and became an executive coach. Jack is a former chairman of the Healthcare Consultants Forum of the American College of Healthcare Executives (ACHE).

Jack started as a hospital administrator before going into consulting with Coopers & Lybrand. In considering the transition, his advice focused first on a few key questions: "Can you 'repot' yourself into a different culture in a different setting? How well does the person confront who they are?" Some people told him he would not like this role when he first considered it. In retrospect, he concluded that those who advised against it were projecting some of their own shortcomings and frustrations, although he admits that coaching has its own challenges.

To executive candidates considering a transition to consulting, Jack suggests it may be important to ask how many of their connections are convertible to new business—it's likely only a small percentage. The pace of consulting is also unique; someone who struggles to adjust to that pace will end up in trouble or dissatisfied—or both. Consulting could also be a bad move, he suggests, if someone has trouble writing or is too meticulous about their writing (refusing to let it go until it is perfect).

Consulting requires influencing skills and the ability to deal with ambiguity, along with the motivation to "get something done." You must be able to consider multiple issues at once. Functioning as a consultant means managing both a team and a client in trying to move things forward. Leadership (an underappreciated skill) becomes more daunting as you move up in consulting, and communication is important for all leaders, especially consultants. In his words, "It does not matter that you know what you intend to be saying if the client does not understand."

For those looking to make the transition, Jack shared what a mentor once told him: "If you are good at what you do, the market will find you."

J. Larry Tyler, FACHE, FHFMA, CMPE

Larry Tyler was never a healthcare executive. Rather, he is a self-made entrepreneur, with a strong work ethic, who never set out to become a consultant but had a strong penchant for sales. His infectious personality propelled him into a becoming a phenomenally successful search consultant and the founder of Tyler & Company.

While sales fueled his growth, Larry started out as an accountant doing audits, which he despised. (Possessed of a wicked sense of humor, Larry once described an auditor as "the soldier who comes in after a battle and bayonets the survivors.") The day he qualified as a certified public accountant, he quit PricewaterhouseCoopers and went to work as chief financial officer for one of their clients. After a series of positions, he was introduced to search in 1978, where he quickly excelled. He started Tyler & Company in 1983, which he grew to over $5 million in annual revenues and five offices (two satellite offices and three main ones, including Atlanta, where Larry started). His reputation grew to the point that his consulting peers elected him chairman of the American Association of Healthcare Consultants—the first search consultant to hold this post. Larry eventually sold Tyler & Company to Jackson Healthcare in 2013, and is now more focused on governance.

In his wide-reaching CEO network, Larry has been close to a few people who have made the transition from executive to consultant, though he believes the shift is difficult for most executives. According to Larry, sales is the issue that prevents most CEOs from making this transition successfully. "CEOs seem to think that because they know a lot of people, this will translate into sales. But it does not." He feels strongly that to succeed in consulting you must be an extrovert. "Introverts are only comfortable around people they know," he says. He also believes that executives should have several options if they decide to take the leap to consulting, in case it does not work out.

Because Larry's experience is somewhat unique, more of his story can be found in appendix C.

EXECUTIVE PROFILES

If we forget our stories, we're going to forget our connection to purpose. Stories connect people to the mission and purpose of the organization.

—Kristin Baird (2021)

Many people enter consulting on a part-time basis. Given this, it is important to make a clear distinction between those who dabble in consulting and those for whom consulting becomes their sole source of income. This research excludes the hobbyists and those who supplement their income with the occasional consulting gig. Many people may dip their toe in the water, but we are focused only on those who chose full immersion into the profession.

When I began this, my working hypothesis (which proved out) was that the transition to consulting had become more popular among executives who (1) were intrigued by the challenges presented by consulting (intellectual and otherwise), and (2) had experienced growing frustration with the limitations of being a full-time executive. Have things changed to encourage this shift even more today? If so, what has changed? Has it somehow gotten easier to make this shift? What were and are some of the challenges; have there been any changes? For some, executive positions in healthcare have gotten more challenging and less satisfying, causing more people to consider alternatives. These and related issues are discussed in detail.

A notable parallel to executives facing this decision is the physicians who are increasingly taking early retirement, reflecting a lack of engagement due, at least in part, to some of the many changes that have affected healthcare delivery. Nearly 30 percent of physicians retire aged 60–65, and 12 percent retire aged 59 or younger, according to one report (Farouk 2019). The mantra among this group has been, "This is not what I signed up for." As a result, I needed to compare a group who had made this transition many years ago with a more contemporary group. Both groups consist of individuals who shifted their career paths to full-time consulting either midcareer or toward the end of their careers.

The careers of the executives I interviewed are exemplary, by any definition. They took full advantage of opportunities that came their way (being opportunistic) while they sought out new opportunities (planning for their career change). These profiles might more accurately be characterized as aspirational examples of what is possible, rather than likely. Given the value of these testimonies, more detailed versions and observations are provided in appendixes A (early pioneers) and B (contemporaries).

Early Pioneers

I reached back to a few of the people I refer to as early pioneers: Ken Ackerman, Reginald Ballantyne III, James A. Rice, and Fred Hobby. Each of these executives had amassed impressive accomplishments by the time they made a career change to consulting. The circumstances of those changes varied, as you will see from the brief profiles here. I should acknowledge at the outset that I identify more with the early pioneers. I mention this to titrate any bias inadvertently applied in this regard.

F. Kenneth Ackerman Jr., FACHE

Case Study: Executive, Consultant, Consulting Management, Elected Leader

Focus: Growth, Systemness, Performance Improvement

Ken Ackerman was in his mid-fifties when he decided to try something else and became an independent consultant as part of a well-known firm. For over 30 years, Ken had served in several positions at Geisinger Medical Center in Danville, Pennsylvania, ultimately becoming the organization's president. He received numerous awards during his executive career, including ACHE's Robert S. Hudgens Memorial Award for Young Healthcare Executive of the Year in 1975.

Ken's transition to consulting began when he joined the successful McManis Associates in Washington, DC, which was in the process of being sold when he started. He stayed on for several years learning the consulting business before joining Clarke Consulting in 1995 as chief operating officer. Ken subsequently became CEO of the organization that evolved into Integrated Healthcare Strategies, based in Minneapolis. The firm was later sold to Gallagher Human Resources and Compensation Consulting (Gallagher HRCC), making Ken a two-time survivor of firm sales as a consultant.

After he left McManis, Ken's consulting practice focused mostly on executive and physician compensation and benefits. His firm offered some benefits-related products in addition to compensation consultation services. Ken received his master of health administration degree from the University of Michigan, which was pivotal to how and where he spent most of his career. He managed all these different jobs while maintaining his primary residence in Danville, Pennsylvania.

Reginald M. Ballantyne III, FACHE

Case Study: Executive, Internal Consultant, Independent Consultant, Speaker, Elected Leader

Focus: Growth, Joint Ventures, Collaboration

Reg Ballantyne's leadership career straddles local, regional, and national health interests. Most of his consulting was as a strategic advisor (internal consultant or corporate resource) to the leadership of several publicly traded for-profit organizations, including Vanguard Health Systems after they acquired Phoenix Memorial Hospital in Arizona. Reg stayed with Vanguard as a senior advisor in Nashville, Tennessee, until it was acquired by Tenet Healthcare in Dallas. On leaving Tenet late in his career, Reg launched his independent consulting firm, RMB III Consultancy, offering businesses and government entities collaborative ideas and ventures.

Along the way, Reg served in a leadership capacity for several state and national entities and associations, including as 1997 chairman of the American Hospital Association (AHA). He is also a Fellow of ACHE and a recipient of ACHE's Gold Medal Award for excellence in healthcare leadership. Other roles included participation on numerous boards of advisors for a variety of private health-related companies. Always civic-minded, Reg also found time to serve as a chairman of numerous regional community and civic organizations. He holds a master of business administration degree from Cornell University and a bachelor of science degree from the College of the Holy Cross. Raised in Long Island, New York, Reg has called Paradise Valley, Arizona, his home since leaving Phoenix Memorial.

James A. Rice, PhD, FACHE

Case Study: Executive, Entrepreneur, Strategist, Author, Speaker, Consultant, Elected Leader

Focus: Strategies, Governance, International Health

Dr. Rice's career includes a large dose of international health. As of 2021, he is managing director and senior advisor for governance and leadership at Gallagher HRCC and chairman of the Akadimi Foundation (www.governakadimi.org). Jim attended the University of Minnesota master's program in health administration. During the Vietnam War, he was given a US Public Health Service Traineeship and a commission as an officer in the Navy Medical Service Corps. He also received a doctoral fellowship from the National Institutes of Health.

During graduate school, Jim's exposure to consulting began with his work on an interdisciplinary team in a US Department of Labor Job Corps program in Albuquerque, New Mexico. For several years he worked in a variety of settings helping to expand ambulatory care programs and facilities. He was then called back to the Minneapolis area by one of his mentors to serve as a senior officer for a new multihospital system that was developing in the region. He worked within this system to help organize a series of mergers and hospital management contracts that became Allina Health. During his 17 years serving in this system, he helped establish Health Central International as an international consulting firm. Jim decided to pursue his interest in international health through a variety of projects abroad. He later became president of the Governance Institute in California, where his consulting work focused on health system governance. His work extended from the United States to a wide variety of projects in at least 34 countries. Along with Frankie Perry, he wrote *Healthcare Leadership Excellence: Creating a Career of Impact* (Chicago: Health Administration Press, 2012). He holds numerous faculty appointments and has received many awards for his far-reaching work.

Fred Hobby, CDM

Case Study: Executive, Association Executive, Speaker, Consultant

Focus: Chief Diversity Officers, Diversity, and Inclusion

Fred Hobby is a true pioneer in many ways. He is generally regarded as the first full-time, fully dedicated chief diversity officer in a healthcare setting. Often the first African American to serve in a position, he played a big role in development and training of chief diversity officers in healthcare organizations.

Fred started in government, serving four years as the executive director of the Affirmative Action Department for the City of Louisville, Kentucky, during which time he was also on the faculty of the University of Louisville. He began his hospital administration career with Humana Inc. in Louisville, as administrative resident. While he held a graduate degree, it was not in health administration.

Fred picked up operating skills while serving in a variety of roles over the years, including positions in Newport News, Norfolk, and Virginia Beach, Virginia, and as CEO of one traditionally Black hospital. Ultimately, Fred's career included executive positions across three states and six hospital systems over more than 40 years. This included ten important years with the Greenville Hospital System (GHS) in South Carolina, where he was encouraged to expand more into his area of expertise. His work at GHS included clinical services and establishing a diversity and inclusion program aimed primarily at Latino patients in the region. This work led to development of a training program that was picked up by the South Carolina Hospital Association.

Fred's work at GHS gained the attention of the AHA, which was recruiting for the third leader of its new Institute for Diversity in Health Management. He was hired as president and CEO of the Institute, where he stayed for ten years. Among his many achievements at the AHA was the development of a certification program for chief diversity officers. In his role, he often served as an internal consultant to the many fledgling programs that began springing up among member hospitals. In 2015, he left the AHA to become an independent consultant with CulturaLink, LLC, a full-service language assistance and health equity consulting company in Atlanta.

Fred also serves on the advisory board of InveniasPartners. Other board work over the years has included two terms on the national board of the Certification Commission for Healthcare Interpreters and serving as the founding president of the South Carolina chapter of the National Association of Health Services Executives. Fred received a bachelor's degree in history and political science from Kentucky State University, and a master of arts degree in sociology from Washington University in St. Louis. He has received recognition and awards from numerous organizations during his career.

Contemporaries

As it has become more common to make a career change from executive to consultant, I approached a second group of executives, the contemporaries, who made the change more recently and had spent at least one year as a full-time consultant. This group includes Chris Morgan, Nicole Denham, and Kim Athmann King.

There are numerous differences between the contemporaries and the early pioneers. Because they are newer to consulting, they have had to deal with more recent changes in the industry. None of these contemporary consultants were known to me before writing this book.

Christopher L. Morgan, FACHE

Case Study: Executive, Entrepreneur, Consultant, Veteran

Focus: Value-Based Strategies

Chris Morgan views himself as a transformational leader, having held literally dozens of administrative positions in seven states and abroad before becoming a consultant. He is the founder and CEO of Health Strategies, a consulting firm that provides population health services to providers seeking to transition to value-based services, including direct contracting with employers. Using mostly a virtual firm model, he has assembled a pool of some 35 independent contractors—consultants who have experience developing several clinically integrated networks and accountable care organizations.

Before founding his consulting firm in 2017, Chris served in variety of hospital administrative positions, both in the military (in the US Air Force) and in civilian health systems. Starting out as a trained emergency medical technician, Chris has followed an eclectic career path that bridges operations, planning, and collaborative ventures. His operations experience covered three deployments abroad (in Chile, Trinidad and Tobago, and Southeast Asia) and two domestically (with the US Veterans Health Administration and the US Department of Defense TRICARE contractor network). He has held a wide variety of executive positions throughout the United States, including executive positions in Danville Regional Health System in Virginia and WellStar Health System in Georgia. His collaborative activities included work with the Mississippi Business Group on Health and at the Vanderbilt Health Affiliated Network.

Chris has a bachelor's degree in business administration and business management from Troy University and a master of business administration degree with a focus on healthcare planning and marketing from William Carey University. He is a Fellow of ACHE and served as ACHE Regent for Mississippi. He has won several awards for his commitment to improving the careers of other healthcare leaders.

Nicole Denham, RN

Case Study: Nurse Provider, Executive, Entrepreneur, Consultant

Focus: Clinical Change and Process Improvement

In 2015, Nicole Denham shifted out of her career as a cardiac critical care nurse to establish COR Consultants. Her 16-year nursing career began at a metropolitan Atlanta hospital that became one of the largest heart centers in Georgia. This organization offered her a varied experience in cardiac services, critical care services, and learning resources. She spent several years managing teams and overseeing cardiac processes within the healthcare system. These experiences, combined with her passion for change and process improvement, led her into the world of consulting.

Since cofounding COR, Nicole has worked alongside healthcare leaders throughout the country in a variety of public, private, and government healthcare organizations. She teams up with her clients for strategic planning, clinical optimization, and training solutions. A certified John Maxwell coach, she uses proven leadership strategies to execute effective change.

Nicole received her bachelor of science in nursing from Georgia State University and a master of health administration degree from Pennsylvania State University. She is an active member of the Georgia Association of Healthcare Executives, a chapter of ACHE.

Kim Athmann King, FACHE

Case Study: Marketing and Communications Executive, Strategy Executive, Entrepreneur, Consultant/Founder

Focus: Business Development and Strategy

Kim King is founder and president of Strategy Advantage, located in Los Angeles. She provides an interesting example of someone who not only made the transition from executive to consultant but also shifted between different consulting paths: After first striking out on her own she eventually joined a large firm for several years, only to boomerang to building her own firm some years later.

Before launching Strategy Advantage in 2002, Kim spent 12 years holding a number of executive positions in strategy, business development, and marketing at both Saint Agnes Medical Center in Fresno, California, and Cedars-Sinai Health System in Los Angeles. She paused her first consulting venture after five years to join one of the well-known specialty healthcare consulting firms, Kaufman Hall, where she served as senior vice president of strategy services for three years. She then decided to relaunch Strategy Advantage, Inc. with a focus on competitive growth. Kim eventually built a new type of virtual firm model including a group of experts as part of a contracted network and a lean core team of internal staff. In 2014, she added a new service to help healthcare leaders and organizations stay on top of the many disruptive innovations in healthcare.

In addition to her consulting work, Kim has also published regularly. In 2015, she launched "Outside the Lines," a biweekly point-of-view email newsletter offering a perspective on lesser known, nontraditional trends and events occurring in and around the healthcare industry.

Kim attended St. Cloud State University as an undergraduate and received her master of business administration degree from California State University, Fresno. Strategy Advantage is headquartered in the Los Angeles area, and Kim maintains residences in California and in Minnesota, her home state. She has been involved both locally and nationally in numerous professional societies, including ACHE, the Healthcare Financial Management Association, and the Forum for Healthcare Strategists.

RECOMMENDATIONS

1. Seek advice from search consultants and executive coaches, as they are key sources of information on career changes. Many are former executives and have had personal experience with such career changes.

2. Approaching others who have experienced a transition to consulting can be highly informative. Paths vary considerably, which speaks to the myriad of ways to make this transition. It is not a one-size-fits-all undertaking.

3. Regardless of the path, such a career transition remains challenging. The profiles included here are all of extraordinarily successful leaders, who are all quick to point out that their path has not been easy. Their advice to others stresses caution and diligence.

4. All those profiled as both early pioneers and contemporaries speak of a rewarding career in consulting. No regrets!

5. The variety of practices from these profiles reflects the expansive growth and reach of consulting into all facets of the healthcare industry.

REFERENCES

Baird, K. 2021. Paraphrased in Q. Studer, "Getting to Always: The Power of Hardwiring Systems in Your Organization." *Pensacola News Journal*, July 29. https://eu.pnj.com/story/money/business/2021/07/29/power-hardwiring-systems-your-organization-quint-studer/5409817001/.

Farouk, A. 2019. "Early Retirement? 5 Factors Physicians Should Evaluate." Career Development (blog), AMA. Published January 4. www.ama-assn.org/practice-management/career-development/early-retirement-5-factors-physicians-should-evaluate.

Pine, B. J., II, and J. H. Gilmore. 2019. *The Experience Economy: Competing for Customer Time, Attention, and Money*. Boston: Harvard Business.

The Road Less Traveled

*Time, which changes people, does not alter the image we have
retained of them.*
—Marcel Proust

CHAPTER 5 SHARED the profiles of executives who successfully
made the transition to consulting. Here, I will summarize some
observations for each the three groups interviewed: the talent people,
the early pioneers, and the contemporaries.

THE TALENT PEOPLE

The interviews of search consultants provide much to contemplate
(exhibit 6.1). Generally, the talent people seemed skeptical about
most executives' preparedness for a career change. Their characteriza-
tions were replete with references to lack of knowledge and people
cutting corners. Further, the feedback they got from people who
made the change did not seem encouraging.

Some former executives succeeded despite not knowing what
was in store, but the talent people clearly believed better preparation would have helped. Search consultants universally promoted
the potential benefit of using an executive coach during the career
change process, and had seen the value. As more executives contemplate a career change, executive coaches will probably become
more popular.

These interviews also seemed to reinforce the idea that some people who had decided to make a career change may have misdiagnosed their situation. A job change may have been a better fit for some.

Exhibit 6.1. Insights from Talent People on Executives Turned Consultant

Timing of the change	Often prompted by job loss or actions of others
Reasons for change	Change of leadership (e.g., board chair, CEO)
	Dealing with voluntary board and the related controversies and conflicts
	Tired of the grind (repetitive, always on stage)
	Loss of control; corporate interference
	Disdain for negative politics of healthcare organizations
	Personal indiscretions
Reasons for selecting consulting	Perceived as main or only option available
	Bought into consulting, including myths
	Grass looked greener
	Seeking fewer work hours and more control over schedule
	Location
Solo or with a firm	Half and half
Perceived risk at the time	Universally poorly understood
Most satisfying result of the change	Control over personal time
	Personal growth
	Exposure to diverse organizations and challenges
Biggest disappointment with the change	Travel
	Sales can be very demanding
	Friends did not return calls

What skills transferred	Public speaking
	Intellectual curiosity, broad interests
	Extensive knowledge about hospital operations
	Listening
What new skills were acquired	Sales (but better to have this before the change)
	Reliance on case studies, research, and experiences
	Computer expertise
Where expectations were met	Challenging
	Rewarding
	Stimulating
Surprises	Travel can be incredibly oppressive
The one thing I would change if I could do it over	Better research up front
	Talking with more people, especially about the realities of consulting
Advice to others: Do	Seek advice from others before the move
	Go to meetings attended by people who can hire you
	Use an executive or career coach
	Make sure you are comfortable with sales
	Consult with your spouse or partner about travel
Advice to others: Avoid	Don't assume your past success assures future success
	Don't do it for the money; you may be disappointed
	Don't be naive about travel

THE EARLY PIONEERS

Early pioneers were just that—*pioneers*. Their stories demonstrate extraordinary energy and resourcefulness as they took advantage of a moment when the industry was ripe for change. For some, the opportunities came to them; others sought them out. Each relied on extensive personal networks and some national notoriety in making several career moves.

> **Early pioneers were just that—*pioneers*. Their stories demonstrate extraordinary energy and resourcefulness as they took advantage of a moment when the industry was ripe for change.**

The early pioneers all picked up skills along the way, and several are quick to credit their credentials from top-rated programs in health administration and reliance on their extensive alumni networks. They all have impressive accomplishments in business and a shared passion for healthcare in its many forms. While they did not all form independent companies, an entrepreneurial bent is clear; they created their own opportunities. They were quick to recognize the unique role that healthcare plays in American society and to claim a seat at the table with other business leaders, both foreign and domestic.

That these early pioneers all pursued their passion for healthcare by following dramatically different paths demonstrates that healthcare has long been a growth industry—it now accounts for almost one-fifth of the total US economy. Opportunities are rich and careers can be fruitful, even where the path leads in many different and perhaps unpredictable directions. Significantly, all these executives ended up in consulting and were very satisfied with this outcome.

None of these executives took a formal, structured course in consulting, even after they took the leap. A few described an apprenticeship experience with some firms. Interestingly, none worked for one of the better-known global consulting firms, where they might have received more formal consultant training. A few noted the important influence of key people who helped them pursue their interests, coupled with certain events that pushed them in new directions.

The diversity of interests among the early pioneers is demonstrated by the distinct branches of healthcare in which they functioned: for-profit hospitals and ventures, international health and high-level strategy with a governance and management focus, executive management of a human resources services and benefits firm, and association leadership.[1]

As these profiles clearly demonstrate, consulting has long been an attractive opportunity for people with the right skill set and knowledge. It may be significant that virtually all the early pioneers have continued consulting past the average retirement age. All have been successful and could easily have drifted into a more relaxed lifestyle. Instead, they chose to continue their trade, and seemingly with less regard for income; they simply enjoy the work.

Although not a dominant theme, wealth accumulation seemed at least part of the reason the early pioneers shifted to consulting; however, most were set financially after their executive careers. There is obviously a difference between making a career change when you are fully dependent on the income thus derived and doing so later in life when motivations tend to be less focused on money.

THE CONTEMPORARIES

The motivations of the contemporaries could be most relevant to the current conditions in the healthcare industry. Times have changed to be sure. One thing that is immediately apparent is that two of the three contemporaries are women. Understanding the history of women breaking into consulting can offer some insights into the ability of consulting firms to change.

Women have always played an important role in consulting, at least in my experience. Two of my first bosses, including as a consultant, were highly accomplished women. However, it was

---

1 Notably, Ken Ackerman and Jim Rice both worked for Integrated Health Systems before it became part of Gallagher.

rare in the past for women to get much beyond the manager ranks. Talented consultants often left the workforce during childbearing years, for example, and faced high hurdles to re-enter the workforce thereafter. Significant efforts have since been made involving family leave and other approaches to make consulting more inclusive, especially in leadership positions. Things are much different now, thanks also to technology gains that have enabled remote work and more progressive policies and benefits. The remote work situations demanded by the coronavirus pandemic have long been the normal work structure for most consultants, and women looked particularly favorably on remote working during the pandemic. Just as firms have made changes to better accommodate women and families, I hope that similar efforts will succeed in helping racial and ethnic minorities gain ground in consulting.

When contrasted to the early pioneers, two primary environmental issues seem most evident from the interviews with the contemporaries: the pace of change and the disruptive nature of changes. Management decisions today must be made faster and there is less margin for error. Executives depend more on access to information (not just data) and informatics, and there is less focus on who or what you personally know. Management is focused on agility. Poise in the face of turmoil has become more important. As disruption has become the norm, comfort with change is an imperative. There are no successful consultants in healthcare who lack comfort with change.

> **As disruption has become the norm, comfort with change is an imperative.**

What can we learn from the contemporaries? First, they characterize their careers as far more challenging than they were before the shift into consulting, and they have enjoyed the recognition that comes with being an expert consultant. All were pursuing new knowledge, driven to become familiar with additional dimensions of healthcare. Each expressed the importance of continuous learning and of mentoring others, as well as the opportunity to innovate.

All three contemporaries are now running their own businesses. Two of the three spent some time with other consulting firms. This raises the question of whether establishing their own practice is more of a motivator today than used to be the case. Starting and running a business is not easy, but joining a consulting firm also has its challenges midcareer. It was interesting that the two consultants who joined established firms both mentioned that the experience, while helpful, also allowed them to identify things from those firms that they did not like and wanted to do differently in their own practice.

All three strongly believe that they made the right move. All had superb executive careers in which they experienced some frustrations at times, and acknowledged excitement about playing a different role as consultants. Not surprisingly, all reflected on the value of their skill in relationship building and their fulfillment in helping others and being rewarded for the effort.

A COMPARISON OF THE RESULTS

While there were some similarities between the early pioneers and the contemporaries, there were some differences as well (exhibit 6.2). Clearly the context has changed, as the industry has changed dramatically since 2000, with more changes in store. And while each case study stands on its own, it is interesting to see what patterns emerge that have conspired to bring consulting more into the limelight. Four things stand out as I compare these two groups:

1. The timing of their career changes is fairly consistent.
2. The necessary skills were acquired largely through their executive experience, not through formal consultant training.

3. No one seemed focused on risk when they made the change, but all acknowledged the complications and challenges when looking back.

4. All enjoyed the rewards of consulting and were determined to continue in this role for as long as their health holds up. Most acknowledged that they could continue consulting well into their retirement years if they wanted.

Consulting to the healthcare industry has become more pervasive. New areas are being forged and new specialties are emerging. These profiles are of prominent leaders, most of whom have developed a niche or specialty. Taken together, they just scratch the surface of the vastly different areas where consulting is now routinely involved with many healthcare organizations. Specialties such as finance, IT, compliance, facilities planning, supply chain management, and revenue cycle management, to mention just a few, have greatly expanded.

Exhibit 6.2. Comparison of Early Pioneers and Contemporaries

	Early Pioneers	Contemporaries
Motivations to change	Responded to an event or opportunity	Realized they could do it on their own
	Reached a point where they had achieved all they could as an executive	Became excited by a new challenge
	Wanted a change	Felt they could be more influential in the role of a consultant
		Became typecast and unable to expand into other corporate roles
Timing of the change	Varied from midcareer to senior executive	They felt they had accomplished most of what they could in their previous position
	Looking for more	Looking for more
		Felt constrained

Reasons for selecting consulting	Natural migration Appealing new learning curve Reluctant to retire	Had established track record of success, including with a few clients Attracted to being a recognized "expert" Ability to innovate and do things their way
Solo or with a firm	Most joined an existing firm midcareer or near retirement	Mixed, but clear bias for own firm
Perceived risk at the time	Not perceived as a real barrier; more a challenge	Limited awareness Not much of a consideration
Most satisfying result of the change	Enjoyed the work, especially meeting and working with new leaders and teams	Ability to set own schedule Became more of a leader Exposed to more parts of the industry
Biggest disappointment with the change	Travel can be oppressive	Wish they had known more about establishing a business Wish they had done it sooner
What skills transferred	Leadership Ability to influence	Leadership Ability to influence Analytics
What new skills were acquired	Sales	Sales Networking
Where expectations were met	Freedom and wealth creation Stimulating	Freedom and wealth creation Stimulating
Surprises	A bit of a lifestyle shock	Need to codify services and approach
The one thing I would change if I could do it over	Nothing	Involve financial and legal advisors from the start Might have done it sooner

Advice to others: Do	Do an honest self-assessment	Develop your own schedule/ routine
	Recognize and understand the primacy of sales	Take the time to find out what you are good at
	Must be adaptable; willing to deal with the unexpected	Talk to others to see what they think
	Cultivate your network and be inviting to others	
Advice to others: Avoid	Make sure you understand the travel involved and talk with your family about it	Develop a plan B
		Don't try to make a lot of money in the beginning
		Don't try to do it all yourself; get advice from others

Another indication of just how expansive consulting has become is Dr. Rice's unique international consulting experience. Ever the advocate for international health, he says that, while globalization is not perfect, it will continue, and healthcare and health gain in a globalized world will require engaged minds and the use of tools that advance knowledge and enhance the performance of teams and organizations driven to accomplish those goals. Consultants are needed to span boundaries across disciplines, service lines, and diverse cultures and people.

Further, the health sector landscape for consulting is transforming, with healthcare delivery clients getting much larger and more complex (Mason 2021). The health sector is rapidly expanding to include artificial intelligence, DNA-guided personalized medicine, new technology firms, and new pharmacology firms. The markets for modern health sector enterprises extend across national borders as knowledge, money, people, and diseases move freely around the globe. These transformations will open new opportunities for consulting endeavors, and require consulting to occur in interdisciplinary and intercultural teams. These consulting teams will need culturally sensitive expertise and knowledge of cross-national labor law, intellectual property rights, and currency exchange complexities.

Dr. Rice's drive to change the world, and the extended careers of the high-powered consultants in the pioneers group, also speaks to my personal experience with the pace of consulting. The role of a healthcare executive tends to involve more unproductive activity or down time than you will find on a consultant's timesheet. I got in the habit of maintaining a timesheet early in my consulting career. It makes you more aware of how you are spending your time, and you become more cognizant of time not well spent. Yes, it can become somewhat oppressive, but it reflects the reality that much of a consultant's time must be paid for by someone else.

Both roles are demanding, but executives take far more meetings than consultants do, and many of my clients would share that only some of those meetings are productive. As I have said elsewhere, a consultant's clock seems to run faster than that of many executives.

Perhaps this generalization might not stand up to more aggressive scrutiny, but the pace of consulting becomes almost addictive; the drive to be productive is always there. When running my own consulting firm, I never worried much when one of my consultants was on the beach because I knew they could not stay there for long; they had adopted the mindset that they needed to be productive—it comes with the territory. I don't know whether this mindset predates the shift to consulting or arises from it, but it exists. Being around a lot of smart, productive people breeds a thirst to be similarly engaged. Once you experience this, it is hard to back off this pace or the feeling of being needed and accomplishing good things. For many, including the early pioneers I profiled, this energy translates into high-energy pursuits in other facets of their lives. For the pioneers, this has included running marathons, maintaining an energetic tennis routine, traveling extensively, taking care of family or a loved one, and pursuing active lives well into their later years.

> **Being around a lot of smart, productive people breeds a thirst to be similarly engaged.**

On the rare occasions I have tried out interim management at the request of existing clients, I found it was hard to adjust my mindset. Meetings and other less productive pursuits seemed to dominate my schedule. I took occasional inventory of my meetings to determine which were really necessary; often, few were. I also became a fan of stand-up meetings, which are short by definition. Consulting thrives on tangible output—completion of tasks on a timely basis, moving on from one project to the next, multitasking.

This may be speculative and more reflective of certain personality traits, but I have observed that people who have spent considerable time in the saddle as consultants find it hard to slow down. The pioneers may have stayed busy well past the need to supplement their income because of their need to feel productive. But at some point in any business or career, things will slow down. Any addiction, if untreated, can have disastrous consequences. Given the level of burnout these days, especially among healthcare workers, it seems fair to suggest that this drive for continued productivity has both positive and negative connotations.

Another interesting observation is that all the interviewees spoke in terms of "mission" and "calling." They all had something to say. They have values, standards—things that are important to them. This was more than an elevator speech; for some, these values were reflected in their motivation for starting their own consulting business—part of their *personal brand*.[2] Leadership style can also be an important consideration. While phrases such as *servant leadership* and being *results-oriented* are helpful, these are too general. Adam Bryant (2021), managing director of the ExCo

---

2 Much has been written about personal brands, especially with regard to consulting. See chapter 3 in *The Healthcare Consultant's Handbook* for more on developing a personal brand in the healthcare consulting space.

Group and coauthor of *The CEO Test*, suggests a key question for leaders that a consultant should also be able to answer: "What are the three values that are most important to you as a leader and a colleague—that is, the consistent behaviors that everyone can rely on from you?" All the pioneers and contemporaries interviewed said something about their personal values and what they considered important when explaining how they conducted business as a consultant.

Finally, a key takeaway from these interviews is the optimism everyone expressed about their career change to consulting and, importantly, the prospects for consulting. The interview format, while structured, allowed the respondents to take the conversation where they wanted. Without exception, the feedback was dominated by positive comments. The only time anything negative arose was when specific questions focused on a few of the dissatisfiers of consulting, including those reviewed earlier (long workdays, bad clients, bad engagements, and inadequate budgets). Some even went so far as to suggest that an optimistic outlook on the industry was a requirement to succeed as a consultant. Based on their collective comments, opportunities will continue to exist, both domestically and internationally, for those who are interested in making the shift to consulting and have the necessary resolve. Approached with the right mindset, along with a little luck, a career change to consulting can be enormously rewarding.

WHAT ABOUT THOSE WHO FAILED?

This informal study has not accounted for people who failed in their attempted shift to consulting. In chapter 9, I will offer a few examples of former CEOs who did not perform well with my clients. Most of them did not succeed in consulting. Researching these unsuccessful shifts is challenging; for understandable reasons, these people tend to avoid the limelight and get absorbed back into the healthcare infrastructure. No one brags about failure. Most of these executives have probably pursued one of the several plan B strategies discussed in chapters 7 and 14.

Failure in consulting takes many forms, but the universal result is that you are not busy enough or do not derive income commensurate with the effort required. Throughout my career I have met many people who chose consulting but never seemed to be very busy. Some clearly lacked the skill or experience to succeed. A few of these people were quite talented but with limited ability to leverage their skills. This usually comes down to an inadequate network or limited ability to get in front of potential clients. Some people who fail in this transition are very capable of delivering a sound consulting product. As noted previously, knowledge and experience, while essential, are insufficient to sustain a successful consulting practice. (See exhibit 8.1 on page 151.)

One memorable example shows just how complicated it can get. Thankfully, this story has a happy ending. It concerns a highly qualified and successful midlevel executive who thought they could monetize their expertise as a consultant. (I have honored their wish to remain anonymous.) This person had given much thought to the move, and shared that preparation with me when we first met. Being a career consultant myself but involved mostly in different segments of the industry than they were, I was really looking forward to working together, learning from their experience, and getting to know this person better. Within a couple of months, this new consultant had left the firm.

As it happens, we stayed in touch. To their credit, this executive turned consultant had realized almost immediately that their expectations and their experience were entirely different. Instead of using their extensive operating experience to bring value to clients—something intended to add a significant new thrust to the firm's service offerings—they ended up caught in the bureaucracy that can invade consulting just like other professions. After a few sales efforts that were successful primarily because of this person's credibility and experience, things went downhill quickly. The fees generated from those sales were credited to other partners who had been with the firm longer. The new consultant's share was a mere pittance by comparison and barely showed up in their compensation. But it got worse: This talented operator was doing most of the work on these engagements and the firm was unable to provide much in the way of support.

The new consultant felt manipulated. The culture of this firm was obviously a poor fit, and the lifestyle changes that suddenly seemed unavoidable were simply not going to work. The politics of the situation were also discouraging. Some of the dissatisfiers of consulting in general came into full view, one being a commute to another location most of the week that made it impossible to become more integrated into the rest of the firm. It felt more like interim management than consulting.

This was not a case of skill gap. This person enjoyed sales, but the points system that applied to compensation was confusing and seemed to favor certain partners over others who were more directly involved in the work. The work was enjoyable, everyone recognized the operator's skills, and most importantly, the client recognized their expertise and was appreciative. But the politics of the firm quickly got to be too much. In the end, this executive turned consultant opted for other opportunities related to technology platforms. The consulting experience had been a big disappointment. Despite preparation, this person ended up with the wrong firm, with promises made but not kept, and had such a negative experience that they decided consulting was not the right path.

Sometime later, this executive also realized that they enjoyed running the show. Eventually, they started a firm with several other executives focused on operating technologies. When I asked about this, the response was, "It turns out I was more of an entrepreneur."

I must acknowledge that this incident alarmed me. How can a highly intelligent person take the necessary time to evaluate their options only to make what turned out to be a bad decision? My former colleague obviously recovered quickly and moved on to other successful pursuits, but this example is one of the things that drove me to pursue this research further. It is a dramatic example, to be sure, but a mistake that I think many others have probably made, and one that I hope can be avoided by following some of the guidance in this book.

I have chosen not to highlight people for whom a shift to consulting did not pan out, but that does not mean they don't exist. I suspect that many more probably fail than succeed in this career move, and still others become easily diverted and remain reluctant to give it full consideration. Not all consulting firms are good places to work. It is important to do your homework before taking the plunge. Obviously, I hope to change the odds. In sharing the profiles before, I made a conscious choice to focus on those who made it and have attempted to explore some of the factors that seem to have contributed to their success. I also hope my contributions might lead to improvements in how many consulting firms operate to more properly reward their people.

The Healthcare Consultant's Handbook offers additional insights on how to differentiate between firms. The best consulting firms embrace a culture based on merit, not political favoritism. Further, they genuinely recognize that their greatest asset is their people, and the good firms find ways to ensure that their people are both appreciated and rewarded for their work.

DON'T UNDERESTIMATE YOUR GIFTS

In evaluating these success stories, no one should underestimate the effort involved or the enviable gifts of the profiled executives. Not everyone has the talent or resolve of these key leaders. They were all highly accomplished before they made the change, and while they may have been less cognizant of the risks inherent in their career shifts at the time, there is a strong argument that they all would have succeeded at anything they attempted. One simple conclusion may also be that consulting attracts people of high energy and resolve.

You do not have to start your own firm to succeed in consulting. The profiled executives who started with a solo or virtual firm model all had a specialized niche, proven credentials, some name recognition, and references. Additional training in consulting skills, while still helpful, becomes less of a factor where specialized knowledge and experience exist. It was also evident that these people had a clear plan for how to pursue consulting—not that these plans were carved in stone. Clearly, some took unexpected turns along the way.

Each of the profiled executives had some experience working with other consultants (even as a subcontractor), not all of which was favorable. These difficult experiences helped inform their specific approach to consulting. Two examples stand out. In one case, the person felt strongly that they sold *relationships*, not engagements. This wasn't mere sophistry; it seemed that this consultant would be reluctant to work with a client who did not approach things the same way. A successful engagement requires mutual trust.

In another case, the consultant made a point of only staying involved with the client to complete the task, and not one minute longer. Training the client operator to take over implementation was built into the proposal. This innovative approach was a direct response to previous experience with other consultants who were blatantly trying to upsell services.[3]

Finally, everyone who was interviewed was eager to share the philosophy and innovations that they believed helped set them apart from their competitors. These differences not only reflected their intent to distinguish themselves from others (i.e., to compete successfully) but also were core to their brand.

So, what do we conclude from this? The contemporaries were perhaps more likely to have been exposed to some form of formal consultant training than the early pioneers, at least training related to enhancing sales. Yet both groups have performed at a high level as consultants. While it's obviously possible to succeed without

---

3   *Upselling* is a retail term that describes selling someone more than they need or want to take the customer to a higher price point. For example, when my son needed a basic pair of sunglasses, he came out of the shop with 12 unnecessary upgrades at ten times the cost. Instead of a $30 pair that would have done the job well, he paid more than $300 with little real value added.

formal training, everyone interviewed supported taking advantage of that training.

I believe it is getting harder to succeed without the formal training that the larger firms offer. If you are a midcareer executive and join a firm that offers this training, it can enhance your opportunity to become an accomplished consultant by supplementing the knowledge and experiences you have accumulated. Access to formal training programs should be a key criterion to at least consider in the selection of a firm to join as a midcareer executive.

As a senior executive, closer to retirement, receiving such training seems less likely, and you are best advised to rely on what (knowledge and experience) and who (network) you know. If you have a particular niche—because of a merger or similar event—that positions you with certain well-defined clients, then go for it. Otherwise, you may find the competition in a crowded marketplace overwhelming.

Consulting is but one of many options a healthcare executive might after gaining significant experience. I have focused on successful transitions to consulting in this chapter. In chapter 7, we will get more granular with respect to executive versus consulting roles and the nature of different forms of consulting.

RECOMMENDATIONS

1. Healthcare consulting may be more competitive than ever before, given the increase in the number of firms, how common it has become, and the needs of the industry.

2. Early pioneers in healthcare consulting enjoyed wide-ranging opportunities; the market in 2021 is more specialized. Midcareer executives today may require more remedial attention to key skills for a career change to consulting to be successful. Yet there remain

opportunities to be creative and innovative in structuring and supporting engagements.

3. The experienced consultants profiled in chapter 5 are clearly overachievers. This may be part of why they were attracted to consulting: to benefit from being part of a meritocracy that would recognize their skills.

4. This book has focused on the successes of others who have made this transition. However, many more people have probably failed in this transition. Learning from the successful experiences of others and understanding the range of paths available may improve the odds of success.

5. Formal training in consulting may become more important as firms refine their offerings and competition intensifies. For midcareer executives considering a career change to consulting, access to formal training programs should be a key criterion when selecting a firm to join.

REFERENCES

Bryant, A. 2021. "What Is Your Personal Leadership Brand?" *Strategy+Business* digital article. Published July 14. www.strategy-business.com/blog/What-is-your-personal-leadership-brand.

Mason, S. A. 2021. *The Healthcare Consultant's Handbook: Career Opportunities and Best Practices*. Chicago: Health Administration Press.

PART III

How?

*How does consulting compare, so I can determine
whether it is the right option for me?*

Once we have determined that a change is necessary and reviewed some of the options available, it's time to determine whether consulting is the right course. To do this, we have to learn more about the different types of consulting, as well as some of the dissatisfiers that come with the territory.

We also need to better understand what is required to manage this transition if we choose to make it. Too many people seem to leave this critical piece to chance. Previous chapters shared the experiences of others who have made this this career change; now we need to go further. I fervently believe that clarifying some of the steps required to navigate this challenging transition will increase your odds of success.

CHAPTER 7

Executive Management Versus Consulting

As a consultant you listen to people's gripes about the company.
As an executive, you are the source of people's gripes.
—Mike Micklewright (2012)

CHAPTERS 5 AND 6 showed that some former executives have found great success as consultants. Times have changed, however. As this transition has become a more popular option, it also has become more difficult. Now that we have covered some of the market considerations weighing on healthcare executives and shared the personal experiences of others, we need to talk about key differences between the executive experience and the consulting experience, and discuss which skills may be transferable. The good news is that some operational experience is essential to anyone contemplating a shift to healthcare consulting. The challenge is that major differences exist between an operational role and an independent consulting role. As an experienced executive with a well-established management routine, you need to clearly understand these differences so you can adapt your routine to better meet the requirements of an independent consultant.

KEY ROLE DIFFERENCES

Exhibit 7.1 lists some of the prominent differences between executive and consulting roles. The primary difference relates to authority and responsibility. Line managers and senior executives are used to having a certain degree of freedom with respect to their specific areas of authority and responsibility. They typically have people who report to them (span of control) and from whom they expect certain results (accountability). As part of an executive team, they share responsibilities with others (collaboration) such that the functions of the enterprise overall are coordinated, and the team has a greater likelihood of success. Certain functions are delegated, and others are owned by the executive. Personnel decisions tend to occupy significant time for any executive, because talent management has taken on greater significance.

Exhibit 7.1. Key Differences Between Executive Roles and Consulting

Dimension	Operations or Line Management	Consulting	Implications for Career Change
Line authority and responsibility	Major	None in client context; limited internally	Different accountabilities
Internal meeting demands	Major; meetings are frequent	Major, often remote, related to client needs and meetings	Greater focus on client than internal needs
Delegation	Frequent; major dependency on others	Exists, but greater personal accountability, especially in solo practice; client is not looking for delegation from the principals	Frequent need to meld client and consulting team skills

Span of control	Extensive	Limited; multiple teams; multifunctional teams that are mostly self-supporting	More diverse teams with potential for more extensive skill sets
Reporting relationships	Paramount	Less important; focus is on teams	Less linear or positional
Accountability	Clearer and connected to responsibility	More shared	Focus becomes the value everyone brings to an engagement
Time dedicated to innovation	Infrequent but increasing	Frequent and essential	Becomes more of a driver; an essential component
New competencies required	Evolves as reform and policy changes take hold	Sales and marketing Writing Client relations	Constant need; strong emphasis on new learnings
Primary deliverable	Meet or exceed operational thresholds	Meet or exceed client-related thresholds	Tracking and measuring progress is essential

An executive's formal authorities or powers might be recorded in a power grid or authority matrix, but the reality may be somewhat different. Unless you are the CEO, there are limitations on your ability to set the agenda and pursue your vision. Even as CEO, truth be known, the board and other members of the C-suite must share and support your vision for it to be fully realized. Inability to achieve a shared vision within a healthcare organization can be a great source of frustration, and has caused many a leader to seek employment elsewhere or consider starting their own firm.

Another key consideration is the volunteer board of directors that is integral to most US nonprofit organizations, including hospitals and health systems. Some years ago, I was introduced to the idea that the most important job of a board of directors is to assess the organization's risk tolerance and apply it to key strategic decisions. I have dealt with nonprofit volunteer boards my whole career, and this description resonates with me. Lack of alignment between a leader and their board regarding risk tolerance was a major source of disruption in many healthcare organizations where I was brought in to assist. Most volunteer boards I have dealt with were far more risk averse than their CEOs. A key approach to risk reduction is knowledge, and many volunteer board members simply lack important knowledge about the healthcare industry. This gap leaves them genuinely challenged to provide informed oversight.

During my consulting career, I have noticed two dramatically different approaches to volunteer hospital boards; the choice between them tends to be mostly influenced by the CEO's style. More enlightened CEOs work hard to attract an independent board that consists of a diverse set of individuals who have broad experience in commercial industry, government, and other parts of the community, including healthcare. The other approach, which unfortunately tends to be more common in my experience, is where the board is stacked with friends and supporters who will be more likely to take direction from the CEO. The latter approach, while understandable on one level, tends to be far less desirable and has resulted in several disasters with which I became quite familiar.

Regardless of which approach CEOs take to building a board, I must admit to a strong sense of admiration for the noble people who are willing to give their time and support as board members.

I only wish they were universally given better access to the tools necessary to exercise their authority. I often ask board members if they are still friends with the person who nominated them; I am only half joking when I ask this.

It takes years as a healthcare executive to develop a sensitivity to volunteer board considerations. Nothing is more important strategically than how a healthcare organization connects with the communities it serves. The board is uniquely qualified to help foster the desired relationship. Understanding the degrees of freedom that exist at each level of the organization and the role to be played by the person in each position is an acquired skill. For the right people, this is among the most challenging yet enjoyable functions of being part of the executive team in a healthcare C-suite.

Culture in a consulting environment is dramatically different than in a healthcare organization. For the executive, at least some of the authority is positional—which is to say that some "rights" come with the title. Not so for the consultant. In consulting, authority is linked more to knowledge on a particular subject or the ability to gain people's trust regarding your approach or the conclusions and recommendations that you make. Consulting tends to operate as a purer form of meritocracy. For the consultant, part of the authority is derived by your role as part of an engagement team, which can vary with every type of engagement. It is not uncommon for a junior member of an engagement team to be given authority to speak on a particular topic or write a particular section of a report for an engagement when they have important experience or knowledge, regardless of their position in the firm. One of the enjoyable factors of consulting is that you may find yourself functioning in vastly different roles, sometimes simultaneously, as part of different engagement teams. The exposure to different challenges can be vibrant and fulfilling, in comparison with executive functions that seem more positional and have more of a tendency to become repetitive and routine.

> **When working with a client, the consultant's role is strictly advisory, with no authority whatsoever.**

The key difference that must be clearly understood is that when working with a client, the consultant's role is strictly advisory, with no authority whatsoever. Finding the solution to a problem is not enough; you must convince the client that it is the right solution, and often show them how to successfully implement that solution. Unfortunately, a consultant is rarely given the opportunity to implement a solution in a healthcare organization, although this appears to be slowly changing. So, for the executive considering consulting, how do the skills acquired in these executive roles transfer into the different culture of consulting?

CONSULTING IS MORE THAN GIVING ADVICE

We should acknowledge the nature of consulting services before we get into a more detailed discussion of skills transfer. A classic article by Arthur N. Turner (1982), published in *Harvard Business Review* with the title "Consulting Is More than Giving Advice," presents a hierarchy of consulting purposes that is still relevant today (exhibit 7.2).

As Turner's article acknowledges, items 1–5 have long been considered traditional consulting purposes. Turner made several insightful remarks about these purposes. For example, when solving a given problem, a key issue for the consultant should be "whether the problem as posed is what most needs solving" (122). Regarding effective diagnosis, Turner remarks that "much of management consultants' value lies in their expertise as diagnosticians" (123). Recommendations, he points out, are only useful if they can be implemented. And when consultants are involved in implementation,

Exhibit 7.2. Turner's Hierarchy of Consulting Purposes

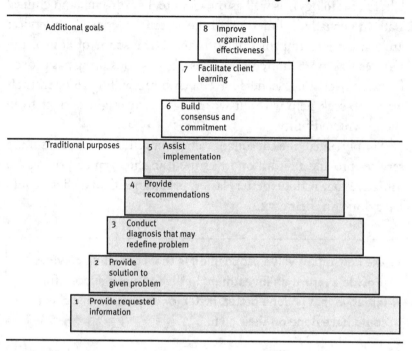

it dramatically changes the engagement. However, a key point of Turner's article is to highlight the higher order functions as ones that most consultants would rather perform, and suggest that there should be more emphasis on process and collaboration. Given the early date of the article, Turner's recommendations have held up well.

Contemporary healthcare consultants are asked to partner with key executives in the organization to solve problems and help reposition the organization to better address its mission in its communities. This consultant–client relationship is built on trust and can include not just operations improvement but strategic repositioning as well. Consultants advise key departments (e.g., lab, IT, radiology), as well as the C-suite, boardroom, and clinical staff. In virtually all functions of the enterprise, consulting services are available to improve performance. The scope of consulting services was more limited in the past, but as consulting has proven its value over time, leaders have been more willing to open their wallet to seek help without worrying that it might detract from their own credibility.

Simply stated, the consultant value proposition is that consulting services provide a return on investment in the form of a successful initiative that is done better, faster, or cheaper than a client could have done on their own.

> **The consultant value proposition is that consulting services provide a return on investment in the form of a successful initiative that is done better, faster, or cheaper than a client could have done on their own.**

Given this simple value proposition, where and how can the executive turned consultant best fit their skills and experiences into this burgeoning field of endeavor?

SKILLS TRANSFER

Is it reasonable to expect that much of what you have learned from your executive experiences will be applicable to consulting? The answer is a qualified yes. The qualification recognizes that much of the management skill set applies to a wide variety of settings. However, the experience of consulting is vastly different from line management.

Managers develop a variety of skills based on their position in a healthcare organization. While some executive leadership skills might be widely applicable, operations and strategy involve a different orientation (short term versus long term) and different skills. The skills that transfer to consulting involve two dimensions: how you were involved in or approached management, and what form of consulting you wish to pursue.

For example, your approach to management is largely a matter of focus and preferences. Are you more drawn to the talent aspect of management roles or to the analytical part? If talent is more in your sweet spot, search consulting might be a logical focus and you could expect to transfer much of what you have learned. If your interest lies in another of the specialized areas of healthcare, such as finance or information systems, then again, much of that knowledge can transfer. However, if you are most interested in organizational behavior or strategy, the skills transfer may be somewhat limited and you will have a steeper learning curve, as firms can vary considerably in how they approach such work. We must get down in the weeds a bit to understand how skills and experiences can match the nature of a consulting practice. A bit of history can help set the stage.

Frederick Taylor is credited with originating the concept of *scientific management* in 1911. This theory was built around Taylor's belief that improved productivity was paramount and that all efforts to organize should be focused on this singular objective. Scientific management was responsible for many improvements in efficiency over the years—so much so that Peter Drucker said America would have been unable to defeat the Nazis in World War II without Taylor's innovations. And while scientific management was among the first attempts to separate the function of management from that of workers, it also began the separation of distinct management functions. Building on Taylor's foundation, Henri Fayol, a mining engineer, reduced management to five functions: planning, organizing, command, coordination, and control. In 1937, Luther Gulick expanded on Fayol's management functions, naming his framework POSDCORB—planning, organizing, staffing, developing, coordinating, reporting, and budgeting (exhibit 7.3).

Exhibit 7.3. The POSDCORB Conceptual Framework

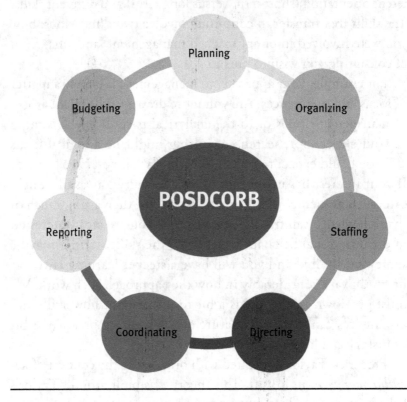

Ultimately, the specific skills that transfer to consulting reflect areas in which an executive has functioned. When I first became a management consultant, a generalist approach was valued; today, we live in an era of specialization. So, broad exposure to the POSDCORB areas as an executive, while interesting, is likely to be reduced to the specialized nature of your consulting practice.

One way to identify and assess your executive skill set is to answer a few key questions about your current work. What strengths do you rely on given your current responsibilities? For example, are you good at delegating? How about communications and writing? Perhaps your toolbox includes planning and conceptualizing

Exhibit 7.4. Comparison of Consulting Roles Based on Scope and Approach

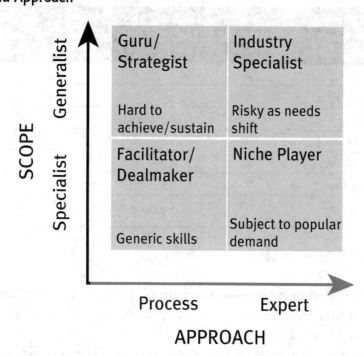

(creativity). Teambuilding is increasingly emphasized as well. How do you feel about deadlines and having your work measured against specific outcomes? Likes and dislikes can apply as well; we tend to gravitate toward things we enjoy and do well.

So much for existing skills. Now, how can we understand the nature of a consulting practice? The distinctions between consulting roles relate to scope and approach.[1] *Scope* is usually described in terms of being a generalist or specialist. *Generalist* tends to be a term less in favor these days, but it was the primary form of consulting when I first joined the industry. *Approach* can be arranged along a continuum from *content expert* to *process facilitator*. Combining

---

1 Consulting practice structures are reviewed in considerable detail in my previous book.

Exhibit 7.5. Transferable Skills by Consulting Category

Consulting Type / Functional Skill	Guru/ Strategist	Industry Specialist	Facilitator/ Dealmaker	Niche Player
Planning	X		X	X
Organizing	X			X
Staffing		X		X
Developing	X			X
Coordinating	X	X	X	X
Reporting	X	X	X	X
Budgeting		X	X	X

these dimensions results in four general categories of consultants: Guru/Strategist, Industry Specialist, Facilitator/Dealmaker and Niche Player, as shown in exhibit 7.4.

Again, consulting practices tend to specialize, and each type of practice requires some unique skill sets. Of course, some skills are more generalizable. One way of determining which skills may transfer from operations or line management to consulting is to match POSDCORB functions to the categories of consulting, as shown in exhibit 7.5.

Another key variable to consider is the structure of the practice: Solo practice may require a broader set of skills related to running the business. For senior executives especially, solo practice represents an opportunity to have your own show built on your unique skills and experiences. The trade-off is that any skills that may exceed yours will have to be covered by other experts on an as-needed basis. Exhibit 7.6 shows how operational or line management skills might translate into solo practice and firm practice.

Exhibit 7.6. Transferable Skills by Firm Structure

Firm Structure / Skills Inventory	Solo Practice	Firm Practice
Delegation	Not applicable except with stringers or trainees	Extremely important
Managing	Relates more to stringers or trainees	Depends on specialty versus global
Execution	Vital	Vital
Planning and organizing	Vital	Vital
Leading and motivating	More applicable to the client than to staff	Depends on the role in the firm
Teaching and instructing	Mostly limited to client	Vital
Thought leadership and innovation	Could be essential in a specialized area	Depends on the firm; some emphasize only execution
Selling and presenting	Vital	Vital
Writing and communicating	Vital (depending on the nature of the practice)	Vital
Coordinating and reporting	Important but simple by comparison	Vital
Multitasking	Vital	Vital
Assessing and evaluating	Emotional intelligence required	Vital
Financing and budgeting	Simple but essential	Can be complicated
Team building and mentoring	Less applicable except for teaming with clients	Vital

Consulting as part of a firm may be more like an executive management position in a healthcare organization, depending on the size of the firm. If nothing else, consulting as part of a firm involves more people and more moving parts. "It gets complicated," as they say. A key to success for any consulting firm is managing people and organizing their talent to be productive. Consulting success is about multitasking and providing leadership. Motivating people and bringing them along in their professional development. Relating to clients, understanding their needs, and gaining their trust, thus enabling you to find the best way to solve their problems. Ideally, you will not only meet the client's expectations but exceed them, and thus be considered for future business—the key to sustainability in consulting.

SALES—THE KEY DIFFERENTIATOR

The most important new skill that is rarely needed as a manager in a healthcare organization is *sales*. In my experience, few executives in healthcare organizations have been formally trained in sales, although this may be changing.

Most instructors would describe sales skills as somewhat generic—something everyone has to do, beginning with selling ourselves to others in basic interpersonal relations. Commercial sales, while similar, requires something more, and selling services differs from selling products.

Sales involves persuasion, and many executives have learned how to write persuasively. Presentation skills, also a core capability for most executive roles, is also an essential part of sales. *Missionary sales* also involves explaining the thing being sold, which is harder than selling the buyer a recognized product or service.

In consulting sales, you are usually competing against others offering a similar service. Although functioning as a line manager involves persuading and explaining things to subordinates, persuading a relative stranger is different. As a manager, you are a leader among leaders, and you have direct reports to whom you have a duty and who have a duty to you. As a consultant, you are the expert. The expectation is that you have relevant experience, usually more than your client, and you have been hired to help create value by sharing your knowledge and experience. You get paid in both situations, but the accountability is different. People pay more attention to someone when they have paid specifically to hear their advice.

Competition in an external sales context is also different from internal competition in executive suites. As an employee, you may represent an idea that competes with someone else's approach. This internal competition tends to be an open forum where ideas are discussed and different points of view are shared, instead of something personal. (Of course, internal competition can also be personal, such as competing for a position that just opened up.) External competition is quite different. You may know very little about who you are selling to and who you are competing against—critical information that can be hard to come by.

Sales is as much about attitude as skill; fear of failure and the inability to handle rejection are toxic. Yet consulting does not exist absent sales.

After knowledge and experience, which are core requirements in the Consultant Value Chain (discussed in chapter 8), sales tends to be the great differentiator in a consulting career. Although you can approach consulting without a sales background, having some exposure to sales and being comfortable with the concept can be a vital factor that will greatly mitigate the fear that normally accompanies this career change.

I have seen many senior healthcare executives hired by commercial firms to help open doors for service or product sales; many of these transitions have been short-lived. Leveraging an existing network of senior healthcare executives can clearly have value to a commercial firm, and some of the profiles in chapter 5 were of executives who did just that. But any salesperson will tell you that there is a big difference between knowing people and translating that list of contacts into a sales pipeline. Further, even where a legitimate pipeline exists, closing a sale can be very challenging. While sales is generally regarded more as an art, there is a growing body of knowledge that can be viewed as the science of sales, as discussed in the next section. Usually, this is the biggest challenge in sales, and it's an unfamiliar challenge for most healthcare executives. Comfort with sales can spell the difference between success and failure in transitioning from an executive position to a career in consulting.

FORMAL TRAINING VERSUS EXPERIENCE

Obviously, there is a lot to consider in terms of skills transfer and what is required to succeed as a consultant. Some skills may be supported by personality traits (e.g., someone who is outgoing and naturally gregarious may find sales and networking relatively easy), whereas other skills may have to be acquired (e.g., presenting, facilitating). Regardless, there is a role for training—or more accurately, a role for *education*. What is the difference? To best explain this, I refer to one of my favorite thought leaders—Nido R. Qubein, renowned speaker, author, and president of High Point University: "Training teaches how. Education teaches why." An example he offers explains this well:

I once ordered an apple pie and a milk shake at a fast-food restaurant. The server smiled and asked, "Would you like a dessert with that?"

This young woman had been trained to act. She had been conditioned to smile and try to upgrade the sale by reciting her memorized lines. And she rehearsed them to perfection.

But she had not been educated in customer interaction. She hadn't been taught to listen to the customer, to think about what the customer ordered and to acquire a feeling for what might appeal to the customer under the circumstances. (Qubein 2019)

Qubein charges us to migrate from "mechanistic organizations" to "thinking organizations." Education allows us to have a vision for an improved future. In many respects, this was my stock-in-trade as a strategy consultant. While not always practical, my job was often to help push the organization beyond its current vision to something greater. I helped convince the leadership that they could do more for their communities, whether that meant forging a relationship with a larger entity, turning around an operating deficit, or replacing an obsolete hospital facility. Creating such momentum in a large, complicated organization involved harnessing a thousand little things, which resulted from daily interactions, from seeing and seizing opportunities when they arose. From developing and presenting an argument. From advocating a position.

Most of us not are not born with these skills. It takes education (not training) to see beyond what our eyes can see, to feel beyond our own personal experiences, to continually strive for a higher level of functioning than we thought possible. This is the essence of vision as a force for change.

Virtually none of the people profiled in chapter 5 are pursuing the type of consulting that I was initially trained for by an elite global consulting firm. The generic training on problem-solving that most global firms offer has evolved into signature leadership development programs that are highly sought after by the best and brightest from top graduate schools. In fact, the elite global firms recruit almost exclusively from the top 25 MBA programs. Because such programs are not familiar to everyone, the training (education) these top firms provide is described here:

These firms hire consultants after already establishing the candidates' various strengths and weaknesses throughout their interview process. Not content to plateau, however, these firms employ rigorous training for all employees and ensure that the consultants expand their talents and fine-tune their specialties. Not only does this extensive training improve the quality of the work, but it also indicates that the firms truly value their employees. . . .

At many consulting firms, in addition to managing client engagements consultants must contribute to the firm's intellectual capital to get promoted. Thus, these larger consulting firms create an environment where information is constantly created and curated. . . .

Within top consulting firms, consultants emphasize a culture of information sharing and collaboration by uploading sanitized information from past consulting projects into knowledge management platforms. This allows consultants to pull from the database to have a more solid understanding of industries and specialties when entering into new engagements. (Cerisano 2015)

One of my more interesting engagements early in my consulting career helps to further illustrate the difference between education and training. A partner at the firm I worked for secured a government contract to evaluate the USDA's meat and poultry inspection system. At the ripe age of 26, one year into the job, I somehow got assigned to this. I even ended up managing much of the day-to-day work toward the end of the nine-month engagement as a result of some untimely staff turnover. Absent formal education on how to interview, organize, write, present, and manage, I had no prayer of completing this work successfully. I knew nothing about the subject and had never worked on a government contract. We had to deal with unions, government workers, politicians, and veterinarians. I had to learn about meat and poultry. I personally interviewed over a hundred people and visited more than 80 slaughterhouses in two dozen states. I ended up at several public meetings presenting on behalf of the firm and dodging questions from the media that were mostly gotchas designed to diminish the study any way they could. It was a completely different experience from consulting in the healthcare industry. The oversight I received, the access I was provided, and the commitment of other corporate resources made all this possible.

Any consultant in any industry must be able to interview, interact, write, present, and otherwise manage client engagements and sell business. Any consultant to the healthcare industry should also be conversant with key trends and the mechanics of the industry. Yet, I believe these skills all come more easily, and are better developed, through formal education and training. Otherwise, why would the global firms invest so much in the development of their talent?

That is not to exclude the greatest of all teachers: experience. Some of the former executives profiled in chapter 5 thrived as consultants because of their experiences as operators and leaders of healthcare organizations. But the combination of experience plus formal training (education) is a formula that cannot be surpassed. Learning consulting skills the right way early in your advisory career can be essential. As a golf pro once explained to me, if you are doing something wrong, more practice will not help. In fact, practicing doing something the wrong way turns bad habits into muscle memory. (I have spent years trying to get rid of bad habits that haunt my golf game.)

Executives who start in consulting seem to have a leg up on their peers when they choose to return to consulting. They intimately understand what they are getting into, as they have *experienced* consulting. They can focus more on the nuances of the firm and the higher order considerations of teams and quality clients. For several people in this category, their secret seems to be that it took them several tries before they found a firm where they were totally comfortable. In some cases, that firm was one they founded on their own or with a partner or two. Consulting is a team sport, after all.

That said, I believe a lack of formal training is responsible for much of the variability often cited as a shortcoming of the consulting profession. Therefore, I advocate formal education and training for an aspiring consultant, and as early as possible in one's career.

Although shifting as a midcareer executive can involve some training, that training is not at the same formative level as an early careerist would receive with a global consulting firm. And senior executives would likely be limited to apprenticeship exercises; they are more inclined to pick a niche path and focus on a specialized practice that leverages their unique experience.

Certainly, corporate training programs are not the only way to accumulate skills, and the apprenticeship model does work relatively well in most cases. Let's be clear: Not for a minute am I suggesting that the consultants profiled earlier are anything but first-rate. They all know their stuff in their areas of focus and have strong client loyalty—key measures of success. This does not occur by chance. Somewhere along the line they picked up these skills, just not through one of the consultant boot camps offered by most medium to large firms. But these people may be among the exceptions. Most of those interviewed agree that it has gotten harder to be successful as a result of growth in the field and stiffer competition. Some would be quick to cite a little luck along the way, bowing to the reality that while many people may possess the knowledge and experience to succeed at consulting, relatively few do.

RECOMMENDATIONS

1. There are key differences between executive and consulting roles. One of the biggest is that executives have authority and consultants have none.

2. While executives have positional authority, consultants must rely on powers of persuasion. These powers can be cultivated through formal education and training.

3. Different types of consulting exist in terms of scope and approach. Similarly, executives may excel in different functions; some of these functions may transfer to consulting, depending on the nature of the practice.

4. Sales skill is the great differentiator in consulting, and one where most executives lack experience.

5. It seems likely that consulting skills will eventually become more common in executives than is the case today.

REFERENCES

Cerisano, R. 2015. "8 Things Top Consulting Firms Do Differently." 9Lenses (blog). Published February 13. www.9lenses.com/8-things-top-consulting-firms-differently/?s.

Micklewright, M. 2012. "Consultant vs. Executive." Quality Insider, *Quality Digest*. Published April 3. www.qualitydigest.com/inside/quality-insider-column/consultant-vs-executive.html.

Qubein, N. R. 2019. "From Training to Education." Nido R. Qubein (blog). www.nidoqubein.com/articles/17/From-Training-to-Education.

Turner, A. N. 1982. "Consulting Is More than Giving Advice." *Harvard Business Review* 60 (5): 120–29.

CHAPTER 8

A Closer Look at Consulting

When you hear the term "consultant," you most likely conjure
up images of suits instructing high-level management on
strategy. . . . A majority of professionals will one day
be consultants instead of employees.
—Jonathan Dison (2017)

You are not alone in considering a career change. According to
the Bureau of Labor Statistics, more than six million people made the
same decision in 2015 and 2016, and "that was before the pandemic
led many to explore different career opportunities, either by choice or
necessity" (Pohle 2021). The pandemic has had an enormous impact
on people looking at an uncertain future, according to a February
2021 Harris Poll conducted for *Fast Company* (Dishman 2021):

- Fifty-nine percent of people in the middle-income bracket
  were actively considering changing jobs.
- Forty-eight percent of workers with six-figure salaries
  were planning a job change, and two-thirds said their
  confidence in this decision had increased over the previous
  six months.
- Sixty-eight percent of employed workers valued remote
  working options; 43 percent of women and 33 percent
  of men rated remote or work-from-home options "very
  important."

Sadly, one of the many byproducts of the black swan event known as COVID-19 has been an enormous rise in furloughs and layoffs. While healthcare has had other things to deal with in terms of public health demands to contain the pandemic and the tremendous strains on the system to isolate and effectively treat those afflicted, the industry has also faced this enormous disruption to employment.

Even those healthcare organizations that did not furlough or lay off employees experienced shocking declines in patient volumes, related mostly to state mandates to prohibit so-called elective procedures (an unfortunate term that those affected would strenuously contest).[1] People caught in this vise had to deal with the scourge of unemployment and the associated free time on their hands, along with the corresponding decline in income. The promise of full employment, long an attraction of the healthcare industry, especially for overtrained nurses and physicians, has hit the proverbial brick wall. What now?

It would be shortsighted to suggest that healthcare could avoid the profound consequences of such a disruption. People otherwise attracted to healthcare tend to be relatively risk averse. Most have had training in the sciences, after all, and persevered through challenging academics to get where they are today. The payoff for their sacrifices should be at least some comfort in secure employment and a fulfilling career helping others. The bloom is off the rose if little job security remains in healthcare. Healthcare executives have long had to contend with the vagaries of high turnover and decision-making that is often steeped in internal politics. Hitching your wagon to a healthcare organization can no longer be perceived as the safe path it once was.

---

1   It will be a challenge to the public health establishment to retrospectively determine the enormous cost in time, talent, and treasure of deferring care for patients who did not suffer from COVID-19, sometimes resulting in greater morbidity and even death. A more holistic view of managing a pandemic is an urgent requirement of the public health community.

THE CONSULTANT VALUE CHAIN

Consulting has become a more common option for those considering a career change. Consulting has a lot going for it. As discussed in the previous chapter, executives have many skills that can transfer to a consulting setting, including newly developed skills in remote work (long a requirement for consultants). Consulting offers flexible hours and more control over your life. A subtle but important element of this process is the recognition that this conversion to consulting goes far beyond possessing some knowledge and experience. This realization led me to develop the Consultant Value Chain (exhibit 8.1) that is discussed in considerable detail in *The Healthcare Consultant's Handbook* (Mason 2021).

Exhibit 8.1. The Consultant Value Chain

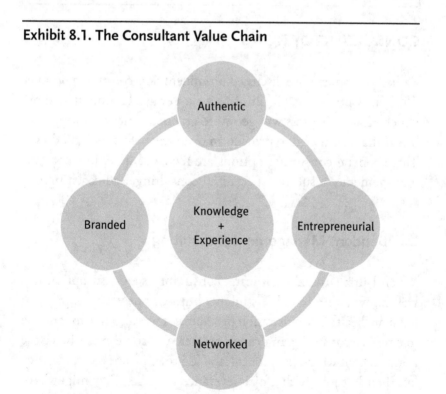

There comes a point of no return in deciding on a career change. The Career Change Decision Framework used to structure this book has guided us to this point. You have assessed your current situation and determined that a simple change of venue will not suffice, and you have considered other ways to leverage your skills. Clearly, the experiences you have accumulated in your years in healthcare have value. You have a network of important people in the industry. You have learned a lot that you believe you can use in different ways. The question is how best to leverage these skills and monetize your experience.

> **The question is how best to leverage your skills and monetize your experience.**

CONSULTING OPTIONS

Earlier in chapter 4, we discussed prominent non-consulting options. There are options in consulting as well. Let us examine these more closely. Later chapters will get more granular, but consulting is so broad that it is useful to provide an overview before we drill down. Three general consulting options are reviewed here: independent management consulting, specialized consulting, and coaching.

Independent Management Consulting

When I first entered healthcare, consulting as a career option was well known among MBA students but was not yet as popular in graduate health administration programs. It was also rare for anyone to embrace consulting midcareer or later. Yes, some executives close to retirement would list "consultant" on their business cards as they left their last jobs with a nice severance package. They might have been invited by a few friends to come spend a day with them to go through a little show and tell. But beyond informal "coaching" or swapping stories (mentoring), it seemed rare for senior executives to join consulting firms to do much more than be part of an advisory board (formal or informal).

This career trend has changed. In part, this may be because most graduate programs now emphasize team elements that are captured in small group exercises. These small groups (sometimes cohorts[2]) can be influential and can even foster a greater level of achievement among the members as they push each other. Perhaps some of your graduate school colleagues or cohort members joined a consulting firm right out of graduate school and speak highly of their experience. (Be cautious, as bragging rights may apply here.) Or perhaps you have hired and worked with several consultants. You were impressed with them and enjoyed the experience. The consultants made a difference, which also impressed you. Alternatively, you may have progressed to the point where a colleague, who knew of your current dissatisfaction, suggested, "Have you ever considered consulting?"

At the same time, the areas of expertise in which people consult have expanded dramatically, including in healthcare. As previously noted, when I first entered consulting, emphasis was placed on being a *generalist*—what is now called *strategic consulting*. The original idea of this label is that you are trained to take on any problem, even in subjects that may be outside your area of expertise or experience. Healthcare consulting, which was largely focused on the limited areas of facilities programming and planning back when it first started after World War II, has expanded to include many specialties:

- Change management and innovation
- Executive coaching
- Finance and accounting

---

2   Cohorts can involve a group that stays together for a period, going through each step in a process as a group. An example is "Joint Camp," where a group of people requiring similar orthopedic surgery (e.g., knee replacement) go through screening together, have surgery near the same day, and go through recovery as a group (which can extend over a lengthy period). I witnessed the favorable results of such a pioneer program under the leadership of Dr. Marshall Steele at Anne Arundel Medical Center, where superior outcomes were achieved.

- Fundraising
- Governance
- Government relations and regulatory compliance
- Human capital and recruiting
- Information systems and analytics
- Management systems design and integration
- Marketing and communications
- Operations performance improvement
- Quality planning and improvement
- Strategy and planning
- Supply chain management
- Training and education systems

The list goes on.

Furthermore, the nature of consulting has become ever more complex as the industry has grown. Significant market factors affect healthcare organizations today. Traditional management concepts, long the lifeblood of commercial enterprise and long panned among nonprofit organizations, have become far more commonplace. Today, management structures and processes among healthcare organizations more closely resemble those found in any commercial enterprise. The distinctions, while real and related mostly to compensation and capital (e.g., access to public markets), are fewer today than they were in the past. The exception to this may be mostly in the public safety net hospitals so vital to urban communities throughout the United States. To be fair, the distinctions in this case seem more likely to reflect limited resources attempting to address the seemingly unlimited needs of the growing clientele that depend on these hospitals.

The continued dominance of the nonprofit model in healthcare organizations is reflected most in their cultures. The profit motive, in contrast, seems profound in its simplicity. Nonprofits depend on donated funds and grants; these become the lifeblood of certain organizations—for example, children's hospitals—without which they simply would not exist. As such, nonprofit organizations incorporate fundraising and a variety of other components that do not typically exist in commercial enterprises.

From a consulting perspective, the essential transformation in healthcare creates an inviting market. Consulting thrives on change. In the healthcare environment, consulting also faces a unique challenge: improving what has traditionally been done while simultaneously adapting radical new approaches to every segment of the industry as it attempts to become more value based. The result is that healthcare management is both highly specialized and ripe for change. Not only must the traditional business of inpatient care improve with new techniques and technologies, but the new core business of community-based ambulatory and virtual care must expand in its aim to make healthcare more accessible and affordable.

Specialized Consulting

Mirroring medicine's evolution into subspecialties, no industry has been more receptive to the specialized solo consultant than healthcare. In the post–World War II push for new hospital construction, consulting focused largely on facilities design and clinical programming. Over time, that has expanded into equipment and supply chain management, debt financing, information systems, and other specialized areas. Since then, the healthcare industry has stood out in its complexity and specialized nature.

The search business thrived on this specialization, and many recruiters have focused on this space. As the healthcare industry changed, general managers required additional training, notably in clinical and administrative areas, so graduate programs sprang up across the country. Global consulting firms began to develop specialized practices focused on healthcare, which tended to include life sciences or provider and insurance-related "verticals." The array of services has only increased over time.

This growing complexity in healthcare fed an increasing need for multifunctional teams to address complicated challenges. These teams are composed of individuals with the skills required to address a wide variety of issues both in and out of healthcare. Most consulting studies in healthcare involve the convergence of many different disciplines directed toward the provision of or payment for health-related services. A study might require familiarity with a particular drug (calling on former drug reps), piece of medical equipment (medical device executives), or work process (management engineers), or the application of the unique requirements of end users (clinical systems and IT specialists).

The demand for management, clinical, and technical expertise has only increased, along with demand for the ability to create alignment overall. Large firms that currently rely on access to such specialized skills will continue to require them in the future. This suggests sustainable demand for people who possess these skills, either as independent contractors or as employees of global firms that have the client base to keep such people busy. More consulting firms appear to be using a hybrid model, employing a critical mass of generalist consultants who work alongside independent contractors with specialized skills.

Specialization can range from administration to clinical and technical areas. The technical side includes information systems and analytics—one of the highest growth areas for employment since 2010, as healthcare has become more automated and evidence-based.

Clinical specialization is nothing new in the delivery of care. What is more recent is emerging consultant specialists who have leveraged their experience developing breakthrough programs such as joint camps, neonatal and high-risk obstetrics centers, and related clinical service lines, representing mass customization of healthcare services to defined consumer cohorts (e.g., cancer patients, women's health, heart services). Clinical service lines are a great example of the convergence of clinical and administrative services in a manner designed to appeal to a discrete cohort of consumers.

Coaching

Executive coaching can be viewed as a form of consulting, but has several critical differences from other forms of management consulting. Whereas consultants advise clients—they are in the advice-giving business—coaches help the executive or leader come to their own conclusions. A coach's role includes helping the client gain confidence and perspective so they can perform at their best in making their own decisions. Ideally, the client becomes more self-aware in the process—their emotional intelligence grows.

Another key distinction between consulting and coaching is accountability. A coach is accountable to the client—usually the person being coached, not their employer. In contrast, the management consultant is ultimately accountable to the client organization that has contracted with the consultant (as one person I know puts it, the name that appears on the check). While subtle at times, there is a difference. The question to ask is, to whom do you owe devotion? You do not coach an organization; you coach a person or a team.

The reference to a *coach* in this case relates to someone who can enhance your performance. This includes your ability to examine the current situation, evaluate the source of your dissatisfaction, and determine what opportunities might be open to you at this stage of your career. "Coaches are in the transformation business," according to B. Joseph Pine II (2020), coauthor of *The Experience Economy*.

While the distinction between consulting and coaching may be blurring, notes Dr. Michael Hein (profiled in chapter 5), a coach who ends up giving advice is potentially diminishing the client's ability to develop these insights on their own. Instead, the coach should be like a catalyst in a chemical reaction—they help promote the reaction but then are no longer needed and the substance (the executive) is forever changed. As opposed to the consultant who may well be viewed as an expert, purists would advocate for coaches to be viewed as a partner with the client. Any expertise a coach may have by virtue of their experience is suspended, or set aside. The client's expertise is the focus. The underlying assumption of coaching is that the client is resourceful, and that the coach's role is to help the client enhance these resources to make sense of their context. The coach can help the client gain insights and "clear the clutter" that can often exist as they assess their context, what options are available, and how they choose to act. While no executive coaches are purists (the typical ratio is probably about 80/20—80 percent theoretical/purist and 20 percent "practical"), the best coaches find ways to interject their experiences into the conversation without it being "advice." There are now career change coaches who specialize in this pursuit. You may find it helpful to secure such a coach.

But the main reason for raising the option of coaching here has to do with leveraging the skill set that most executives will have developed from their administrative experiences. Obviously, there are many dimensions to coaching, but for our purposes *coaching* refers to helping others perform functions similar to those you performed as an executive. While coaching can involve more specialized things—skills development, dealing with job separations, coping skills, and so on—it can also be somewhat of an apprenticeship function, helping people succeed in jobs identical to the ones that you have held. Most executives get involved in evaluating, and yes, coaching their subordinates. Some of this may be related to succession planning, or simply staff development. The transition from executive to coach can be easier than executive to consultant.

On behalf of those who have received formal education and training to become certified executive coaches, I would be remiss if I did not raise the same point that I am raising about management consulting in general. There is a difference between someone who has received formal instruction to be an executive coach and someone who simply hangs out their shingle with a new title. For example, Jack Schlosser of Desert Vista Advisors had a long and distinguished career as an executive search consultant with Spencer Stuart. He took advantage of one of the many training programs for executive coaches and became certified. When we spoke, he was quick to point out that a trained executive coach has access to tools, including diagnostics, that can be helpful in working with individual clients attempting to make important changes. So, while becoming an executive coach is perhaps a more natural transition from an executive position than becoming an independent management consultant, it would nevertheless be beneficial to receive some formal training and education.

CONSULTING SKILLS IN THE C-SUITE

In his book *The Consulting Economy*, Jonathan Dison (2017) provides an expansive view of consulting, suggesting a "workforce revolution" is coming, with companies shifting to a "flexible workforce solution" where contractors (which the author equates to consultants) are preferred to full-time employees.[3] Jonathan Dison starts his book with an example of someone who worked for a company for 22 years, only to be laid off during difficult times. Having worked with Dison on a consulting project when she was the client, she sought out his advice, not thinking that consulting was an option. Dison hired her to be a consultant, noting that although she lacked confidence she had already exhibited strong project management skills, along with other skills that related to the kind of consulting Dison did. His central thesis is that "in the near future, **nearly all professionals will be consultants or contractors**" (emphasis in original).

This is a bit of an extreme point of view, to which I do not fully subscribe. What does resonate with me is the recognition that future executives will increasingly be required to possess some of the skills normally ascribed to consultants. As evidence of this, a growing number of career consultants have competed for and won prominent executive positions in healthcare. Perhaps this reflects the complexity of these executive jobs and the expanding collaborative cultures, discussed in some detail in chapter 3.

---

3   It is interesting to speculate on the impact of COVID-19 on this. Will employers be inclined to support a more temporary/flexible workforce in the future?

C-suites are driven by the cross-functional teams that are prevalent in consulting organizations. As of 2021 there are only a few isolated graduate courses focused on consulting, but it seems likely that this number will grow as building blocks such as analytics become more common, and as sales continues its slow evolution toward being a recognized field of academic study. Over time, perhaps the lines that currently separate executive management from consulting will begin to blur a bit, which would be a good thing. This might also help bridge the gap that makes becoming an independent management consultant so challenging for people who have functioned for any extended time in the capacity of a CEO, as discussed in the next chapter.

RECOMMENDATIONS

1. It is now time to see what committing to a consulting option would mean, including the desire to eliminate the potential regret of not giving it a try.

2. The ongoing transformation in healthcare creates an inviting market for consulting, which thrives on change.

3. Three general forms of consulting exist: independent management consulting, specialized consulting, and coaching. There are some important differences between these three types.

4. Coaching, while a common function as an executive, is different in several important ways in the context of becoming an executive coach.

5. It seems likely that education for executives of the future will include the development of some skills similar to those commonly required of consultants today.

REFERENCES

Dishman, L. 2021. "Is Now a Good Time to Change Careers? More Workers Are Feeling Good About It." Career Evolution (blog), *Fast Company*. Published February 23. www.fastcompany. com/90607167/is-now-a-good-time-to-change-careers-more-workers-are-feeling-good-about-it.

Dison, J. 2017. *The Consulting Economy: How to Manage Your Career in the Coming Workforce Revolution.* Carson City, NV: Lioncrest Publishing.

Mason, S. A. 2021. *The Healthcare Consultant's Handbook: Career Opportunities and Best Practices.* Chicago: Health Administration Press.

Pine, B. J., II, and J. H. Gilmore. 2019. *The Experience Economy: Competing for Customer Time, Attention, and Money.* Boston: Harvard Business.

Pohle, A. 2021. "How to Change Careers: Find What to Pursue Next." *Wall Street Journal*, February 4. www.wsj. com/articles/how-to-change-careers-find-what-to-pursue-next-11605824886.

CHAPTER 9

CEOs Face Some Unique Challenges

*My greatest strength as a consultant is to be ignorant
and ask a few questions.*
—Peter Drucker

WHEN I WAS employing a virtual model in my practice, I had
the advantage of experiencing many different experts in action.[1] By
this time I had an established track record of assembling consulting
teams composed of other career consultants and collaborating with
other firms on a variety of projects. I also had occasion to bring a
few former executives into engagements. I found that my experience
with CEOs turned consultant was more variable and risky. Several
worked out, but a number were disasters.

These were all highly accomplished executives with stellar careers. I
would put these former executives up against anyone in terms of executive performance and results—but not when it came to consulting. I
found that experienced executives can go horribly wrong when asked
to function in the role of a consultant. These experiences contributed
greatly to my desire to better diagnose what may have gone wrong and
to try to help future CEOs better navigate this transition. This chapter
discusses a variety of thorny issues that may arise. A companion case
study in appendix D demonstrates how these issues may show up in a
consulting engagement. Together, I hope they will help you examine
your motivations for this career change and to avoid similar problems.

---

1 See chapter 8 in *The Healthcare Consultant's Handbook* for an explanation of different
consulting models.

CEOs HAVE MUCH TO OFFER

One of the great joys of a career in healthcare consulting has been the exposure to many immensely talented CEOs. (To be fair, there were also a few duds along the way.) No two of these CEOs came into their positions in the exact same way, and their skill sets were diverse as well. I have also observed talented people who did not succeed in one organizational culture but who were immensely successful in a different one. Fit is important. An operational turnaround situation, for example, is very different from a thriving growth environment. Business is cyclical, according to many experts, and each phase of a business cycle draws on different skill sets. Few people straddle all these skill sets well.

Before I suggest some particularly common traps for CEOs, it is important to acknowledge that anyone who has reached this level of experience in healthcare likely has much to offer in terms of knowledge and experience. The CEO traits that are most attractive relative to consulting are listed in exhibit 9.1. Let's examine each of these briefly.

Exhibit 9.1. CEO Traits Attractive to Consulting

Traits	Knowledge	Experience	Implications
Experience as client	A user's perspective How different firms operate	Participating in numerous and varied engagements as a client	Ability to empathize Implementation experience Feel for cultural differences
Comfort in a fishbowl	Been there, done that	In comfort zone Delegating successfully Taking ownership	Familiar with being on stage

Communication prowess	Clarity of vision and ability to present and advocate	Dealing with crises and sensitive issues	Not likely to be caught off guard
Ability to gain consensus	How to delegate decisions How to let the process happen	Respecting the gifts of each team member	Knows when to lead and when to sit back
Team building	Attributes of high-performance teams	Ability to attract and retain good people	Knows how to achieve alignment
Comfort with complexity	Intimate understanding of what makes healthcare complex	Managing multiple issues in a complex environment	Has the judgment to set priorities and not allow complexity to be a barrier to success

Experience as a Client

I have encountered some CEOs who see hiring a consultant for help, much less for implementation, as a sign of weakness. Thankfully, this attitude is rare and probably reflects a broader insecurity. Even where they may not have this specific fear, some CEOs are comfortable hiring a consultant to help figure things out but reluctant to delegate any part of implementation to an outside firm. This leaves consultants desperate to know how well their recommendations were implemented.

As an experienced healthcare executive, you possess a profound understanding of consulting that, frankly, some consultants lack. Simply stated, you have lived through numerous consulting engagements and *experienced* different firms (styles) and the impact of their advice on your organization—both good and bad. This user's perspective is invaluable. Consulting firms have been known to expend considerable resources trying to better understand this perspective—setting up advisory boards, speaking at bag lunches, making site visits, and more—in an effort to raise their sensitivities and understand what approaches work best under different circumstances. Your experience living through these experiences has real value and could be a driver for your future consulting practice, although you do not want to overplay this hand.

A fundamental tenet of consulting is that recommendations must be successfully implemented. Failure to implement makes the overall engagement a failure; finding the solution to a problem is of little value if the solution is not put to use. It is hard for consulting firms to survive when their recommendations are not followed. A former CEO's ability to bring this dimension to a consulting team can be of great value if positioned properly.

Comfort in a Fishbowl

If we were to be invited to eavesdrop on the healthcare CEO locker room, what complaints would we hear? As likely as not, it might be the weariness associated with being on call 24/7. As long as you're in town, the phone can ring at any time. A certain notoriety also comes with this position. For many communities in the United States, the local hospital is the single largest employer. You are noticed in the grocery store or at your favorite restaurant. You can delegate certain things, but that only goes so far.

It follows that the best executives not only become comfortable with notoriety, they thrive on it. It is part of their calling. It helps them take ownership. Ownership is a hard attribute to imitate, but CEOs understand it. This understanding is a major asset in consulting. Ownership is also one of the things that makes CEO turnover so difficult to manage. We will come back to the negative aspects of ownership later.

Communication Prowess

Not all CEOs write well, but they have learned when to speak and when to listen. The position requires it. Many consultants never learn this lesson well. Given that the CEO attracts so much attention, they tend to learn quickly that much can get accomplished at times by sitting back and letting others do the talking. Group meetings are the lifeblood of many executive suites. CEOs learn to be productive and gain consensus through such meetings.

There is a caveat here, however. As noted in a March 2021 LinkedIn post by Restart Agile, "the ability to listen requires deliberate cultivation. Few people need it more than senior executives, who tend to focus on presenting their own opinions as forcefully as possible, rather than on listening to what others have to say." A classic *McKinsey Quarterly* article offers concrete advice for executives who want to become better listeners: Respect others, stay quiet so they can speak, and challenge your assumptions (Ferrari 2012).

The discipline of communication covers many fronts, one of which is dealing with crises and sensitive issues. Experienced CEOs are unlikely to be caught off guard. They have access to resources and are comfortable speaking across a broad array of events in front of diverse audiences—an important skill.

Ability to Gain Consensus

Leading requires the CEO to occasionally get out in front of the team. An experienced CEO learns to do this sparingly, as it can defeat the desire to gain consensus from a bottom-up process.

Not all CEOs are capable of achieving consensus. Although getting out front may be common in commercial enterprises, nonprofit organizations tend to operate more on a consensus basis.[2] Most healthcare CEOs have experience operating in a

---

2 This may relate to the nature of the volunteer board; there may be a reluctance to alienate any of these people, who are donating their time and who may bolt if they feel disrespected.

culture that considers consensus a noble pursuit, although such a culture can be rightfully criticized for sometimes emphasizing conformity over innovation. Similarly, consulting generally involves seeking consensus: no easy task. There is no substitute for experience leading within such a consensus-based culture. The CEO experience is perhaps unique in its exposure to the many nooks and crannies of such a culture.

Not always easy to understand and generally difficult to achieve, operating within a consensus platform requires some unique collaborative skills, including the ability to persuade people of all stripes and interests. Any experienced CEO in healthcare can boast of considerable experience with this level of discourse. It takes patience and can become counterproductive if not managed carefully. Granted, not all CEOs operate as consensus leaders; few management decisions ever come down to a vote, and I have heard more than one CEO say, "This is not a democracy." But the good ones know how to lead by consensus when required.

Operating within a consensus platform requires some unique collaborative skills, including the ability to persuade people of all stripes and interests.

Team Building

Good CEOs lead good teams. They attract good people and retain good talent—often, talent that extends into areas beyond the reach and knowledge of the CEO. Successful CEOs recognize this, respect the gifts of each team member, and take pride in assembling and leading such a team.

Done right, this skill can be carried over into consulting. A key element of team building is knowing when to lead and when to step back. The best CEOs use this to their advantage. At the end of the day, it is about alignment. Nothing is more important to a team than alignment around common values and goals, whether in a provider setting or in consulting. Like a sheepdog, CEOs know how to tend to the flock and pay attention to different members of the team. No one is born knowing how to cultivate goodwill. CEOs adopt approaches that work for them, recognizing that different people require different approaches.

Comfort with Complexity

The emerging science of complexity has implications for management, and is especially important to successfully managing the transformative changes required of healthcare. The best healthcare CEOs learn to be comfortable with complexity. Healthcare organizations are complicated; healthcare is complex. There is a difference, and managing expectations based on these differences is important.

Much of what we manage in healthcare is complicated. Applying pressure in one area can lead to unintended consequences in others. Systems theory applies, and some level of uncertainty always exists. Executives who seek a black-and-white world have likely been quickly chased away from leading a healthcare organization. Comfort should not be allowed to block curiosity or reduce the resolve to solve problems, but it must be tempered with the reality that some problems are best left to tomorrow, as today already has enough challenges. CEOs are confronted daily with a plethora of challenges and learn to sort through a defensible list of priorities, both for them and for the organization.

Executives who seek a black-and-white world have likely been quickly chased away from leading a healthcare organization. Comfort should not be allowed to block curiosity.

Clearly, CEOs bring a wealth of valuable experience with them as they consider a transition to consulting. However, they may also confront a number of traps that are easy to fall into as a result of their experiences. Those traps are covered in the rest of this chapter.

TRANSITIONING TO CONSULTING CAN BE ESPECIALLY CHALLENGING FOR CEOs

There are a number of critical differences between executive positions and consulting—some are so critical that one could suggest the cards are stacked against CEOs attempting to make this transition. Without a clear understanding of the situation, some CEOs may find traps such as these lethal to their career change:

- natural conflicts of interest;
- confusion over the different roles of entrepreneurs, consultants, and operators; and
- the need to unlearn some behaviors that were valuable in the CEO role but do not necessarily transfer well.

I have had some time to reflect on what happened when former CEOs did not work out as members of the consulting team. I tried to coach these executives regarding the difference between being the decision maker and the advisor. I accept some responsibility for these failures. There is a fundamental difference between driving the agenda as CEO and serving a client who has their own agenda. In retrospect, I probably underestimated the transition involved.

I selected these executives because I knew them and had worked with them before, though not necessarily as a consultant to their organization. Usually, they had been through a challenge that was similar to one my client was facing. I usually knew that key differences existed between the organizations that they led and the client in question, and that recognizing these differences was a hurdle the CEO needed to factor into their approach to this engagement, although I somehow failed to get them fully to accept that point.

To be clear, *failure* is not a label I choose randomly; it was the label my clients used to describe the involvement of these former executives. In every case, I had been very clear up front that these were previous CEOs who had in-depth experience with a particular issue I thought would apply the client's situation. Also, these engagements involved more than a cameo appearance by these former CEOs, as I asked them to lead work around a key issue and come to a set of recommendations, functioning as a consultant facilitator. Each former CEO did a good job of describing their experience and the process they went through, but they often failed to connect with the client in a way that translated into a positive client engagement. In other words, they interacted with the client as a CEO, not as a consultant. In hindsight, I would say that they failed to recognize that it was no longer their show; it was about the client. A consultant may manage the conversation, but they are no longer in charge. Clearly, this is a subtle distinction, and it can be a tough transition to make. Once someone has had a taste at the top, it can be difficult to shift gears to a role that demands a different approach.

One consultant friend emphasizes the need for consultants to "replace anecdote with research" (or evidence). Just because something worked once for you in your capacity as a CEO does not mean that this can or should be replicated elsewhere. How does this approach compare to how others have done it? How do you know this? What are the important variables to consider? This is the art of consulting, which any engagement must rely on in order to make the necessary team connections. The consultant that walks in with a baked solution before listening to the client will quickly be exposed and is likely to experience some serious blowback early in the process.

This blunt assessment suggests that CEOs may have some unlearning to do. James A. Rice, PhD, who was profiled in chapter 5 as an early pioneer, has an interesting take on this: CEOs require "a splash of cold water." He cautions not to move precipitously, and advises CEOs to consider five "R Factors" that can interact to make the transition difficult: respect, relationships, resources, rejection, and resilience. I have expanded on these five factors in exhibit 9.2.

Exhibit 9.2. Rice's Five "R Factors"

Respect	Many CEOs and C-suite executives think respect is earned by virtue of their position. It may or may not be "earned" at all. While titles can carry significant influence in health systems, they carry little weight in consulting organizations. Watching a typical internal consultant team meeting, you would be hard pressed to tell who holds what position. The conversation is entirely driven by knowledge and experience earned in diverse consulting projects with many clients. Good ideas are good ideas, whoever provides them.
Relationships	Like celebrities, CEOs travel in admiring company. People are always trying to single them out and sell them something. Relationships develop but it is always hard to determine which ones are about the position and which are genuine friendships. In either case, these relationships may have no correlation with selling consulting services.
Resources	CEOs have an executive assistant to help them stay organized. They get good at delegating. There are few such support positions in consulting. Administrative assistants were common in a consulting career years ago, but they rarely exist anymore. Any one unable to type, for example, will soon be frustrated. Consultants must be willing to do much more for themselves than is expected of any CEO.

Rejection	CEOs get used to being "right" and being supported to get grand plans implemented. They are flattered and get invited to exclusive clubs. They are sought after and pampered. Consulting can be a rude awakening. Rejection is not only possible in the pursuit of new business, but likely.
Resilience	Over time, CEOs may begin to coast in their positions. It is an occupational hazard. Perhaps the biggest danger is getting comfortable to the point that you lose your innovative and problem-solving edge. Becoming a consultant means losing the ability to make arbitrary decisions in favor of defensible analysis and persuasion. This can be frustrating.

Dr. Rice goes on to suggest that, at least until recently, men may have been more susceptible to these frustrations than women. For years, too many men have believed that "the job defines the essence of who they are." There is much in the literature regarding the negative psychological impact, particularly for men, of job loss. For many men, it challenges their fundamental view of themselves. In contemporary markets, shifting an executive career to consulting can invoke similar concerns for anyone. In short, these frustrations should not be taken lightly when a senior executive begins to consider the potential transitions involved in a shift to consulting.

Looking back on my attempts to bring in former CEOs as consultants, I think my failures to better integrate them into consulting teams came down to two things: inability to help them make the transition from decision maker to advisor, and the implicit belief that one size fits all (i.e., because something worked for well for them, all clients had to do was approach this issue the same way). Clearly, that did not resonate in these specific cases. Reduced to one key source of failure, these former CEOs lacked *authenticity* as a consultant with these specific clients. While each had a proven track record as an executive, with experiences that were clearly relevant to the issue at hand, their approach with these clients did not convey the level of authenticity required to fulfill the role of independent advisor. When it came to client acceptance, it was essential but insufficient that I respected these former CEOs and was comfortable introducing them into the process. I was left to pick up the pieces.

These hurdles represent profound issues that I have found to be especially challenging for former CEOs to successfully navigate. Few of the former CEOs involved in these client engagements went on to a successful consulting career. It is easy to dismiss these as one-off situations, but I have concluded that there is more to it than that.

Comparing Entrepreneurs, Consultants, and Operators

Being entrepreneurial is one of the four elements surrounding the core of our Consultant Value Chain (see exhibit 8.1). However, consulting should not be confused with being an entrepreneur, though they can feed off each other. There are important differences between an entrepreneur, a consultant, and an operator. Role confusion is a genuine concern; the danger comes from trying to function in a different role without understanding the differences. I have spent some time in each of these spaces and have thus come to appreciate the differences. I will expand on those differences here (exhibit 9.3), as they may interest you as you consider career options.

Entrepreneurs are creative risk-takers who start businesses, often with their own money at risk. They learn or invent what is required to start a business and then launch it. But what is required to start a business is not necessarily the same as what is required to sustain that business; that is the fundamental difference between an entrepreneur and an operator.

Entrepreneurs have access to capital and are driven to some extent by the drama of success and failure; the outcome has consequences. Entrepreneurs remove barriers to success, sometimes rudely; they do not let things get in their way. Failure is not an option, and success tends to be rather black-and-white. They make their money primarily

Exhibit 9.3. Comparison of Entrepreneurs, Consultants, and Operators

Category	Responsibility/Motivators	Critical Success Factors	Source of Income	Key Implications
Entrepreneur	Launch Take creative risks Remove barriers to success Create value Enjoy the thrill; the risk and reward	Focus on start up Accumulate capital Make money for others Build a track record Get to breakeven Position to be acquired Have a clear exit strategy	Equity growth	Can be rude and impetuous in removing barriers Not out to make friends Creates value through organic or external growth Can be impatient
Consultant	Advise Add value Stay within their expertise	Knowledge and experience Successful clients Trusted advisor status Recognition/personal brand	Fees	Sustainable business requires repeat clients Dependent on references Needs to make measurable impact High energy
Operator	Meet operating goals Do it the right way Ensure superior performance .	Handle short- and long-term considerations Build a sustainable business Perform to key performance indicators	Salary and bonus Sometimes equity	Hires and retains staff Grows the business Builds resilience Can be opinionated

from growth in equity. The goal is accumulating capital, some of which can be applied to the next start-up. They are grasping for the proverbial brass ring of riches and the satisfaction of conquering the market. Entrepreneurs focus on the short run and on overcoming the myriad of hurdles in the way—regulatory, logistical, financial, talent-related, and so on. They are not out to make friends; their metric is making money.

Much has been written about founders needing to give way to a true operator (manager) over time or risk getting stuck in the starting position. Serial entrepreneurs recognize this, and stay in a leadership position only long enough to turn the business over to an operator and move on to their next start-up. While those who have started businesses have knowledge and experience to offer others, they usually have a choice to make about being either an entrepreneur or a consultant. Few succeed at being both because the roles involve different outlooks and personalities.

Stories abound of entrepreneurs running over people as they pursue the path to success. I have seen this personally. Failure means financial loss—including loss of investment, not just income. Having spent time with several entrepreneurs, and having been one at times myself, I know they are not always easy to be around. It takes a certain mindset to always be seeking other people's capital knowing that it may not be returned—all entrepreneurial ventures involve risk.[3]

Consultants have different drivers. They tend to be more focused on the recognition that comes with success (personal brand) through the accumulation of knowledge and experience that they leverage by advising others who seek their help. Depending on the nature of their practice, consulting can involve a lot of gray areas. Success is derived by the success of the client. Most consulting income is from fees. Entrepreneurs and consultants both know the critical success factors of a business and share a drive to succeed. Most consultants

---

3   I confess that accepting an angel investment from a young couple—for whom this was a big investment—for a venture I was leading and which ultimately failed (at considerable financial loss to me) is a memory that will always haunt me.

run their business considering both the short and long run. Preserving and enhancing their brand is a key success factor for consultants.

The operator is somewhere between the other two, and more like a CEO. Operators tend to function in a more binary world of right and wrong. In private enterprise, the operator can participate in both equity and fees (or salary). But the key for operators is their focus on the long-term success of the business. More than meeting payroll next week, operators are focused on building something by growing the business and beating the competition. Where entrepreneurs have incredible focus on just a few things, operators must learn the nuances of virtually all components of the business, both short term and long term. No detail is ignored, especially when it comes to attracting and retaining talent. They develop a unique organizational culture and style.

With the lack of barriers to consulting, either an entrepreneur or an operator can be tempted into the field. But the differences can sometimes lead to disastrous results. Entrepreneurs can often get away with functioning, at least temporarily, as a consultant. They tend not to have the patience to do so for an extended period. Impatience is an important attribute driving serial entrepreneurs; there is an urgency to all that they do. They are in and out of a business. The operator has a different orientation.

Operators find it hard to function in the role of consultants in my experience, except for operations improvement studies. They tend to take pride in the operating success they have enjoyed and to believe that there is only one way to effectively do things—their way. The more competitive the business, the more this seems to be the case. I have seen this play out with dire consequences. One situation involved an exceptionally talented operator who clearly knew the ins and outs of a particular business—generally an asset in any client interaction, so long as the focus is on operating performance. Unfortunately, operators also tend to hold strong opinions about how a business should be operated as a standalone business. It can often be inferred from their delivery that *everyone else does it wrong*. Healthcare is complicated.

What Can Go Wrong

Inability to see the big picture. One of the complications in health-care is the realization that most healthcare organizations operate more than one business. They tend to support a portfolio of businesses, all of which must be interrelated (systemness) at least to some extent. Each of these businesses should ideally be competitive with other alternatives in each space (e.g., rehab services). This can be a delicate situation, and there can be a different dynamic present for operators, as illustrated in the following example.

I was teamed up with an operator associated with a highly competitive and growing healthcare business. This operator knew their stuff and, as is typical of most successful operators, had a commanding personality. Sharing the limelight was challenging for this person. During one challenging engagement, their operating orientation became more evident, and it was clear they were used to being in charge. OK so far. However, leaders encourage debate, and operators require performance—a subtle but important distinction. There were multiple dimensions to this client engagement, as it was about more than just this line of business, and when the operator's expertise intersected with that of other members of the consulting team, the operator became openly argumentative. Again, that is OK, as long as it takes place off stage.

Interactions within the consulting team generally encourage consideration of different points of view. Diversity of opinion is central to the quality of the resulting product. But having such a debate in front of the client is toxic and sows confusion. The fallout was immediate. The client lost confidence in the consulting team. For the remainder of the engagement, the client was on edge, questioning everything the consulting team recommended. Every interaction seemed to anticipate another open disagreement among the consultants, almost as though the client was baiting the consulting team into additional controversies. It did not take the team long to realize the winds had shifted and there was no finding a new path to success. The damage was done. The engagement was terminated prematurely.

This engagement is an extreme example of the risk, but an operator who lacks formal training in basic consulting skills can easily come across as a bull in a china shop. When legitimate attempts to educate the team become disruptive or the operator is perceived as arrogant, it can have dire consequences for the engagement. Operators can tend to stand out from the team in ways that are not helpful. Lacking muscle memory in the basic skills that the rest of the team has conquered (organization, presentation skills, conflict resolution, teamwork, delegation) can make them difficult to work with. This reflects poorly on the team and can be perceived as unprofessional by the client. The open disagreement among the consultants on this engagement was perceived by the client as "not getting your story straight."

An executive who gets thrown in the pool with experienced swimmers runs the risk of sticking out and underperforming. It does not always end this badly, but the risk is there. While I do not wish to generalize this to all operators, some of the behaviors that may be required to be good operators can prove difficult to overcome in the role of consultant, even with more training.

Do it my way. Another way of interpreting such behavior is that operators tend to want to do things their way. Their focus tends to be on performance, and they are surrounded by people looking for direction ("do this like that"). This attitude is more common when the business becomes commoditized, requiring training (what to do) rather than education (why to do it). Where the market sees little difference between competitors, superior performance is rewarded and more emphasis is appropriately placed on doing things better than others. While a CEO would generally have a broader focus than performance, the operator may be much like a CEO who has functioned in that capacity for two or three decades, becoming set in their ways and less receptive to innovation.

> **Insensitivity to differences in context between clients may be the single greatest danger a former CEO must overcome to function in an advisory role.**

Insensitivity to differences in context between clients may be the single greatest danger a former CEO must overcome to function in an advisory role. The danger is the implicit belief that most healthcare organizations have a lot in common, and their past successes can be easily replicated anywhere. These executives tend to consider any deviation from the way they did things to be inferior rather than innovative. As the skeptic once claimed, "All organizations would be great save for one key thing—the people."

Creating dependency. Consulting is personal. If nothing else, the people factor is, by definition, different in every consulting engagement. People will struggle to succeed in the role of an independent consultant unless they are willing to pay attention to the people factor. Successful consultants are attracted to meeting new people and figuring out how to influence their thinking and actions. Consulting advice only has value to the extent that it is accepted by the client and produces the intended result. To that end, it is often better to serve as a facilitator who helps the client develop the solution themselves, thus developing the confidence needed to tackle the next challenge. This is far preferable to the client developing a dependency on the consultant for all the answers.

I must admit I have known more than a few consultants who seem to thrive on the *dependency approach* to consulting, as it can lead to a long-term relationship with more future work. This can also be characterized as the "black box approach," where the consultant pushes their brand as having found some magical, proprietary solution to every problem. I much prefer helping the client to become more self-sufficient.

One size fits all. Functioning in the capacity of interim CEO on several occasions allowed me to see how the expectations were different for CEOs than for consultants. There is a difference between making a recommendation and making the decision. CEOs can become used to making the decisions, and sometimes these decisions seem arbitrary. I liken it to a parent defending a decision to an inquisitive child: "Because I said so." That may work for some parents (only temporarily mind you), but it's far less successful for seasoned executives.

There is another subtle component to this. CEOs who have been with one organization for an extended period of time tend to lose their appetite for seeking alternative ways of approaching things; they become set in their ways. Men may be particularly susceptible to this. Rice and Perry (2012, 21) suggest, "Many male leaders assume that their effectiveness must be shaped by an authoritarian or even autocratic management style." We are all a product of our experiences.

In smaller organizations, one of the limitations is less exposure to alternative ways of thinking and operating. The concern is that the CEO turned consultant may take for granted that people in the client organization possess the same skills and orientation common in the organization they led for many years. Said differently, it is easy to overlook the subtle accommodations that take place over time, allowing the organization they led for many years to be molded to suit the CEO; it becomes comfortable. Teams get used to each other, to the point they can finish each other's sentences. Roles are clear and complementary, and expectations become comfortable and predictable. As noted before, such exposure over an extended period of time can easily morph into the belief that one size fits all. The result can be truly disastrous for the transition to consulting.

Lack of empathy. Empathy is often touted as an important attribute of a skilled consultant. Understanding client cultures is one area where this tends to be difficult for some consultants. Again, experience gained from being the client helps CEOs foster empathy and humility.

Most consulting engagements, at least in healthcare, tend to end before implementation. The client team is left to implement the recommendations, and the consultant misses out on the back end of the engagement process. This may be shocking to executives, but experienced consultants are keenly aware that the process is often truncated in this fashion, as most clients tend to feel that they are capable of implementing most recommendations coming out of a consulting engagement.

MANAGERIAL BEST PRACTICES ARE CHANGING

Consultants have long been involved in helping management teams adopt more enlightened practices. Consultants who do not recognize and adapt to these changes run the risk of being accused of offering advice for a world that no longer exists. To help you avoid this, I offer a few managerial best practices that future management consultants should understand.

Collaborative Leadership

A charismatic model of leadership, or what medicine refers to as *hero medicine,* while old school, has tended to dominate managerial practices in healthcare. While all effective leaders can benefit from some charisma, this hero model is being intentionally replaced by more collaborative styles (Goman 2017).

The complexity of current times demands much from leaders. In fact, the traditional models do not really work well under changing circumstances. Quint Studer (2020, 14) puts it well in his leadership handbook:

The fact is, "command and control" is on its way out. Right now we are in a period of struggle as many members of the old guard still want to lead in traditional ways, while newer leaders try to figure out new models and structures that work well. As younger generations replace the older one, more change will occur. One thing's for sure: followers can no longer be passive order takers or "yes men" and "yes women." Good followership is active, dynamic, and creative. It gets noticed and rewarded.

A more collaborative approach is required: one that recognizes the inability of one person to meet the many, and at times conflicting, requirements of leadership. Consulting is a team sport. Today's CEOs did not invent the hero model; it was modeled for them by their mentors, and it was common at one time. But CEOs who employed this style of leadership will find the transition to a consulting career challenging.

High-Performing Teams

I have seen many teams that developed such extraordinary familiarity with each other and so honed their interactions that it had taken their conversations to another level. While this environment is intuitively attractive (who doesn't want to be comfortable in their work setting?), on closer examination I found the cultures of these organizations to be mostly stale and uninspiring. It may seem counterintuitive, but more often than not these teams had lost their edge when compared to other teams that exhibited more dynamic tension, and they tended not to innovate. Worse than that, innovation was often discouraged. Conformity (sometimes confused with *loyalty*) was the behavior that was rewarded. An unfortunate result is that such teams often close themselves off to new members. This becomes obvious when a new person is added to the team and quickly notices that openly disagreeing or offering another point of view on some issue is met with disdain (sometimes overtly, other times more subtly).

High-performing teams benefit from dynamic tension when staffed with executives who seek challenges and enjoy the level of engagement that such cultures demand. This isn't just my observation. Microsoft, for example, partnered with IDEO to identify five attributes of successful teams:

1. **Team purpose**—*Keeps teams focused, fulfilled, and aligned on achieving their objectives.*
2. **Collective identity**—*Fosters a sense of belonging and helps team members work together as a unit.*

3. **Awareness and inclusion**—*Enables teams to navigate interpersonal dynamics and value everyone's perspective.*
4. **Trust and vulnerability**—*Encourages interpersonal risk-taking in teams.*
5. **Constructive tension**—*Serves as a generative force for new ideas, driving better outcomes. (Spataro 2019)*

Practical Onboarding

When a former CEO joins an existing consulting firm, the consulting team is likely to intercede on an engagement before the CEO is exposed to any client work. During the first assignment, the engagement team will begin preparations for the work based on the accepted proposal. The former CEO will be immediately subjected to interactions with a group of overachievers who have been taught not only critical thinking but also how to structure an argument and defend it. Most if not all of the engagement team members will have far more consulting experience than the CEO. Just as the culture that the CEO just left had a preferred way of doing things, every firm has a certain culture-bound way of approaching things that becomes part of their brand. This takes time to learn and understand.

When CEOs first get exposed to these internal consulting processes, they tend to be overwhelmed by the talent and abilities of the people associated with the firm. (I have occasionally had the wow experience of watching a highly skilled consultant exercising their skills in ways that were reminiscent of an artist with their palette and canvas.) One of the attractions of consulting is being surrounded by highly capable people who are both experienced and motivated. This can be both shocking and invigorating, depending on the circumstances. Nothing quite compares to great feedback from a colleague after a sensitive client meeting: "Wow, you were sure on your game in there."

In contrast, can't you just picture the dynamic exchange between members of the engagement team and a know-it-all former CEO who has a long track record of doing things their way? The results will answer the age-old question of what happens when an unstoppable force meets an immovable object. Fortunately, any firm with experience in onboarding an executive will understand these challenges and will actively coach the former CEO to navigate these transitions.

Getting plugged into an engagement team is a good example of what happens when a senior executive is immersed into a culture that is neither familiar to them nor perhaps consistent with their previous team experiences. Such a group does not seek nor embrace a charismatic leader; rather, it values experience and insights from settings relevant to the services being sought by the client in each situation. As in the overall marketplace for consulting, executives with relevant management experience will bring value to the dialogue that is part of every consulting engagement. But where relevance is not obvious, they will be confronted with the same challenge as every other consultant—what value can they bring to this team?

Highly Educated, Autonomous Teams

Management team members today are more well-read and educated than in the past and are eager to make a contribution. The charismatic style of management, while effective in the past, appealed more to followers than leaders. The current crop of managers coming out of graduate programs were trained to lead, not to follow.[4]

For those CEOs unable to separate themselves from the executive chair, frustration can develop when the consulting team—much less the client—does not accept or is otherwise unable to adopt a

---

4 I have been around long enough to see some ancient models of management play out. Take, for example, the CEO who was coddled to the absurd point that that they did not have a driver's license or know how to drive a car when they retired from the organization where they first started as administrative resident some 50 years before.

recommendation from the former CEO who was used to "doing things his way." When their recommendation is rejected, especially in a client situation, these CEOs turned consultant tend to become jaundiced and end up criticizing their client as being less capable. It is truly hazardous for a consultant to become critical of their client. While subtle perhaps, this point is so important to understand that I developed a detailed exercise to shed more light on this challenge (appendix D: Case Study of a Failed Engagement).

Sharing the Ball

I am reminded of a conversation I had some years ago with Mark Alarie, a close friend who played in the NBA and was an All-American basketball player at Duke (where I was a freshman walk-on player during the Pleistocene era). When we first met, years after he had graduated, I told Mark that, as good as his team was I really wished he had shot more, as he was an exceptional scorer. His response has stayed with me over the years: "You have to understand that there was only one ball."

In team sports, a leader's connectedness is often such that everyone in the organization has what they need to act in ways that are likely to realize the aim of their shared goal (winning the game). The leader helps set the framework—the why, and the what.

Managing in complexity involves the manager, as opposed to the leader, deciding the how. The player with the ball ultimately determines where it goes based on the actions of the team and their competitors. And Mark was not the point guard; Johnny Dawkins was. The team had great success because of the skills of each player, but Johnny, who had the ball most of the time, had to know what he was doing. Everyone was so talented that it was hard to stand out on that team (as evidenced by the fact that Johnny was honored as the Naismith Player of the Year). The team did well because Mark, Johnny, and their teammates understood and were comfortable with their different roles. Johnny knew how to share the ball—how to anticipate what other teammates were doing and get the ball to the open player. He also knew how to move without the ball.

In contemporary management, CEOs must learn to move without the ball. Vision and culture must encourage innovation and trust that allow this higher level of functioning—this *shared consciousness*.[5] In my experience, just as sports teams work hard to create a shared team culture, there is no substitute for a well-managed enterprise strategic planning process and the contribution that it can make to creating such an aligned culture. Involving a coach for a sports team, or independent consultants in such an enterprise process, is paramount if the undertaking is to avoid being diverted toward unconscious bias or debilitating politics.

Credibility Through Diverse Experiences

Like athletics, much of executive coaching deals with helping executives gain comfort and skill with the roles they are asked to play. The new consultant will have much to learn about how to integrate into a consulting team and work with a client. Working with multiple consulting teams makes this even more challenging. Imagine if a college athlete had to work every other month with a new team, taking on varying roles in each. That is both the fun and the challenge of consulting. While it's not for everyone, it can be quite stimulating. There is little to no chance of becoming bored.

Coaches see things others miss. When you are in the moment, especially as an elite athlete or proven professional, muscle memory kicks in. You know what to do next because you are in total sync with the group. Even though it may not be true, it feels as if you have been there before. This muscle memory is created through practice and repetition, coaching, and open interaction within the group.

---

5 A phrase deployed by Gen. Stanley McChrystal (2015, 154) and his coauthors to describe his goal of a team that shared "fundamental, holistic understanding of the operating environment" and the organization while preserving individual team skill sets.

While an individual's experiences are almost always useful at some level, a diverse set of experiences from many individuals is even more useful. And, though it may be counterintuitive, it can be even more useful if some of those experiences were failures. It stretches credulity when every experience someone describes is a success; it comes across as inauthentic. Management careers simply don't work that way.

If one CEO has been at the same organization for more than 30 years ($n=1$) while the other has been with five different organizations ($n=5$) in the same period, who is more likely to make the better consultant (much less CEO)? While I prefer not to generalize, as personality also has some influence, I would tend to have more confidence in the person who has been immersed in a number of different cultures. Being sensitive to the differences, as well as having the experience of interacting with different teams facing a variety of challenges, clearly adds richness to their experiences. This variety is one of the attractions of a consulting career.

Compressing Time

Consultants must make a connection with the client team—quickly. There will always be some tension between the consultant and the client team; it is a necessary dynamic to this fascinating exchange. However, failure to connect with the client team is an existential crisis for the engagement.

CEOs get used to having an engaged team, as members of the team are obligated to work with the CEO. But that is an internal team in an organization where the CEO has positional authority, not an external team where they have no authority and can only advise. The more a team is together the more connected they tend to be. Consultants, in contrast, come and go, and have relatively little time to connect with a client team. In their attempt to connect with a new client team as consultants, some former CEOs I employed simply failed to recognize this challenge. The clock for a consultant runs faster than for an executive. You don't have a second chance to make a first impression.[6]

MORE COMPATIBLE ROLES

Ideally, drawing attention to the pitfalls of prior CEO experience allows you to address these issues and avoid these traps. But all is not lost for those who have succumbed to the vagaries of being CEO. There are other roles wholly compatible with this experience and orientation. As noted previously, both interim management and coaching can be an easier transition and will take advantage of your prior executive experiences.

That said, nothing can mask arrogance or a sense of superiority that clouds the sensitivities necessary to any advisory role. The first step to enabling a transition to any of these roles is the realization that you are no longer the CEO. Functioning in an interim capacity changes things, just as the role of coach changes things. Interim management is not the same as having a permanent line management position. Telling a story about how you dealt with an issue as CEO at a certain organization can be valuable and people will pay attention, but the first role of consulting is to listen. Where experience comes into play—and it always comes into play (sometimes in the form of a bias)—is being able to place the story in context of the situation that presents to the client. Understanding what is similar and what is not can make all the difference.

For the former CEO, resist the temptation to frame all future consulting engagements in the context of your previous experiences or to express such experiences with undue bravado.

---

6   Clint Eastwood is famous for only allowing one take when he directs a film; there are no do-overs.

For the former CEO, resist the temptation to frame all future consulting engagements in the context of your previous experiences or to express such experiences with undue bravado. Clients prefer to discuss their situation with you, not hear about your experiences. Limit such references to cogent examples of what can happen. Be careful not to set yourself up as the hero CEO who was always able to overcome obstacles and make the right decision with no mistakes. Confidence is one thing; hubris is another. The consultant who attempts to rest their credibility solely on their personal achievements as CEO is surely on the path to early retirement.

RECOMMENDATIONS

1. CEOs have some unique skills that can provide great value as a consultant.

2. There are also some traps that can expose some habits common to executives but toxic to consulting. Some of these traps can be subtle, such as a tendency to dictate how things are done.

3. Having broad experience as a CEO in several different organizations is an antidote to having an attitude that can come across to clients as inauthentic. Looking forward, it is important to incorporate managerial best practices into your consulting engagements.

4. Humility[7] is an important component of telling any story, and a critical element of being authentic and likable. Resist the temptation to frame all future consulting engagements in the context of your previous experiences or to express such experiences with undue bravado.

---

7   See Kaissi, A. 2021. *Humbitious: The Power of Low-Ego, High-Drive Leadership.* Vancouver, B.C.: Page Two Press.

5. Other types of consulting can still work for the executive who is unable to shed some of the difficult traits that can come from holding the position in one organization for an extended period; executive coaching is one. But executives making a career change to all such positions will benefit from additional training and education.

REFERENCES

Ferrari, B. T. 2012. "The Executive's Guide to Better Listening." *McKinsey Quarterly* digital article. Published February 1. www.mckinsey.com/featured-insights/leadership/the-executives-guide-to-better-listening.

Goman, C. K. 2017. "Six Crucial Behaviors of Collaborative Leaders." Leadership Strategy (blog), *Forbes*. Published July 11. www.forbes.com/sites/carolkinseygoman/2017/07/11/six-crucial-behaviors-of-collaborative-leaders/.

McChrystal, S., T. Collins, D. Silverman, and C. Fussell. 2015. *Team of Teams: New Rules of Engagement for a Complex World.* New York: Portfolio/Penguin, 2015.

Rice, J. A., and F. Perry. 2012. *Healthcare Leadership Excellence: Creating a Career of Impact.* Chicago: Health Administration Press.

Spataro, J. 2019. "5 Attributes of Successful Teams." Microsoft 365 (blog). Published November 19. www.microsoft.com/en-us/microsoft-365/blog/2019/11/19/5-attributes-successful-teams.

Studer, Q. 2020. *The Busy Leader's Handbook: How to Lead People and Places That Thrive.* Hoboken, NJ: John Wiley.

PART IV

WHEN?

When will I know that consulting is the appropriate option
so I can finish preparing to launch this change?

YOU NOW KNOW a lot more than you did when you started this journey. You have answers to many of your original questions, and probably some new questions as well. Your view of the future is balanced with the reality of what a career change involves. There clearly are risks and traps, but you understand these better and have crossed off many of the concerns through further research—notably, by talking with others who have given you some sound advice.

You feel confident in your exploration up to this point. While you suffer no delusions in your outlook, you remain enthusiastic about your career pursuits. It is time to explore specific opportunities and make a go/no-go decision. Your support group is set up and your network is poised to help you make the shift. You are clear on the commitment required and ready to take the plunge. Once you are sure you can avoid common mistakes, it's time to launch.

CHAPTER 10

Avoiding Common Mistakes

Anyone who has never made a mistake has
never tried anything new.
—Albert Einstein

As a consultant you are going to make mistakes. Period. Thoughts to the contrary are not realistic. While they may not be mistakes technically (e.g., perhaps you will never offer bad advice), things can and will go wrong. A client may misinterpret something you said. A team member may be difficult and you may not handle the stress well. You might get emotional about an issue and let your guard down. These things can and will happen. You are going to make mistakes. The best you can hope for is to make small ones while learning from the mistakes of others. Your apprenticeship will likely surface mistakes that your mentor has experienced.

The Healthcare Consultant's Handbook reviews in some detail the personal attributes that might suggest an affinity for consulting. A high level of energy and a thirst for learning are among the most important attributes. Another involves a certain level of impatience with the sometimes slow pace of an executive job, and the corresponding boredom that can accompany this. But there is a danger in this as well, if you are to pursue a consulting career: Aggressive impatience might involve striving for perfection. In my experience, many consultants (and yes, I include myself) tend to be perfectionists and their own worst critics. Managing expectations is important in this regard.

COMMON MISTAKES FOR NEW CONSULTANTS

Advice for consultants is nothing new. The original edition of *Consulting for Dummies* offered the ten biggest mistakes a consultant can make (Nelson and Economy 1997):

1. *Not listening*
2. *Failing to establish rapport*
3. *Letting your ego get in the way*
4. *Being inflexible*
5. *Overpricing your services*
6. *Underpricing your services*
7. *Having one primary client*
8. *Turning down work*
9. *Taking current clients for granted*
10. *Failing to market for future business*

Try to avoid these mistakes and make new ones. And always recognize that, with the right attitude, most mistakes can become a positive learning experience.

I believe there are several common mistakes when someone is making a career change to consulting:

- Trying to achieve too much too soon
- Overextending your capabilities
- Assuming that people will buy
- Expecting it to be easy
- Expecting too much from your personal network

These mistakes can be tricky to spot, so you need to understand them well. Let's address each one in turn.

Trying to Achieve Too Much Too Soon

The pace of consulting usually represents a big change from executive jobs. Time is money when you charge by the hour. You are immediately up against a budget, and you will often be below or above this budget. Learning to manage your time is critical. Consultants have a low tolerance for wasted time. In fact, being productive often determines the success or failure of each consulting engagement. Going down too many rabbit holes or otherwise not managing our time wisely can be catastrophic given a tight budget. Budgets related to client engagements can simply be inadequate because of ineffective internal budgeting or an aggressive client that is pushing costs down. We are all hostage to our experiences when it comes to completing a certain amount of work in a given time frame. A key contributor to this problem can be impatience and the desire to lock in a client engagement irrespective of budget shortfalls.

Don't expect to be the best consultant right out of the gate. Yes, you should be able to draw on your experiences before you became a consultant, but most consultants have also accumulated plenty of scars along the way. Now it is your turn. I hope there will be no permanent scars, and you will move on with a valuable lesson. But let's face it, this is easier for some of us than for others.

If you are expecting that you will somehow avoid all the mistakes others have made, that is a worthy but unrealistic goal. Give yourself time to acclimate. Be willing to develop, or at least consider, new work habits that might be better suited to the consulting grind (e.g., daily timesheets). Recognize that, while you may be a fast learner, you need time to adjust. Success in consulting is never an overnight thing. Be patient with yourself. Ask lots of questions. Do not make the mistake that many consultants have made, assuming that you must have all the answers on day one. Often, firms give some slack in a budget for a new consultant. Take advantage of this to learn the ropes. (PS: It gets easier.)

I learned an invaluable lesson from an early mentor, Bob Tschetter. I was relatively new to consulting and had the privilege of accompanying Bob as we started a strategic planning process for a midwestern community hospital. Mind you, Bob was the leader of the Health and Medical Practice for Booz Allen. The Big Cheese. This was our first meeting with the CEO, to kick off the process. This was also my first strategic planning engagement. I was in "sponge mode" trying to take in all that was happening around me.

At one point during this fascinating exchange the CEO asked Bob a question. Bob's response: "I don't know." That was it. I was shocked. I thought consultants were supposed to have all the answers. I was expecting a sharp retort: "Well, why did I hire you then?" I feared the engagement was over before it started.

Contrary to my naive mental image of consulting, the conversation not only continued, but took an interesting turn. For that CEO, the consulting team immediately became more human. There was an instant connection. We did not suffer the hubris he had feared, or think we had all the answers. Implicit in Bob's response was that we would find the answer together. That was the purpose of the strategic planning process. After that, the client saw the consulting team as authentic, not disposed to hyperbole. Willing to acknowledge gaps in our knowledge, with the caveat that we would find the answer.

As a new consultant, this translates nicely to your interactions as a member of a consulting team. Asking questions of your peers is not a sign of weakness. Quite the opposite: It is an acknowledgment that you lack experience and are interested in learning best practices so you can execute them consistently. And when you make a mistake, which you will, be willing to forgive yourself and move on with the knowledge that you will do better next time.

While consultants tend to be overachievers and have all the corresponding energy that entails, it helps to slow down during this time. Embrace the training available to you. Work with a mentor or observe experienced consultants, recognizing that what works for them, given their background and personality, will not always be the right approach for you. Observe the differences of approach—be a student of the game. The way another consultant approaches a structured interview may not be comfortable for you.

Finally, set some realistic benchmarks along the way. If you need to get comfortable with something, set aside the necessary time to do so. Do not rush this. Better to learn it well than to learn it quickly. Ask questions. Seek help. Consultants are almost always willing to help others; after all they went through the exact same process themselves and got help from others along the way. This is the very essence of the profession.

Overextending Your Capabilities

Consulting involves a certain entrepreneurial spirit, especially where sales is concerned. Not everyone in consulting likes to gamble, yet pursuing a competitive bid involves taking a chance and allowing for the possibility of losing. At the same time, there is sometimes a strong temptation to take too many chances.

True confessions: I don't take losing well. I never learned to do this, either as an athlete or a professional, and I have no intention of ever becoming a "good loser." People say not to take things personally, but it is hard to lose without taking it personally, at least on some level. Especially when you really wanted to work with that client. You clearly sent them the best proposal. They should have selected you. Perhaps you didn't know that they had worked with a competitor many times before and you were merely used as a stalking horse. Ouch.

While it may be exhilarating to gamble on a game of chance, there comes a point where it is not healthy. Time is limited, and one must be selective in their client pursuits. If you chase everything, you may gain a reputation for responding to every opportunity, but you may also gain a reputation for never winning.

When I was starting out with my own firm, I worked closely with a firm that sent a proposal in on every opportunity that presented itself. The founder's theory was that they would win their fair share; in fact they set their budget based on winning a certain percentage of proposals. I became convinced over time that some opportunities were far superior to others and that certain opportunities were simply not worth pursuing.[1] Where you have a separate marketing department, they may pursue engagements that do not really interest the consultants who would have to work on them.

Screen your opportunities carefully, and only go after those that are reasonably in your sweet spot. Do not extend yourself too far beyond your capabilities or your capacity to satisfy a client need. More than a few times we have ended up grateful that we lost a bid, after seeing the mess left for the firm that won the engagement because of the difference between what the client asked for and what they really wanted. There is no denying that you will occasionally come across a client from hell. Make no mistake, there are clients you do not want to have.

A client of mine liked to joke about unlikely scenarios: "Dog catches car." The visual for this can be entertaining, but in consulting this can be a disaster. Imagine taking on an important engagement with a favorite client and having limited experience or skill with which to satisfy a specialized need. Nothing can kill a great relationship faster. You can waste enormous amounts of time and resources pursuing something that is beyond any reasonable level of risk. Failure can occur for a number of reasons—for example, being prohibited from collecting critical information required to form an opinion on something. Think that client demands are always reasonable? Think again. Their expectations often exceed the proposed budget or scope. Beware the trap. While it is tempting to stretch yourself under the right circumstances, stretching resources or capabilities should ideally be done with the full knowledge of and mutual risk-sharing by the client (i.e., "there may not be any obvious answers, but we are willing to go at-risk together and see what we can come up with").

---

[1]   As an example, I would not propose on a strategy study without first having a face-to-face visit with the client. Unlike other types of studies, strategy involves a significant level of trust and familiarity. I did not believe it was possible to establish this without having a chance to meet, get to know each other, and share expectations before deciding if there was a fit.

Assuming That People Will Buy

One of the trickiest mistakes that people make is getting the false impression that you can sell, when in truth, people are just being polite. Sales skill is the great differentiator for most executives in the consulting business, as they tend not to have much experience with it. Many people don't enjoy trying to sell something. A career change to consulting is infeasible if you have a strong aversion to sales. There are nuances to effective sales. No one is impressed with people who emphasize "sizzle" over the steak.

> **A career change to consulting is infeasible if you have a strong aversion to sales.**

I believe this is the single biggest mistake people make in trying to shift to consulting. Having knowledge and experience, while essential, is simply not enough to guarantee that people will be willing to pay for your advice. Taking on responsibility for managing an organization is not the same as offering advice to an organization. And you aren't really advising an organization; you are advising a CEO, a management team, or some component of an organization. This exposes you to the people side of the business. By definition, that means uncertainty.

We are all familiar with window shopping. Retail has great lessons in this regard. The talented merchandiser knows how to stage items in a window or on a shelf to maximize appeal. Much of this is art, but there is science as well (e.g., analytics). It comes down to managing the experience and making it intentional (not by chance). For some goods and services, buyers need to find a way to handle the product or experience a service before they make a buy decision.

There is no substitute for managing the consulting experience. It does not happen by default. You must make clear what you are selling. You must make clear the value proposition to the client—how things will be better than before. You must make clear what it will cost them to receive this service. And last but not least, you must receive some indication from the client that they are willing to pay for this service. This last item is easily overlooked. In my opinion, a verbal commitment is never sufficient. Except for speeches, I always get some form of payment up front for any consulting engagement. I am less concerned about the amount or manner of payment than I am about an actual payment.

To some extent, insisting on an initial payment ensures that the accounting department recognizes you as a legitimate entity and is willing to cut you a check. I have had a few instances where the CEO's promises did not carry the expected weight with accounting, and they demanded a separate contract or purchase order from what was already negotiated with the CEO. Ouch! Better to find out now than after expending time and energy and running the risk of not getting paid. I have occasionally insisted on a larger down payment for an engagement (e.g., a leadership retreat) where it was well known that the client was struggling financially. I have found that payments can be significantly delayed in such situations.

The real test here is a required breakthrough in the transition to consulting. The underlying question is both profound and simple: Are people willing to pay for your advice and services? There are two key components to this: Are you credible, and are you selling something of value?

The question of your credibility resides in how people respond to you. Are you clear on what you have to offer? Do you have your elevator speech worked out? Can you make people listen, hold their attention? Do you have interesting things to share? How do you know this? Have you tried it out on people? Have people bought from you in the past? Were they pleased with the result?

This is about authenticity. We are all familiar with the snake oil salesmen selling potions that allow you to run faster than a bullet and leap over tall buildings. The internet has become a haven for snake oil salesmen. How do you avoid being seen as just another one of these? This goes to your credentials and your references. While there are no licenses required to be a consultant, professional credentials can help here. Being a Fellow of the American College of Healthcare Executives lends credibility, as does fellowship in the Healthcare Financial Management Association and a few other granting agencies in healthcare.

Of these different supporting elements, client references are probably the most important. Testimonials are a particularly useful type of reference. Who has used your advice before to their advantage? Are they willing to talk about it in their own voice? Will they speak to a prospect on the value of your services? Not all clients turn into positive references. They may all be positive, but not all are willing to take the time to be a reference for you. Try to find out which ones are willing to do so before you cite them as a reference. It is a deal killer to use someone as a reference only to find out that they did not take the call from your prospect!

Regarding the value of your services, the test is straightforward: If what you are selling has value, you will find buyers. If it is not selling, you can try to alter the services or the sales pitch in the hopes of finding future buyers, or you may need to focus on different types of buyers.

I shared these questions with you under the implicit assumption that you are going into business for yourself. I want you to understand the hurdles involved in addressing this issue. Alternatively, getting help with sales is often why people join firms and why most people do not initially strike out on their own. Once someone has some years of experience and has learned the ropes of getting people to pay for their services (and provide references), it becomes more possible to entertain more of an entrepreneurial approach to consulting, including pursuing a solo practice.

Expecting It to Be Easy

I have come across several people who assumed the transition to consulting would be relatively easy. Likely, a well-meaning friend had misread their situation and remarked, "Well how hard can it be?" For example, sometimes a CEO leaves their position, and the former employer retains them to finish several ongoing assignments. Some people may misinterpret this as launching a new career, when it may have been nothing more than a way to work off a separation agreement or counsel someone out of the organization.

It bears repeating that the advice of friends can be a mixed bag. Friends who naturally encourage you to find out if consulting is right for you may inadvertently imply that they are willing to hire you as a consultant, when that is not really the case. Saying that they think you would make a great consultant is not the same as saying, "I have something specific that I would like your help with and that I am willing to pay you for." And although this sounds implausible, I have been convinced through several personal experiences that when friends say they need your help with something, they do not necessarily mean they plan to pay you for that help.

Friends can, and some will, take advantage of your experience with little or no regard for the reality that this is now how you make your living. The only rationale I have been able to come up with to explain this behavior is that your relationship in the past has involved you giving them the benefit of free advice. They have never paid you for it before, so why should they have to do so now? This may seem strange, but I have learned that other consultants have also experienced this phenomenon and are equally challenged to offer an explanation. Over the years, there have been half a dozen or so people I have grown close to, at least professionally, who have never paid me for my advice and yet who continue to ask me questions that others pay me to answer. In some cases, I have simply had to cut them off after calling this to their attention.

> Over the years, there have been half a dozen or so people I have grown close to, at least professionally, who have never paid me for my advice and yet who continue to ask me questions that others pay me to answer.

Expecting Too Much from Your Personal Network

One of the critical dimensions of the Consultant Value Chain is networking. Care and feeding of a professional network are essential for a consultant. When making the transition from executive to consultant, you may wonder if your existing network can translate into any consulting business or if you will have to develop a new network focused on consulting. It takes time to develop and sustain a network. Clearly, some people are better at this than others.

I don't think you have to have an existing network that will translate into significant consulting business, but it could certainly help. More likely, your existing network will open doors to others who might benefit from your services. Think of it as a referral network that you can rely on to convince others that you can be trusted and that you have legitimate skills. People in your existing network may function best as references.

Many people assume their existing network will generate a sustainable level of client business. This assumes that your network can recognize you in a role that did not exist when you were forming the network. Your network was not built around your role as a consultant; it was built while you were a healthcare executive. As you were not selling anything when the network was formed, it would be naive to assume that the network will automatically translate into buyers. Some might convert, but these are likely the exceptions.

When I first got started in my own consulting practice, I had been a healthcare professional for about five years, two of which were spent with Booz Allen. These jobs had exposed me to a relatively large number of people in a short time. But aside from a small number of clients who helped me get started, virtually none of the business that I subsequently developed came from my initial announcement to this network. Instead, I was introduced to others by some of the people on this list. Often, my future clients were people that I met at meetings or through mutual friends.

Based on my experience, I believe you will probably require a new network to sustain a consulting business. This makes it important to increase exposure through writing, speaking, alumni associations, and other means.

HOW TO AVOID MAKING THESE MISTAKES

Rather than leave you with only the negative thoughts about common mistakes, I want to suggest a few actions you can take to avoid these mistakes. First among these is to adopt productive work habits. A critical success factor for any new consultant is productivity. If you are with a firm and your time is allocated to multiple projects, you must divide your time wisely. Earlier, it was suggested that CEOs bring to the party some familiarity with sorting through priorities for an organization. Setting priorities is an indelible trait of high-performing teams. Frankly, not all consultants set priorities well. John Boitnott (2018) has some advice to address this concern that involves applying some useful productivity habits, adopted from elite consulting firms:

1. Tackle your hardest tasks early in the day, and save the easiest things for later.
2. Prioritize using the Eisenhower matrix (exhibit 10.1).
3. Avoid distractions and meetings by being the first one in the office.
4. If you need resources, ask; and explain the possible impacts if you don't get them.

Some would argue that starting out as a solo practice is a mistake absent formal training and/or consulting experience. Most experienced consultants would tell you that they learned these skills either from being part of a firm that had relevant training programs or because of extensive client experiences. Your inexperience with consulting can be offset through several approaches, one of which is to join a firm (discussed more in chapter 11). As suggested by several of the former executives profiled in chapter 5, a sponsor

Exhibit 10.1. Eisenhower Priority Matrix

Not Urgent		
Urgent		
	Important	Not Important

can be extremely helpful under an apprenticeship model. Starting without either a firm or a sponsor invites a level of risk that may be hard to overcome.

CRITICAL SUCCESS FACTORS FOR CONSULTING

A career change to consulting involves a number of critical success factors. Several of the most important factors are summarized here; others are discussed in more detail in my previous book.[2]

Commitment

Making a career change requires resolve. We are not talking about sticking your toe in the water. You have already done that by talking to friends, spending time shadowing a consultant or visiting a firm, or finding some other way of trying out the consulting experience. The time to take the plunge is quickly approaching. A real opportunity for a career change may come only once or twice in your career. Should you let this opportunity pass, you may regret it.

---

2 See chapter 4 of *The Healthcare Consultant's Handbook* for more on the essentials of consulting success.

If you don't feel ready to commit yet, examine why. Perhaps you skipped a few steps in the Career Change Decision Framework. If so, it may be time to circle back and cover these, at least to some extent. Perhaps you are not one to embrace change easily. (Who is?) As we have noted, shifting from an executive management position to a healthcare consulting position is a major change that cannot be taken lightly. Do you have doubts? Good. I would be more worried if you had no doubts, as that is not very realistic. That is not an excuse for lacking commitment.

Lack of commitment may result from holding out hope that key issues with your current situation get resolved. If this is the case, you should set a reasonable deadline by which the situation must be resolved, one way or the other. A career move under those circumstances runs the risk of failure; any latent regrets about the status quo may drag you down if not addressed. Resolve any lingering doubts first, lest you be tempted to enter consulting with less than a full commitment.

Being committed may or may not involve a contingency plan or plan B. While you might get differing views on this point among experts, I prefer forging ahead without much thought to a plan B. If you are truly committed to a career change, it is important to eliminate disparate thoughts that could be distracting. (See chapter 11 for more information on this.)

Making a career change will affect a lot of people besides you. You may have to move to a new city. You may not be able to manage other changes at the same time. A career change of this magnitude requires your full attention; you must be all in. Time to institute the 25/5 rule (Bariso 2021). List your top 25 goals and then circle the five most important things on the list; cross off the rest. In other words, "switch your focus from what you *could* be working on to what you *should* be working on" (italics in original). Manage the other life factors affecting you at this time so they do not detract from your ability to give this career change your full attention. The hardest and most important point of the 25/5 rule is ignoring items 6–25. This is emotional intelligence—trying to neutralize these other life factors to the extent possible.

A Realistic Time Frame

There is a difference between timing and time frame. Timing is about now versus 90 days from now or two years from now, or last year. When do you pull the trigger? What's the biblical phrase? "If not now, when?"

Time frame, in this case, relates to how long you need to experience consulting to make a sound judgment on whether it is working out for you. As mentioned previously, the most common failure of entrepreneurs, bar none, is to pull the plug too soon. How much time is required before you will know if you have made the right decision?

This time frame will vary by person and circumstances. The consulting experience is often described as being pushed into a pool and asked to swim. Some elements of this transition can feel like that—the learning curve can be steep (and not soon forgotten). But other elements are far more subtle. In *The Healthcare Consultant's Handbook*, I presented the case of two new consultants who had similar backgrounds and started consulting around the same time, with the same practice, in the same firm. One consultant felt they had a good experience while the other had mixed reviews and changed jobs at the end. They each remained in consulting, but with different types of firms and practices that better corresponded to their individual preferences. Attitude was identified as a critical variable in this case. This gives rise to an important consideration that you should be aware of *before* you embark on this journey.

Consulting may turn out to be an excellent career move for you, but you may initially find yourself at a firm or practice that is not the right fit. Rare is the career consultant who has stayed with just one firm (unless it's their own firm). A key reason for this is that it is hard to judge the culture of any firm before *experiencing* it.

In addition to corporate culture, you need to be aware of the context of your experience during the transition. Different circumstances can affect the feedback that you are getting. In the case study just mentioned, a bad client experience clouded the early months for one of the two consultants. This may have had nothing to do with their skill set; the negative experience may have been totally independent of the consultant interactions. Expectations are important. Not everyone who is new to consulting can realistically expect every assignment to go well right out of the box.

There will be challenges; that is the nature of the business. It is less an issue of circumstances and more an issue of how these circumstances are handled. Done right, there will be a clear separation between feedback that is relevant to the consultant and feedback that is beyond the control of the consultant.

That some clients are more fun to work with than others should come as no surprise. Some engagements are more rewarding than others. As one manager put it to a consultant after a tough day, "If the client wasn't experiencing some problems, they would not have called us in the first place."

Try to see the big picture and separate yourself from the circumstances. Some consulting engagements can take years. Most are shorter—months or weeks. In the beginning, you will likely complete several engagements with a variety of teams and clients that will give you a broad exposure to consulting. How long this will take depends on the nature of the practice, the types of engagements, and the clients involved. There will be a variety of experiences under the best of circumstances. Every client engagement is unique at certain levels, notably the people involved.

Regardless of the form of consulting you embrace, it seems advisable to take at least six months to a year to determine whether this is the right move for you. Anything less runs the risk of reflecting more on the firm or on specific clients or engagements than on your choice of career.

A Formal Feedback Loop

Setting up a formal feedback loop before this transition can be helpful. In addition to your job performance, you should also want feedback on how your new job is affecting those around you. The shift to consulting causes significant lifestyle changes, not least of which are travel and absence from home. How are you feeling about this, and how are those around you feeling? While technology has made it much easier to stay in touch while on the road, travel can still be grueling. How are you holding up? Are there things you can do to address travel-related issues? Keep in mind that you will get better at travel with experience as there are skills to being a road warrior and moderating the impact of travel. You can likely pick this up by observing members of your team who have been doing it for years.[3]

You should also review your career goals. Did you commit them to writing before making this decision? If so, how are you doing on those? I would not advocate pulling out those career goals before 90 days into the new position. There is too much going on to involve such a distraction. Give it a chance to take hold.

Ideally, you will complete several client engagements and get feedback from those before you begin to evaluate things. When you do, you must have not only client feedback (some of which you will experience in real time) but also feedback from team members you worked with on these engagements. What did you learn? Was this hard to learn or did it come naturally? What was the biggest surprise? (This can often be the source of some of the richest learning.) How did you manage this? Was the approach to the engagement successful? How did people respond to you? How satisfied were you with the outcome? Would you do some things differently if you could do it over again? If so, what? Over time, this type of introspection should become muscle memory for you. Failure to do a postmortem on each engagement will stifle your growth as a consultant. To those people who were destined for consulting, this type of evaluation should come naturally.

---

3 The COVID-19 pandemic caused significant changes in the acceptance of operating on a remote basis. I may be in the minority on this, but I believe people will find that operating remotely simply cannot compete with the interpersonal interactions of on-site presence, especially for certain types of consulting where process is involved.

Confidence

Throughout my writings, I emphasize authenticity as an important attribute for successful consultants and an important part of the Consultant Value Chain. To be authentic in consulting—or in an executive position—one must exude confidence. Confidence is contagious; people who report to a confident person will likely develop confidence on their own over time. A leader who lacks confidence will not lead for long. Followers tend to sense whether people have this quality or not.

Any professional must display confidence. For example, a presenter is first challenged by the need to give the audience confidence that they know what they are talking about. Even more basic but no less important, they must demonstrate that they are comfortable presenting. We learn that public speaking is drama, and it is important to first put the audience at ease. Once this drama has been overcome, the audience can relax as they have now been primed to listen. We are left to convince them that we know what we are talking about and have something important to share, that what we are discussing has value.

Before shifting to consulting, it is vital that you have a vision of doing so with which you are comfortable. How do you want to come across to clients? What do you want them to say about you? From this vision or brand, with proper experience, will come confidence. This might be best described as being comfortable in your own skin as a consultant.

Visioning is used to mean many things. One variation that I subscribe to comes from the sports world—for example, a golfer envisions a shot before they attempt it. Any athlete will tell you that there is power in vision if channeled correctly. You must be able to see yourself comfortably in a role if you expect others to do so. This is not an idle statement. Unless your personal vision is clear in this regard, consulting may not be in your future.

> **You must be able to see yourself comfortably in a role if you expect others to do so. Unless your personal vision is clear in this regard, consulting may not be in your future.**

It will also be helpful for you to test this vision on others. I once saw myself as a serious basketball player, but I lacked a number of things—including the necessary size—to advance to the next level. This is where feedback from others can be helpful. It can be a challenge to see ourselves as others see us. Can friends and family see you comfortably in an advisory role? Why? Why not? Has sharing this vision with others built your confidence or raised more questions?

Consulting requires a person to go at-risk, fully disclosing their thoughts and views to the client. There is drama involved, and sometimes fear of failure. The client always has the right to reject the consultant and/or their advice. It takes conviction to present such advice with confidence. Invariably, such advice is challenged and must be defended. A consultant learns quickly to rely on their skills and on objective evidence (to the extent it exists) to develop and retain confidence in how they approach their craft.

There will be doubts at times, and losses to deal with. This is part of the consulting journey. One of my favorite quips about consulting is, "Occasionally wrong, but never in doubt." Confidence is key, and it can be bolstered by faith and a supportive personal network. I have often relied on my faith when things got tough; others have come to the rescue when my confidence was shaken or I was dealing with some difficult client situations. Things can and do go wrong in consulting engagements, just like anything else in life. While consulting may be attractive, in that clients tend to pay more attention (and money) to outside experts than internal advisors, it is no panacea for career challenges. It takes a certain strength of character to survive as a consultant. Anyone who suggests otherwise probably lacks experience.

RECOMMENDATIONS

1. Being aware of common mistakes made when shifting to consulting can help you avoid those mistakes.

2. There is risk in any change of this magnitude; try to manage it carefully.

3. Develop a feedback loop that includes others. It is important that others be able to see you in the role of advisor; otherwise you may be deceiving yourself.

4. To be authentic, confidence is critical, which requires being comfortable in your own skin as a consultant.

5. Focusing on the critical success factors will set you on the road to a successful transition.

REFERENCES

Bariso, J. 2021. "Why Emotionally Intelligent People Embrace the 25-5 Rule." Productivity (blog), *Inc.* Published June 27. www. inc.com/justin-bariso/productive-emotional-intelligence-25-5-rule-how-to-achieve-more-focus-avoid-distraction-get-more-done-be-more-productive-warren-buffet.html.

Boitnott, J. 2018. "Maximize Your Productivity with These 4 Changes an Elite Management Consultant Would Recommend." John Boitnott (blog). Published March 15. https://jboitnott. com/4-changes-elite-management-consultant-tell-make-maximize-productivity/.

Nelson, B., and P. Economy. 1997. *Consulting for Dummies*. Foster City, CA: IDG Books.

CHAPTER 11

Making the Transition with a Firm

The distinguishing feature of a professional services organization is that it does not sell tangible products. Instead, it has production processes that are wholly dependent on expertise and skills of its human capital.
—Gladwin International (2021)

You can transition to consulting by joining a firm or starting a solo practice. These approaches differ considerably, as noted in exhibit 11.1. All things being equal (which they never are), joining a firm is the easier way to go. It's a trade-off between degrees of freedom (solo practice) and access to resources (firm). More important than this is your overall motivation for a career change; if you are driven to pursue personal interests with a minimum of interference, then the solo practice route will win.

Both options can work, so I delve into more detail on some of the key components required to have a successful launch under both models. This chapter deals with joining a firm (the more common model). Chapter 12 addresses solo practice.

The first question you will face when joining a firm is which firm. Part II of *The Healthcare Consultant's Handbook* discusses how to evaluate firms as a new consultant. The same issues discussed there apply to the experienced executive, and then some.

Joining an existing firm essentially involves outsourcing basic administrative functions. Said differently, you rely on others to

Exhibit 11.1. Joining a Firm Versus Starting a Solo Practice

	Join a Firm	Start a Solo Practice
Initial steps	Onboard to new firm Develop branded bio	Secure legal and accounting services Develop business and marketing plan Finalize brand collateral Set up digital footprint Secure office space Finalize infrastructure Set up banking relationships Develop announcement Launch website Connect with network Develop initial prospects list
Critical success factors	Right firm/culture Meeting firm requirements Ability to join a team Sales support Investment capital (optional) Network willing to help Access to infrastructure	Investment capital and access to capital Personal brand Network willing to buy Access to infrastructure An existing book of business Right credentials
Differentiators	Develop internal relationships with other partners in firm Work your network, fostering your new identity	Get marketing information into circulation Solid references Prospect with potential clients
Pros	Internal focus (easier to manage than external) Onboarding to existing systems Instant launch through corporate resources	Maximum freedom and independence Limited expenses

	Access to talent	
	Access to benefits	
	Far easier to get started	
Cons	Possibility of a bad fit or oppressive corporate culture	External focus (takes more effort than internal)
	Excessive bureaucracy	Need to make decisions
	Lack of innovation	regarding space,
	Absence of thought leadership	infrastructure, business relationships
	Lack of capital	Time-consuming
	Internal politics	start-up
	Compensation may get out of alignment with productivity	Likely requires new network

perform basic business functions that you otherwise would have to perform yourself, on at least some level, as a solo consultant. There is nothing wrong with this, but it is only a start. Ideally, you expect more from such an association than fundamental business functions (e.g., rent office space, access to technology, pension fund, health insurance, support staff, finance and accounting, bill generation, proposal writing). Available functions could vary depending on whether you join the firm at a principal (executive) level (with or without ownership) or at an associate level (a step down from principal).[1] Let's examine each one.

CONSIDER YOUR LEVEL OF ENTRY

Unless the firm is bringing you in for broader managerial reasons (e.g., to shore up certain administrative functions), starting at the principal level carries with it the clear expectation that you will generate new business *immediately*. The amount of new business

---

[1] See chapter 9 in *The Healthcare Consultant's Handbook* for a more complete explanation of different consulting tiers.

expected and how fast it is generated will vary considerably. Some firms may expect you to initiate new business on your own; others might expect you to help close new business by participating with other consultants.

If your new firm expects *lead generation*, you are responsible for finding new prospects rather than just pursuing some existing relationships (e.g., generating a new engagement with an existing client). If you are joining a global firm, they will probably expect you to generate new business on the order of several million dollars per year. In other words, you should bring an identifiable book of business with you. You have not previously functioned as a full-time consultant, so the hiring firm is essentially placing a value on your network. Most firms will go at-risk with you and link compensation directly to sales growth. Lead generation is usually valued higher than pursuing existing relationships, as new leads represent new growth for the firm.

If your compensation includes some credit for sales, it is probably with the recognition that the firm will invest in training to enhance your sales skills and create even more value through your network. Because you lack direct consulting experience, you will probably be surrounded by associates with the skills needed to help deliver on the services being sold while you gain experience and learn to deliver some of these services on your own. This could entail several months of training and mentoring.

At the associate level, firms rely less on lead generation and more on your ability to lend additional credibility to business the firm is already generating. You will spend more of your time on project management and proposal writing, on prospect visits, and on activating and expanding your network.

MATCH YOUR INTERESTS TO FIRM ATTRIBUTES

Given the different levels of entry that are likely to be open to you, how does one determine the right fit with an existing firm? There is no simple formula. So much of it is "look and feel" (often referred to as "culture") and it is probably best characterized as opportunistic. But if you have some time to consider options and can open a few doors to different firms, you should consider how these firms differ along several fronts. A simplistic view might separate key functions into service lines (practices), sales and marketing, infrastructure (including document production), thought leadership, and training. Fit is likely to be determined in these areas, and will be driven by need and interest.

Need relates to the skill set you bring to the party. If you are confident with basic consulting processes and skills, then training might be less of a consideration. If training is essential, then need might drive fit. (But you should also consider interest.) Assuming that you are serious about this career change, training should probably be a strong consideration when choosing a firm. What training resources are available? What track record does the firm have in this regard? Have others gone through this training and done well, or are you a guinea pig? How supportive are the partners? Are you becoming a partner or do you expect to become one soon? Is there a clear path to partnership with measurable and attainable targets?

Thought leadership is a bit more elusive. Admittedly this is more in the strategy realm and may not be relevant to you, but for those who thrive on innovation and seeking new solutions, thought leadership becomes a priority. In my experience, healthcare consulting firms rarely excel at this. It takes time and resources that most simply don't have. For those that do, it is a key differentiator. (Thought leadership is McKinsey's lifeblood.) Some firms dabble, while others have a routine method of communicating key trends and innovations. It should be relatively easy to determine which firms are really good at this and which display window dressing: Look at what has been posted on their website over the last two or three years. It will quickly become obvious which firms have invested in thought leadership to the point that it is part of their DNA.

FIND A SPONSOR

When you join a firm, where will your support come from? Who will "host" you and show you the ropes? Is it the recruiter who found you? If so, is the recruiter independent, part of the firm's staff, or a partner of the firm with decision-making authority? In an ideal world, you should have a clear sponsor with clout and influence who will squire you through your first year or so. You will look to this person to do a few critical things:

- Open their network
- Answer your questions
- Help you understand how the firm does things
- Manage relationships
- Best fit your skills to specific engagements
- Leverage your network
- Promote your brand and interests
- Help you pick up the skills as necessary
- Help you develop good work habits
- Critique your efforts (sales and fulfillment)

When you review this list, it is hard to imagine having to navigate these things without a sponsor.

Having a sponsor is important to any new job. In this respect, breaking into the C-suite is similar to breaking into a consulting firm. As noted previously, Dr. Diane L. Dixon (2020) published some important research on breaking into the C-suite with a focus on racial and ethnic minorities. This research involved interviews with racially and ethnically diverse hospital and health system CEOs. Among her important findings was that access to sponsors is important, especially in "providing opportunities that deepen leadership development and lead to promotions" (55). Dr. Dixon devotes an entire chapter to "the essential role of sponsorship." She likens sponsorship in the C-suite to having someone who helps you get into an elite club. The executives interviewed said their immediate boss often filled this role and described their sponsors as "authentic and sincere"—and very often white men, who tend to dominate most healthcare C-suites. A related study by Charas, Griffeth, and Malik (2015, 61) defined the "sponsor's benefit as tangible: It is measured by the economic expectation that 'if you help me, I'll help you'—a traditionally male attribute."

EVALUATE TEAMS AND TEAM BUILDING

Consulting is a team sport. As a result, the best firms are the ones that do teams well. Teams are so important to effective consulting that this section goes into some detail regarding breakthrough research.

When General Stanley McChrystal and colleagues published *Team of Teams* in 2015, it rapidly became a bestseller and an emerging classic on management theory. In this book, McChrystal revisits his command of the Joint Special Operations Task Force in the 2000s during the war in Afghanistan. His group discovered several principles that, when combined with traditional organizational theory, translate into profound lessons for students of management. McChrystal and his colleagues observed that the world was becoming complex, which is more than being just complicated. In complex systems, it is not always possible to predict how a change in one area might affect another area. In other words, complexity defies predictability and demands adaptability.

A more detailed discussion of many other fascinating elements from this book exceeds our purposes here, but their work has some insights relevant to consulting teams. Among McChrystal's realizations was that his new command had "developed tremendous competencies for dealing with a world that no longer exists" (209). Nothing is more threatening to future business development as a consultant than a review that labels your work "dated." You don't want to end up in this position in a consulting environment.

So much of consulting has to do with managing change. Where a consultant's work is preserving the status quo, it likely has little value, especially in the fast-changing world of healthcare. McChrystal found that managing change in a complex world exceeds the ability of any one person—hence the dependency on teams. Or in his case, a team of teams.

Change is ubiquitous in healthcare, which has implications when evaluating firms that you might consider joining. How do they form teams? How do they manage teams? How are teams connected to individual client needs? How do teams evolve? What does the firm teach about teams? In short, it is not enough to know how the firm is doing now; you need to understand how the firm is adapting its processes and investing in its future. Where is the firm likely to be in five years? Will it grow with you to respond to the future needs of the industry?

What services do the firm's teams offer? Are these services relevant to the fast-changing world of healthcare? How do they stay relevant? How do these services compare to competitive services? Do the firm's teams seek new knowledge (thought leadership)? If so, how is this shared within the firm? Outside the firm?

In short, the more you know about how teams are formed and operate within a consulting firm, the more you will know about the firm's adaptability and its ability to respond to future issues confronting healthcare. When visiting these firms, try to get a feel for how important teams are to the practice, how well they onboard new people, and what it takes to meet team requirements (in their many forms). The focus of teams is one of the most important differentiators to help you determine if a firm is right for you—or whether you might be better advised to consider solo practice, as discussed in the next chapter.

MAINTAIN AWARENESS

Finding the right firm is hard enough. Even harder is managing the learning curve. The transition into consulting can be overwhelming, and it's easy to get lost in the process. You will be exposed to new ways of thinking, new people, and new approaches to managing issues and people. The culture of the firm is likely to be different from anything you have experienced in the provider space. There is a lot to soak up, and much of it involves trust.

We are all familiar with the metaphor of the boiling frog. The same phenomenon can easily occur to a new consultant at any level. Anyone transitioning into consulting is likely to feel some heat. The temperature may increase a little at a time over weeks or months, so gradually that you don't notice it because you are immersed in the culture of your new firm. There are good and bad aspects to this, but it's best to avoid getting cooked.

This will be an exciting time and all your senses will be on full alert. It can be an adrenaline rush, to be sure. This process will have tremendous appeal to the adventuresome spirit. But therein lies the problem: You want to avoid getting caught up in all this and losing sight of your initial goals. To counter this possibility, I suggest the following five steps.

1. Have a Monitoring Plan—and Execute It

I am not sure which is more important, the plan or the monitoring. A one-page written plan specifying key goals and objectives is a crucial reminder of why you are making a career change in the first place. You may feel like this should be self-evident, but you will forget some of this along the way. Having it in writing helps you retain some of your original focus.

A plan is not enough, though; monitoring is critical. I know a person who occasionally pulled a card from his wallet with a few key objectives written down. You are likely to get lost or overwhelmed at times, or to lose perspective. Monitoring against a written plan keeps you grounded and reminds you of things that might easily get lost in the fog of the new consulting adventure.

> **Monitoring against a written plan keeps you grounded and reminds you of things that might easily get lost in the fog of the new consulting adventure.**

2. Enlist a Skeptic

One of the truly insidious threats of being a CEO is being surrounded by people who say what they think you want to hear. I have witnessed a few extreme examples of this among clients that got their organizations into terrible trouble. There is no substitute for involving someone outside the immediate environment to bring some objectivity to your evaluation process, as well as to ask the hard questions.

A true assessment involves critical thinking. Enlist a skeptic—a disinterested third party, perhaps. This could be an executive coach familiar with the frustrations you were experiencing in your previous job and who understands the process you went through to get here. You may be challenged to convince this outside reviewer that everything is working out. Ask them if what you are sharing is real progress. Ask for their help determining whether you are meeting some of your initial goals and objectives. What areas have not yet been tested? How are you going to do that? What have you brought up with your peers? What have you left out? Are you missing anything?

3. Keep a Written Record of Important Feedback

Most firms use a personal development plan and a formal evaluation process for each team member. In the bigger firms, formal evaluations happen after each engagement, on a set schedule (e.g., annually), or both. I recommend taking the time to summarize each engagement and write down at least one key thing you learned.

Committing this to writing is a great way to get a sense of the progression of learning, and to look back to measure how you are feeling and where additional needs might lie. Pausing occasionally to review these notes is a great habit, as the fast pace of consulting tends to blur things and you can easily lose perspective.

Take note of the challenges and the successes, what worked and what didn't. This exercise—which helps you distill the experience for yourself—is also important to helping the firm gather and disseminate new knowledge.

4. Schedule Regular Time Off

While most executives are used to being on stage, it takes a different kind of energy as an expert consultant. You may get stressed and not even notice it. In my experience, being on stage also comes more naturally to extroverts (who are used to thinking out loud). It comes down to how much energy is consumed; the introvert can do it just as well but may expend considerably more energy in this work. It can be important to regulate this carefully.

When I first started in consulting, I felt the pressure and I was all in; I was attracted to the adrenaline rush (this is not true of everyone). As this was shortly after graduate school, I was just forging my personal work routine. One of the things I committed to right away was long hours of intense concentration. I consciously decided to forgo lunch and become the poster boy for "keeping your nose to the grindstone." The result was that I felt guilty going to lunch. Silly, right? I did at least take a vacation every few months for a week or so. Invariably, I would crash for the first two or three days of vacation. I often would get a small cold. Over time, I figured out that this was my body telling me to slow down a bit. I learned to pace myself and use less energy as I got used to the stage.

An extension of this "hair on fire" mindset can apply to paid time off (PTO). My daughter, many years later, as a new consultant, shared with me as she was preparing to embark on this career path that she was not planning to take any PTO as she felt this sent the wrong signal to her peers. This reminded me of my initial attitude about lunch, which I shared with her as I am sharing with you now, and told her that over time I learned that employers do not look at PTO this way. I suggested instead that new consultants look around them—everyone is working flat out. You will find no slackers (the system gets rid of them very quickly). What you will find is people who are burned out. This has become a far greater concern to most consulting firms. My daughter soon learned just how important it was to use PTO, even if it's just an extra day on the front or back of a business trip to see something or someone not related to work.

Scheduling some concentrated time away periodically to dial things back is critical. Take some of this time away to pause and assess your progress. What is working? What is not? What adjustments might be warranted? Are we on track? How will you know how you are affecting others? Are you getting the feedback and training you need? What else that you are not currently getting might be helpful? How is the pace? You get the idea.

5. Understand Your Compensation Structure

Up to this point I have been somewhat critical of the unrealistic expectations people can have of consulting. While I recommend starting with a firm to help make the transition easier, things can go wrong. No firm is perfect, and there can be some negative forces that you will need to manage. The reader should be patient in reviewing this section as it covers some important nuances that can be consequential.

The ideal is a balance of risk between the firm, which is about to invest in you, and you, the executive about to change careers and join that firm. You are used to a certain level of compensation and no doubt hope to at least get close to that point, if not surpass it. That is certainly possible, but the cards can be stacked against you depending on how the firm works. You are likely to take a pay cut at first, corresponding to the initial lack of productivity, with a large upside as you progress. A base-plus-bonus compensation program is the usual approach.

Two important factors will affect your earnings potential: your specific role, and how the compensation formula reflects your contributions to the firm. Role comes down to how much of your time the company expects to be billable (conversely, how much of your time is required for infrastructure and related management functions). The more of a leadership position you hold, the less you should be required to bill clients for your time. However, most roles in most firms require substantial billable time, with smaller firms requiring 70–80 percent billability even of their leaders. A practice leader can reduce that target by 10–20 percentage points, depending on the size of the practice (in terms of both revenues and number of consultants). This figure may also be impacted by the amount of time required to be involved in sales, which is also not billable time.

At a high level, I think of compensation as consisting of two major elements: fixed and variable. Your base salary is the fixed component—what you will be paid regardless of performance. Everything else falls into the variable component, often labeled "bonus." On a more detailed level, the compensation formula generally considers four things: billable hours, sales (revenues), bonus (discretionary), and equity (optional).

- *Billable hours.* Billable time is fairly straightforward. Some firms will even agree to pay you a percentage of billable revenues (e.g., 70 percent). Everyone has a billing rate (e.g., $300/hour), but must be able to produce what is sold within the budget parameters of each engagement. Said differently, your hourly rate will reflect the productivity with which you deliver your piece of the deliverable. During an initial onboarding or transition period, you will occasionally have an artificially low billing rate—or, more commonly, additional unbillable time is built into the budget as you learn the ropes.

- *Sales*. Sales gets tricky. This is where culture comes into play. In a true meritocracy, compensation will be adjusted over time to reflect everyone's contributions. The larger the book of business you represent, the more you will be compensated. This simple logic can get lost in what can become a rather complicated points system or something similar. Most disconcerting is when you have brought credibility to a firm in a certain area by lending your brand to the firm, but the compensation package does not reflect this.

- *Bonus*. Bonuses are generally related to performance, and usually come from discretionary moneys left over after covering overhead. Smaller firms cannot afford as much overhead as larger firms, and managing overhead is a challenge. Many smaller firms merely allocate the infrastructure and administrative tasks (e.g., accounting, marketing, practice management) among the partners without regard to compensation, and then divide the proceeds at the end of the year, with an allowance as necessary for capital support (e.g., software and licenses). In medium to larger firms, it is common for a practice leader to receive some compensation based on the performance of the practice they are managing.

- *Equity*. Where partial ownership is in play, at least part of the compensation can be designated according to equity shares. This can work in two ways. The first and simplest is sharing profits at the end of the year based at least partially on the amount of equity held by each of the partners. (e.g., 10 percent ownership translates into 10 percent of profits). Another possibility is a "buy-in" option: A partner can buy part of the firm by earmarking part of their compensation toward this. A valuation formula is applied, and the owner-elect can designate certain dollars toward this buy-in. Usually, the option to buy equity is tied to achieving certain performance and/or seniority thresholds.

Many of the medium to smaller consulting firms use a partnership model, and compensation tends to skew toward existing partners. It can be difficult for a new person to be fairly compensated under a partnership model. In some situations, existing partners have enjoyed a long-standing relationship with an existing client, which is treated as a "franchise." When this occurs, that partner takes a cut out of any future business sold to that client, regardless of how that business was actually sold. I have personally experienced this. This is a slippery slope to manage that can become quite oppressive, which deserves some additional discussion.

The best approach to compensation is where the aim of the firm becomes most transparent. It is challenging to create a compensation system that balances the legitimate need to enrich existing partners while also being attractive to potential new partners. If the firm is skewed too much toward existing partners, then it will be difficult to recruit new partners. (This is one reason many small consulting firms go out of business when the founding partner retires.) Where compensation reflects a desire for new recruits, it involves an investment and subsidization (with a start-up period) targeted toward onboarding new partners and investing in future growth. Signing bonuses have become a common part of compensation in most consulting firms, as well.[2] Don't sell yourself short in this regard. Cash is king, as they say.

One of the truly deceptive parts of consulting can be a compensation formula so complicated that participants don't really understand how to maximize their compensation. Even that orientation can be controversial, as true team players would prefer to optimize their compensation (a shared approach), rather than maximize it (an individual approach), because shared risk should be reflected in any compensation system—especially a true partnership. Regardless of the specific compensation system being used, you must be able to trust how it is administered. There are always choices to make, and the hope is that you will understand the system and believe that your

---

2 For more insights into consulting compensation and benefits see chapter 9 in *The Healthcare Consultant's Handbook*.

interests are being recognized along with those of your partners. A progressive compensation system will recognize that adjustments are always necessary for individual circumstances.

So it's critical that you step back from the precise compensation formula and see the big picture. Which behaviors are incentivized and which may be ignored? Factor in benefits as well (e.g., healthcare, disability, retirement) as these also have value. The most sensitive variable may be the amount of ramp-up time required to onboard the new consultant. This can vary substantially, so the system has to be able to adjust accordingly. The compensation formula is a remarkably complex part of the business, but one that is important if you are to have a rewarding experience. Don't rush this. It is important to get it right before you start. In my experience, you will have limited ability to adjust later.

As noted in chapter 6, don't underestimate the gifts you are bringing to the table. Yes, making a career change will require some new learning and involves some risk, but there should also be a clear opportunity for growth. As your skills grow along with the business that you generate, you should be appropriately rewarded. The upside should be clear from day one and should represent a genuine incentive to produce. Any confusion that might exist should be clarified before you sign that final agreement; otherwise, it can come back to haunt you.

From the firm's perspective, they will subsidize bringing you on board at a certain level for a certain period of time; but at some point they expect a crossover, where your earnings for the firm begin to exceed what they have paid for your services. As much as possible, both parties are trying to get compensation to coincide with this crossover point. Truth be known, this is as much a matter of chance as of skill.

From the new consultant's perspective, the aim is clear: In making this career change you want an incentive to succeed, and you want to understand exactly what is required of you and how you can expect to be rewarded (both financially and in other ways). You are about to commit significant time and energy to your new profession. There should be no confusion about what is expected or how the upside works. You should not be worrying about compensation along the way. Obviously, ownership can neutralize this issue somewhat. Regardless, there is no getting around the fact that the compensation formula can remarkably complex with many sensitivities.

I hope the advice in this book helps you find a firm that matches your interests and risk tolerance, but we have to acknowledge that it doesn't always work out. Through no fault of your own, you may find that you have landed in the wrong culture, or even that your trust was misplaced. If this happens, you do not have to give up on consulting completely. Recovering from a bad choice of firms can be complicated, and changing firms is not easy, but it can be done. Chapter 13 has specific advice to help you through this difficult situation, although I sincerely hope you won't need it.

Finally, be aware that poaching in consulting can be extremely aggressive. If you build up a large book of business, people find out. If you become disenchanted with your current situation, don't be surprised if a recruiter gets you on the phone and presents a few interesting options.

RECOMMENDATIONS

1. Starting with a firm and finding a sponsor will be the best approach for most readers.

2. Pay close attention to finding a sponsor and to the emphasis the firms you're considering place on teams and team building. How these firms treat their alumni is also a useful reference.

3. Have a monitoring plan in place to assess your progress—one that includes someone from outside the immediate environment. Commit important feedback to writing. Avoid burnout by getting away regularly.

Pay attention to compensation and make sure that you understand what behaviors are being incentivized.

4.   Don't underestimate your gifts as you negotiate your compensation package. Your onboarding time with the firm will be more limited than the new careerist who starts out in consulting right out of graduate school. The firm should be willing to invest in your development and provide an attractive upside that recognizes your accelerated progress in building the business.

5.   Being part owner can address many concerns about compensation, but also comes with different obligations. Make sure you are joining the firm at the right level for your desired risk, commitment, and compensation.

REFERENCES

Charas, S., L. L. Griffeth, and R. Malik. 2015. "Why Men Have More Help Getting to the C-Suite." *Harvard Business Review* digital article. Published November 16. https://hbr.org/2015/11/why-men-have-more-help-getting-to-the-c-suite.

Dixon, D. L. 2020. *Diversity on the Executive Path: Wisdom and Insights for Navigating to the Highest Levels of Healthcare Leadership.* Chicago: Health Administration Press.

Gladwin International & Company. 2021. "Professional Services & Management Consulting Search and Selection." https://gladwininternational.com/professional_services_and_consulting.php.

McChrystal, S., T. Collins, D. Silverman, and C. Fussell. 2015. *Team of Teams: New Rules of Engagement for a Complex World.* New York: Portfolio/Penguin.

CHAPTER 12

Starting a Solo Practice

As a consultant, offer a service that is not readily available from any other source. Providing a niche opportunity that others are not adequately serving, or expertise and skills superior to others, will help ensure that there's demand for your services. It makes little sense to offer a service that is readily available in the market, perhaps in an oversupply situation.
—Phillips and Phillips (2004)

STARTING YOUR OWN practice is the same as starting a new business, but in the case of solo practice you are doing it alone. You are both the owner and the producer/employee. It is hard to imagine a riskier proposition, especially from the standpoint of baring your soul. It is the essence of entrepreneurship.[1] You are putting yourself out there for all to see. You don't want to hide your successes, but you can't hide your failures.

Shortly after launching my own firm, I had a memorable conversation with my father over a lunch where I barely tasted the food. I was a month or two into my new solo practice and was beginning to have doubts. I had just turned 30. What had I done? Was this a big mistake? Was I just kidding myself? My father answered my questions with his own. "Scott, isn't it too soon to be asking these questions? It seems like such a natural role for you. Have you really

---

1 There are many paths to this outcome. See chapter 10 in *The Healthcare Consultant's Handbook* for three exemplary solo practice profiles.

given it enough time? You seem to enjoy the work so much." His words were very reassuring.

In retrospect, it took some time to focus my practice and develop some unique skills. I was trained as a generalist, so switching to a specialist role took some effort. I knew I was a strategist, but circumstances caused me to shift from general strategic planning to a focus on mergers and consolidations. This eventually led to a concentration in service line development, and so on. Practices evolve.

COMPETITIVE MARKET SHIFTS

As Phillips and Phillips (2004) suggest, a niche play is probably the easiest path to pursue in consulting. This can include a unique experience, methodology, outlook, technology, or other factor that allows a client to succeed in a certain task. If you have doubts about how well you can convince the buyer that your approach is unique, there are a few approaches you can try.

An internet search will help you determine what else is available in the market related to your area of interest. You have likely done this already if you are actively contemplating going out on your own. The question you must ask is whether you have researched thoroughly. I have found asking someone else to do the search and seeing what they come up with to be a helpful alternative. Beware the tendency to fit the findings to your preferred narrative. For example, are there red flags that are inconsistent with how you see the market evolving? You must be cautious not to ignore these signs.

Several of the consultants profiled in chapter 5 mentioned the importance of having the right credentials, but this only gets you through the door and it must be based on an accurate picture of how the market is changing. To compete successfully, you need a clear picture of what comes next and qualified references of how your service has proven value. This may be the single most important hurdle for a new solo consultant. Starting without the ability to refer to a few success stories is nearly impossible. Sometimes you can carry over what you did as an executive, but that will not likely sustain you for long. You probably won't be very selective with your client list at first—you have to start somewhere. Over time, you will tend to favor those opportunities that stand the best chance of becoming good references for future business. You will no doubt have clients that will not be references for you even if you have a successful engagement. It's not that you did anything wrong; it's simply not how they play.

Still, there is no substitute for an active referral network. Well-established firms recognize that it helps when referrals are from prominent leaders at organizations that have favorable recognition in the market. Fortunately, prominent executives take pride in having a large and active network. The best executives take their networks seriously. Networks provide significant benefit over time, including referrals to the best and brightest that can help with challenges that are common to the industry.

One of the more interesting things we are learning about human nature from observations of the experience economy is that people are compelled to share experiences that stand out—both good and bad. Word of mouth remains one of the most powerful influencers of behavior. We activate our grapevine when we experience an exceptional event. A classic example is sharing a great retail or hospitality experience: "Wow, they really took great care of me." Unfortunately, such research also points out that we feel particularly moved to share negative experiences. This is where branding comes into play. As Warren Buffett has famously noted, "It takes 20 years to build a reputation and five minutes to ruin it."

Another important market consideration has to do with your logical pipeline for new business. Your marketing budget is limited, as is your ability to gain traction in the market, given the myriad of other firms that offer similar services. Becoming a subcontractor to one or more prominent firms to offer your specialized talent might be a good way to expand your network. Working out a formal arrangement with one of them ahead of a launch could secure your ability to lock in future collaborative business.

Of course, a key here is your ability to secure an exclusive arrangement (i.e., the firm uses only you for that service). While challenging to obtain, the ideal arrangement would eliminate the potential internal competition from your partner firm (i.e., they would only pursue such work when you are involved). This is not easy to accomplish unless it involves technology or patents that afford you some legal protection, and a lot can go wrong. For example, a potential partner firm once called us to ask us to join them in a proposal. When I inquired further, it turned out that we were merely being considered to join them in the proposal along with several others. They were not inviting us; they were inviting us to be considered. My read on this was that they were actually more interested in learning my approach rather than forging a new relationship. I declined. In another instance, I went through the normal vetting process and sent the potential partner a copy of my bio, which they included in their proposal. We discussed it further and I decided not to participate, as I was neither qualified for nor interested in the project. They put my resume in their proposal anyway. This can be a slippery slope.

You may decide to differentiate your firm by stratifying the market and specializing in a certain clientele (e.g., small rural hospitals). There is nothing inherently wrong with this approach. For example, I have known a few consultants during my career who have secured a dominant position serving children's hospitals. This is a particularly intimate group, unique in its reliance on donor contributions, and it tends to behave in a somewhat closed fashion. Just be sure with such a niche play that you have the appropriate infrastructure and marketing to maintain continued visibility and traction with your chosen subgroup. Out of sight, out of mind.

Secure references can be critical (so make sure your references aren't all about to retire from their current jobs). You are depending on this insular network to secure future business, so you must invest the care and feeding required to keep this network active. Everyone has a network, but many networks are dormant because of neglect. Do not let that happen to you, especially around a launch.

FEEDBACK WON'T TAKE LONG

You will quickly know whether you are busy or not, and your clients will quickly determine whether you will get paid. Failure is not only an option, it is a certainty if things are not done right.

In many respects, the key to success in consulting is that you have checked off all the boxes regarding other options along the way. You are clear on the risks and determined to succeed. You are also clear that you have the resources and stamina to give it a reasonable chance for success. Following the process outlined in this book, while no guarantee, should give you some comfort in that regard. It can guide in your preparation and help you manage expectations, which is a big part of what is required.

> **In many respects, the key to success in consulting is that you have checked off all the boxes regarding other options along the way.**

Weaning yourself from a regular paycheck is unsettling. One of the executives interviewed for this book tells a story of how he deposited checks from his clients but neglected to set up any regular payment schedule. His wife, who took responsibility for paying family bills, would occasionally ask if he could pay himself. After several similar exchanges, he eventually started paying himself on a regular schedule.

Resilience is critical, as there will always be surprises. It is said that many people lose a golf match before they ever hit the ball. Having a golf handicap helps set expectations given past performance, but an even more critical factor is being in the moment. If you expect to lose, chances are good that you will. If, on the other hand, you not only expect to win but you work hard to justify that optimism, it is at least an even bet you have a chance to win. There are no compromises here.

SECURE A LEGIT BOOK OF BUSINESS

After checking off the boxes to get to this point (refer to the Career Change Decision Framework in the introduction), the next important thing is to begin with a tangible book of business. This gives you a head start. Ideally, you have already secured one or two clients, even if they are relatively small engagements. You might have a retainer for 6–12 months. That is how I started in 1981. You must not take this lightly. Just as sales training emphasizes closing the sale, you should not count any opportunities as a book of business until you have a signed contract in hand and an initial payment. Many of us in consulting have made the mistake of assuming a verbal agreement is adequate.

Having an existing book of business when you launch does several things. First, it ensures that you will not be idle—the curse of an entrepreneur. It is important to start out with a commitment to an existing client. And that is the second point—you will have at least one client reference going forward. It has been my experience that clients who are genuinely pleased with your work will take it upon themselves not only to share that good experience with others but to help you get in front of some of their contacts. Nothing is better than word of mouth from a marketing perspective. No amount of advertising or cold calling can supplant a solid client referral.

Finally, there is one other subtle point about starting out with an existing client engagement. As simple as it sounds, it provides you with a response to the question that you will undoubtedly be asked, both by people who care and by potential clients you are trying to sell to: "What are you working on now?" Responding with "nothing" is the kiss of death. Remember, clients must defend their choice to hire you, and healthcare clients are notoriously risk averse. No client wants to invest in a start-up business.

Too often when the search consultant confronts a candidate who spent some time in his own firm, "Smith & Associates," Smith is forced to confess there were no associates. You must be able to respond positively to similar questions, preferably with a client engagement or two that are in your sweet spot. Sometimes the mere mention of someone you are working with will suffice. When client confidentiality keeps you from identifying the client by more than attributes (e.g., "working with a large academic medical center"), speaking to the nature of the engagement is key (e.g., "working on a physician governance model"). It helps establish your bona fides. Of course, when you have a book of business at the start, that client already knows your bona fides. It is a breakthrough worth celebrating when you secure your first client who did not know you before you became a consultant. But beware of imposters.

It has happened to everyone in consulting at one time or another: We think we will get the opportunity to work with a client, only to find out that the opportunity has gone to another firm. We were counting on a client moving forward with the next assignment, only to be told that something else has come up and they are going to have to postpone for the time being. Or, one of my least favorites: The CEO or engagement sponsor decides to leave or is fired in the middle of a big assignment.[2] In one situation, a friend of many years had long indicated a desire to work with me, but once again failed to do so, even though I had some unique and relevant experiences that were particularly applicable to their situation. All these things have happened to me, and they profoundly hurt at the time. The point is the absence of a clear book of business can be an existential threat when starting an independent consulting practice.

Securing any business includes making sure that there is agreement on scope (i.e., a signed scope of work statement) and payment (i.e., cost and schedule). As silly as it sounds, I have never forgotten how on several occasions I literally had to camp out in the office of a CEO to get a check for my services when I was starting out. Mind you, in all these cases I had a signed proposal and SOW. In one

---

2 In one unfortunate situation, employee accusations of misbehavior by my client CEO were on the front page of an urban newspaper for weeks, abruptly ending an ongoing strategy engagement in which we were heavily invested the prior year, which was very consequential—for both me and the client.

case, after several attempts over several weeks, I finally approached the chief financial officer, with whom I had done a fair amount of work, and asked, "Do you want to own a consulting business?" My attempt at humor was intended to make clear to him that continuing to delay payment for my services was going to result in my going out of business, as I would be unable to pay my bills (including payroll for other consultants). Note: I tried to keep this a firm issue and not a personal issue (not making it about "putting food on the table").[3]

The point is this: one can easily be deceived that a prospective client has a legitimate opportunity for work when this is idle talk. One is especially vulnerable to this deception when just starting out. Lacking experience with closing on such business, you can easily misunderstand intent versus reality. When running a solo practice, it takes a lot of introspection not to take such events personally. But many things can go wrong. The client in question may have good intentions and want to secure such business with you, but not have authority to enter into such an arrangement. Maybe they were just trying to be encouraging and not state an intention. Until you have the signed contract and an initial payment (not one or the other but *both*), you have not booked that client.

As noted previously, I recommend that you have two or more clients secured before launching your practice. These do not have to be huge engagements, but they should keep you busy for a reasonable period and allow you to cover some key operating costs (short of personal salary) and expenses (travel, etc.). Beware clients who ask you to devote time and effort at no cost to see if they would consider hiring you. While it can work (perhaps a visit), at least in principle, I believe that this is not a good way to start. The client must be willing

---

3   This reminds me of a rather embarrassing episode in my career where I was attempting to do some additional work for a client; the client favored another firm that had political ties to them but was far less qualified to do the specific work (at least as far as I was concerned). I was so incensed at the client's decision that I found myself writing a personal letter in which I mentioned their decision would prevent me from putting food on my table. A more mature friend helped me see the error of my ways and I managed to stick the draft letter in the drawer and move on.

to cross the threshold of paying you for your services, otherwise the service can be misconstrued as doing a favor for a friend.

Inexperience in securing a consulting contract should never be underestimated. Once, when I briefly considered whether to expand the business into executive search, a colleague asked me if I was sure that my existing strategic consulting clients would also be willing to hire me as a search consultant. This question stopped me in my tracks. The fact is, I was not sure they would, and this resulted in my not formally extending into search. I had a few occasions that I did so where existing clients had a need for which they asked me to help, but closing on such business and completing it successfully was considerably different than the kind of consulting that I was used to doing.

Finally, do not be deceived by well-wishing friends who promise you future work. Friends and family may want to be encouraging and recognize that consulting might be a good opportunity for you; however, they may not fully understand the chasm between the desire to become a professional advisor and the willingness of others *to pay you* as an advisor. I suspect that not recognizing this chasm has been the reason for many false starts. To avoid this, one must be disciplined in securing an adequate level of business to get started (proving that at least one or two people are willing to hire you), which will extinguish any doubt that people are willing to pay for your services and that this is not just a pipe dream. At least one consultant interviewed for this book suggested that being hired by a stranger who did not know you before is the purest way to test out your ability to function as a consultant.

> Friends and family may want to be encouraging and recognize that consulting might be a good opportunity for you; however, they may not fully understand the chasm between the desire to become a professional advisor and the willingness of others to pay you as an advisor.

KEEP YOUR GUARD UP

A consultant friend of mine tells this story from when they were with one of the large specialty healthcare consulting firms many years ago. There had been numerous contacts between the firm officers and a large health system prospect for an engagement so big that it would have involved a big chunk of the firm. The conversations had all been very favorable, and all indications were that the engagement was a go. But when it came time to sign the contract, the client unilaterally reduced the budget by almost 50 percent—without significantly modifying the scope of the engagement. This came as a complete surprise and was equivalent to millions of dollars, which would leave many people who expected to work on the project out in the cold. Much preplanning had been done after the initial proposal, as the engagement involved literally dozens of people. There were also accounting ramifications. The embarrassment to the partner in charge never really went away. Some would say that it ultimately led to their leaving the firm.

The mistake the partner had made, which is easy for anyone to make, was violating protocol and booking the business before having a signed contract. The fallout was swift and immediate. The budget change was so disappointing that some senior members of the firm at the time were surprised that the firm proceeded with the client engagement under these circumstances. It may seem like overkill, but closing a sale is so critical that you should never let down your guard.

THE RIGHT IMAGE IS CRITICAL

A plethora of books give solid advice about starting a new business, including a consulting business.[4] In the prologue of her excellent book *Entrepreneurial You*, Dorie Clark (2017), from Duke University's Fuqua School of Business, points out "the dirty secret of

---

4   See, for example, Melinda F. Emerson, *Become Your Own Boss in 12 Months* (Avon, MA: Adams Media, 2015).

today's entrepreneurial economy: being excellent, and even being well known and respected in your field, just isn't enough."

Some experts would have you become a certified business consultant, though this credential carries little to no weight in healthcare. Rather than amassing "recommended" credentials, the key is to strike the right balance between what is necessary to establish the desired image and what is practical from the standpoint of managing risk and effectively completing the work that you hope to generate. While not necessarily direct trade-offs, this balance prompts important questions related to infrastructure/image and risk management, shown in exhibit 12.1.

Looking back, these are some of the key things on which I focused. Do you intend to remain in solo practice or is this simply a preliminary step to forming your own firm? While you do not have to decide this up front, you do need to be aware of the difference. Over time, your clients will tend to push you one way or the other. It may also depend on how specialized your practice is.

Managing your digital footprint has become an essential part of any start-up business. Every firm should be launched using all forms of media. This is not a time to be shy. Stake your claim loud and clear, and do not disappear after the first push. Maintain a digital presence. Malvey and Sapp (2020) speak to unique selling points as a key to digital branding. Like the elevator speech that you pull out in short bursts of conversation, your unique selling points need to emphasize exceptional skills and/or laser-like focus. You need to cast your net with the right bait for the kind and size of fish that you seek. Your elevator speech, your selling points, and your digital presence should all lead to actions with clear deliverables and value. The value proposition should form the core of any communication.

"Out of sight, out of mind" has long been an essential tenet of professional services. I confess, attending meetings (there are way too many in healthcare) has long been controversial among consultants. Asking which group to join and how to participate will get any group of consultants energized with a wide range of opinions. My view is simple: As with many things in life, meetings will only be as good as your investment in them.

I have joined several associations over the years, and even worked for one (the American Hospital Association). I still belong to a few. Without exception, those groups that were most beneficial were the ones where I devoted time and was willing to keep up with correspondence and meetings. My impression is that most consultants see little to gain from such affiliations, but my experience has been different. Although healthcare is a massive industry, it tends to function as a small community in most instances. There is no substitute for knowing key people and having the means to interact with them. I was indeed fortunate to meet several prominent leaders early in my

Exhibit 12.1. The Solo Practice Start-Up Checklist

Infrastructure/Image	Manage Risk
Decide between work from home or an external office.	
Decide whether you will outsource or hire support.	
Have a clear vision and an elevator speech.	
Standardize your approach to billing, proposals, and testimonials.	
Incorporate, and select your legal counsel, financial advisor, and bank.	
Have a firm launch plan with a clear indication of scope and approach.	
Stoke your network regularly and consistently.	
Have clear metrics in a dashboard that you monitor daily (e.g., contacts made, calls).	
Choose your pipeline tracking systems.	Decide whether you are willing to engage in competitive bid situations.
Have a marketing plan, with execution beginning with an announcement on day one.	Decide whether you will require a visit before submitting a proposal.
Decide whether you will be in the lead on all engagements.	Decide whether you are willing to become a subcontractor.
Designate an advisory group.	Set up at least one key advisor who agrees to function in this role.

career, which led to name recognition as part of a broad network. Name recognition goes a long way in this business.

While I do not subscribe to the view that you must have a large network to start, it certainly can help. What is important is that the network grows and remains vibrant. The nature of the network will depend heavily on the nature of the practice. It should focus, at least somewhat, on key levers that result in lead generation. I have found that maintaining a prospects list is critical and requires literally daily attention. This takes some discipline, especially when you are selling while completing the work you have already sold.

You can easily conclude that you lack time to attend to this. Someone said to me early in my career that the most important time to pay attention to the prospects list is when you are the busiest. Thankfully, this advice stuck. I am not sure how they reached that conclusion, but it was probably the recognition that there is nothing worse than finishing an intensive period of work only to find that you have no more work waiting. This liability is peculiar to solo practice. I confess there were numerous times when I completed a large client engagement (some of which lasted more than a year) only to find that the next one came along very quickly. This did not happen by chance. Although I was grateful for the work I had, I found that it was important to maintain an edge and be constantly seeking the next opportunity. In a firm where others are also doing some selling, managing the prospects list is a shared responsibility. It only takes one dry period to hammer home this message. Being "on the beach" is the curse of the busy consultant.

Clearly, one of the draws of having your own firm is being as busy as you want to be. And while I will concede that this is possible, at least theoretically (e.g., "I want to average 20 hours per week of billability"), in reality I believe this to be a myth. I think you will find that your clients will dictate just how busy you get. Of course, you can cut off starting new engagements, but this becomes harder when you are engaged with a client who has a need for additional work. You have the right not to take on additional work (as indicated in writing as part of your consulting agreement with the client), but exercising this right is something else. If you were the client and paid good money to a trusted advisor, it would be easy to expect them to accept additional work, especially if the work is related to their sweet spot. You see the dilemma.

MAKE TIME TO GET AWAY

Starting your own firm is all-consuming. At least initially, you will be on high alert and will find it hard to think about much else. But there is a danger here. I have known many people with their own firms, many of which carried their own name (e.g., John Smith & Associates), and some of these folks made no distinction between personal time and professional time. I do not subscribe to this approach. I acknowledge that it is difficult to resist this, but I have found that it is important to get away. Even if you might be vulnerable to temptation, your family and friends will expect otherwise. How does the saying go? All work and no play . . .

But this is about more than that. You need down time. You need to read a book with no relevance to how you make your living, or visit an interesting place, or try your hand at a new hobby. To deny yourself time for such pursuits is clearly shortsighted. Clients often want to discuss more than business issues. If there is no more to you, it will be a short conversation, and it may be challenging to make connections. Better to be more well-rounded and able to carry on a conversation involving a variety of issues. You do not have to talk about politics, but small talk is not so small in my experience. Embrace it. Time spent away from work is essential to your ability to remain an interesting person, worth getting to know.

I have a good friend who has that gift. He is interested in everything and everyone. He seems to believe it is an insult not to be able to engage in conversation on any topic someone might raise. He took this as a personal challenge. He happens to also be a physician. I once witnessed him engage with an older woman for at least a half hour about gardening. Mind you, I am not sure he has ever watered a plant, but sure enough, he clearly had read an article once that discussed the impact of some of the inclement weather on various plants. Small talk truly is a gift.

RECOMMENDATIONS

1. Your ability to differentiate yourself is important, whether in a firm or solo practice, and feedback will not take long; the market tends to respond quickly.

2. Solo practice does not mean starting from ground zero. You must have a book of business at launch.

3. Do not make the mistake of letting down your guard. Stick to sensible policies as you take on your first clients.

4. Having the right image is important from the start. Fixing your image later is much harder.

5. Getting away is critical; burnout is a certainty absent some time away.

REFERENCES

Clark, D. 2017. *Entrepreneurial You: Monetize Your Expertise, Create Multiple Income Streams, and Thrive.* Boston: Harvard Business.

Malvey, D., and J. L. Sapp. 2020. *Your Healthcare Job Hunt: How Your Digital Presence Can Make or Break Your Career.* Chicago: Health Administration Press.

Phillips, P. P., and J. J. Phillips. 2004. "Building a Successful Consulting Practice: Opportunities and Challenges." ROI Institute. https://roiinstitute.net/wp-content/uploads/2017/02/Building-a-Successful-Consulting-Practice.pdf.

PART V

WHO?

Who do I need to involve in this process to provide assurance and
guidance along the way?

CONSULTING IS PERSONAL. What works for me may not work for you. The key is to know what your needs are and then manage the experience according to your preferences.

You have had help along your career path until now. Why should things be any different this time? Having a support group of people who can tell you what you may not want to hear is critical.

In his video "The Power of Vision," Joel Barker shares a story about a man driving down a country road. As the man passes a car traveling the opposite direction, the other driver yells, "Pig!" The first driver is still stewing about this encounter when he rounds the corner and runs into a pig. What he thought was rudeness turned out to be a warning.

We bring a lens to everything, which means we all have some blinders. It is like critiquing a piece of art: Others notice things that you may not. A group can be immensely helpful by adding dimensions to your understanding of a piece of art, or a progress report, or a piece of feedback.

In the end, the market will determine your success or failure. That is one of the most exciting things about consulting—and the most humbling. If you are in this business long enough, you will probably lose some engagements you feel you should have won. You may also win a few you were more likely to lose. Some engagements will go well, others not so well. You will come to rely on yourself to bolster your attitude when times get tough. Staying healthy will go a long way toward sustaining your resolve to succeed. Welcome to consulting.

Chapter 13. If Things Don't Work Out
Chapter 14. Let the Journey Begin

If Things Don't Work Out

*Handling failure, rejection, or disappointment in a productive
way can be as beneficial to career development as a huge
accomplishment—it's all about how you set your sails in the
unpredictable seas of the professional world.*
—Lindsay Danas Cohen (2013)

I HOPE FEW readers will need the contents of this chapter. Obviously, though, any career change involves risk. It does no good to deny this, and we must be prepared for the possible problems.

There are three possible points of failure in your career change. The first would be the failure to try at all. You addressed that one by launching into consulting. No regrets. The second potential failure is discovering that you have joined the wrong firm. This demands special treatment, which we will discuss. The third potential failure is a determination that consulting is not for you, whether in a firm or in your solo practice. This chapter discusses what to do in each of these situations, when things don't work out.

RELY ON YOUR NETWORK

It is hard to imagine a more vulnerable position than to attempt a dramatic career change only to fail. You can take some satisfaction in knowing you at least tried, and we can hope you have no regrets, but panic can set in when you start thinking about what to do next.

Before addressing this, let's be clear on how we know that the run is over. There probably is little chance of the boiling frog phenomenon here; more likely, you are experiencing the Mike Tyson "punch in the face" phenomenon. The purest form of feedback is a lack of client work, but you could also come to the realization that you do not like the firm you are with, or recognize that consulting work is not what you hoped.

While consulting always involves fluctuations, not being busy enough will catch up to you at some point. If you are with a firm, it may be when the firm notifies you that you are performing below expectations for sales, billings, or both. This should not come as a surprise, as you should be closely tracking your progress. You know better than anybody if you are busy or not. In a sense, a solo practice is no different; if you are not busy over an extended period, you will be unable to pay your bills. Either way, it is time for plan B.

Alternatively, you may determine that you love the work of consulting but you are with the wrong firm. Or you might have plenty of work, and even like the firm, but find that you react negatively to the pace, the travel, or to having too many poor client experiences. You are not gaining the satisfaction you were seeking. You are no longer convinced that this is the best way to pursue your career goals at this time.

Regardless of the reason for coming to this difficult conclusion, it is time once again to rely on your network (which should have grown somewhat). Just as you did when you started, you must get back to those who made the journey with you and make clear that you need to be "replanted," as one search consultant put it. You have some choices to make.

You might choose to start the discernment process over again, but you will likely feel a greater sense of urgency at this juncture. You are trying to avoid being stuck on the beach for too long. This is where your earlier preparation is valuable. Your financial reserves remain intact for just such an occasion. Yet, you still need a regular income stream in the not-too-distant future. Find out through your network whether any new opportunities have arisen.

Finally, you came into this process with a support group. That group should still be active and willing to help you. You have involved them along the way as part of your monitoring plan, so this change is probably not a great surprise. Everyone realized at the outset that this was a possibility.

So, now what? Following are the most likely scenarios, along with some tricks of the trade that can be helpful at this juncture.

CHANGING FIRMS

I would much prefer to leave this section out of the book, but that would be disingenuous. I dearly hope that following the guidance in previous chapters has resulted in a good match between your interests and the firm that you have joined. I wrote this book (along with the previous one) to help you focus on the right things and make a sound decision. But sometimes it simply does not work out. You may even have placed your trust in someone and been severely disappointed. I can readily identify several people in my career who would fit this label. Whatever the reason, recovering from a bad choice of firms will have you navigating a number of difficult issues.

Ideally, you will discover this during a 60- to 90-day probationary period and sever the relationship with little hassle. Leaving after such a short time should eliminate some discomfort. Mistakes happen and everyone moves on. But what if it gets more involved and this discussion is occurring six months, nine months, or even a few years later?

If it takes this long, the good news is that you have found your calling and consulting is everything you had hoped it would be, and more. The bad news is that you are in the wrong place. Again, no firm is perfect. Some invest considerable time and effort to continually improve infrastructure and work processes; others don't. Consulting staffs are demanding, and the pressure can be great. People come and go. There are no guarantees. Culture is rarely what it seems on the surface, and it is genuinely hard to determine the cultural fit until you have lived it up close. Perhaps things were not as promised, or a colleague was mistreated, or a key person is hard to be around. So, while you remain excited about consulting and are committed to moving forward in the profession, the firm you are with, for whatever reason, is not the right place for you. Regardless of the reason, and there could be many, you may need to leave the firm.

While it is cold comfort, both you and the firm are likely to recognize if it is not working out; it is rarely unilateral. Still—and there is no way to sugarcoat this—leaving can be difficult on many fronts. It can be done, though, and it is done all the time. There are two scenarios: The first is that you decide to leave before deciding what you will do next or what firm you may join. The advantage of this approach is that it may make things a bit more amicable than otherwise might be the case (e.g., if you are leaving to work with a competitor). Because of the noncompete clause in your existing contract, some people simply take a sabbatical for a year and then rejoin the workforce.

The second possibility is that you intend to continue consulting, perhaps even working for a competitor. This can make things quite uncomfortable, and red flags will be raised quickly. I have known a number of people who have taken this path, notwithstanding the difficulty in doing so. The following guidelines may help here, but legal advice is critical in this case.

- *Abide by your contract.* Assume the firm will enforce all elements of your contract, most notably the noncompete clause. They will likely be very unhappy if you have entertained discussions with a competitor, and they will be particularly sensitive about how others in the firm will react. It is quite possible that you will find their approach to this situation to be somewhat intimidating. Don't let them intimidate you. Some empathy will help here. The key people in your firm will find it difficult to accept that you are going to a competitor. They will feel betrayed and will share their disappointment. Emotions will run high, and there may be hard feelings. Abiding by your contract is one of the best ways to cope with this.

- *Be prepared to lose ongoing work.* Competition does not always bring out the best in people. I have seen firms that, on being informed of the decision, immediately acted as if the person leaving never existed. It should not be handled this way, and I like to think that most firms would do better than this, but you must be prepared for the worst. Their main concern will be how to finish the work for your existing clients. Don't be surprised when you are informed that you will not be allowed to complete this work (never mind the fact that your involvement may be essential to a successful outcome). The firm will ask you not to contact these clients once you have made it known you are leaving. Obviously, this gets terribly uncomfortable. I can only say that clients understand these things happen, and you will likely find a way to reconnect with them at some point.

- *Have a written separation agreement.* Because things can go south quickly, I recommend that you work out a written separation agreement clearly spelling out things that might be important to you (and to the firm). This should include a mutual nondisparagement clause at a minimum. You also need to eliminate any looming issues related to compensation, benefits (including pension), pending sales, deliverables, client relations, and so on. Some labor lawyers specialize in such agreements.

- *Understand that things move fast.* Once this process starts, it can be surprising just how fast things progress. The loss of control can be disconcerting. The existing firm often wants you out of sight and out of mind as quickly as possible. They may work hard to keep you from interacting with other staff once you have decided to leave.[1] Frankly, if this happens, you do not want to stick around either.

- *Protect yourself.* The contents of the separation agreement exceed our purpose here, but understand that this is the last opportunity to clear things up and avoid future misunderstandings. Get legal help with this because some things may not occur to you. Try to build in some protection against retaliation. Some firms can go to extremes in this regard. Imagine leaving a firm and several years later finding out that they have removed your name as primary author of a groundbreaking article you wrote while under their employment. It is a mystery to me what the firm sought to gain from such an action, but I am clear on the serious ethical questions it raises. It is amazing the lengths some firms will go to in their attempts to neutralize the impact of people leaving the firm. I much prefer the approach that recognizes and celebrates people's contributions and expends effort to stay connected to alumni. Personally, I place high value on firms that emphasize solid alumni relations (not just window dressing).

- *Rely on your receiving firm.* While this process is always challenging, it can be easier if you know what firm you are joining. The receiving firm often has access to resources (e.g., human resources and legal experts) that can help you manage this process, as they have likely done it before. Leaving a firm to work with a competitor is a sensitive matter, and the risk of a lawsuit is quite high if this is mishandled. I am familiar with a few situations where

---

1   I am strongly averse to this approach and have stuck my neck out twice to send a company-wide email saying thanks, being complimentary of my time with the firm, and giving my personal forwarding information, without discussing where I was going. The common approach, where nothing is said other than "He has left the firm," and no forwarding information is given, does not work for me. My approach violated company policy, but at that point I did not care. In both cases, things turned out fine.

legal challenges have gone on for years. Your receiving firm can help considerably. Keep in mind, however, that you remain obligated not to share proprietary information about the firm you are leaving.

I have been on both sides of this issue. I have counseled people out of my firm as the owner, and I have left firms where I was not an owner. Even where I have been generous as the owner and given people time to find a new job, things do not always work out. I was reminded of this when one senior person, after being given six months to leave, ended up going to work at our archrival firm. That firm gleefully announced the "coup" of poaching one of my principals before we could make our own announcement. Unfortunately, the principal—who was still on the payroll—had not had the opportunity to inform us first. The violation of trust greatly affected our relationship going forward. Some friction is unavoidable under these circumstances, but it's better to make a clean and timely break than to have things play out over an extended time.

If you do your homework and have a strong support system, it will minimize the likelihood of choosing the wrong firm. *The Healthcare Consultant's Handbook* discusses how some firms have handled departures.[2] How firms treat people who leave is one of the most telling indicators of corporate culture and should be considered during your evaluation process.

What if the firm is fine but consulting in general is not working? If you follow the advice in this book, you have been at it for at least a year, so you will have some client experiences to fall back on. Would you consider working for any of these clients? No doubt, consulting has connected you to people and places you did not know before. How has this grown your network? Some advice is in order depending on the next path you take.

---

2   See chapter 11 of *The Healthcare Consultant's Handbook*, "Joining the Right Firm."

RETURNING TO OPERATIONS

Most executives who contemplate consulting consider returning to executive management as their most natural plan B. They came from line management, so one would think that there should be minimal barriers to returning. Remarkably, this may not always be the case.

Carson Dye of Exceptional Leadership (profiled in chapter 5) offers the perspective of a search consultant who secures a set of candidates to be presented to a client. Carson generally recruits for the chief medical officer position, but he also has considerable experience with CEO searches. He coaches each candidate to stress their respective strengths so they can compete successfully. He notes, however, that these structured interviews tend to be short and rather direct. Put yourself in the shoes of the client, who must conduct three interviews with candidates in a day or two. There is only time enough to tell one story—your story. In other words, having to tell two stories is a liability. Executives who have tried their hand at consulting and are now returning to operations must fill in the gap between their last line position and now. This involves two stories (i.e., executive path and consulting) and places those executives at an immediate disadvantage, not so much because they failed at consulting, but because there is a lack of bandwidth to cover the second story.

You are asking a lot of the listener to have them follow you through two stories. You will be compared to the other candidates, who have one simple, progressive story to tell with no gaps (e.g., from position 1 to 2 to 3). This might vary by position; for example, such a detour might be more of an asset for a chief strategy officer position, where the candidate has shown some initiative and benefited from the entrepreneurship involved. Many would consider such experiences to be helpful to someone charged with strategic initiatives.

Jack Schlosser of Desert Vista Advisors (also profiled in chapter 5) approaches the interview process for returning executives a bit differently. His advice is to explain what you were thinking when you tried consulting and why. People will want to know what you learned. What will they hear when they ask for references related to your consulting experience? A consistent and honest story will be particularly important. Use your network. Consulting is part of your story, but not all of it. Have a story that makes sense, reinforced by some compelling takeaways. Make it an asset, not a liability.

Where you have been is important; it shows your footsteps. Do you make a change every few years? If you change jobs too often, a potential employer will see some risk in that. If, however, you made a conscious decision that fits nicely into where you were at the time and where you are now, it can become reinforcing; a logical stop along the way that yielded some clear benefits.

In some cases, another approach might be possible. Depending on how much time you spent in consulting, you might be able to invoke the "gig worker" angle: You accepted an interim assignment and always intended to return to operations at some point. Another common refrain is wanting more stability than the fluctuations you experienced in consulting. Consultants who migrate into a client organization are not uncommon, nor is it unusual to have a boomerang experience and return to consulting after a short interlude (e.g., as an interim manager).[3] Rather than telling a second story, you could also explain that things have changed on the personal side to set up your return—for example, "My kids went off to college and now I am free to pursue other interests."

Compared to other exit strategies, returning to operations would generally seem to involve fewer barriers. However, returning to the position you left at your former employer probably does not make much sense. A similar position elsewhere could be an attractive alternative. Just be sure to give yourself plenty of time to make such a move. Before the COVID-19 pandemic, changing jobs typically took around 12 months.

---

3   See chapter 11 in *The Healthcare Consultant's Handbook* for a more complete discussion of the Boomerang Experience.

TRYING INTERIM MANAGEMENT

Some experts feel strongly that you should not have a plan B if you are committed to consulting. I lean in this direction. In my mind, interim management does not really qualify as a commitment to consulting, as it represents a time-limited hybrid role that is not intended to be sustainable. Interim management also involves some temporary authority, which is contraindicated for a traditional consulting assignment. Further, it resembles operating performance more than the skills that would be involved in a consulting engagement.

True interim management is a rare opportunity to successfully implement some changes that otherwise might be impossible to execute in a particular organization.[4] I once helped design a physician employment model for a hospital. After completing this work, the client realized they had no one in-house to follow through with this initiative. Timing was critical to take advantage of this opportunity, and I was willing to help get this up and running on an interim basis. While I would not recommend a steady diet of interim management in a consulting practice, an intense desire to help a client succeed can sometimes get the best of you.

If you are looking to remain in this position over time, interim management may not be the right approach. A true interim position should not last more than 6–18 months and should be contracted, not employed. The intent is to accelerate change for the next person, who can then concentrate on securing things from a more permanent position. Interim management is often described as keeping the chair warm for the next occupant.

Operating successfully at this level requires experience and a clear understanding that the position is time limited. Consulting skills can be important to success, in that you need to understand how to fully implement the initiatives that are identified. This could be characterized as a "skunk works" designed to foster rapid adoption of

---

4   See chapter 3 in my previous book for a more detailed discussion of interim management.

some critical changes—changes that may require actions concerning difficult issues that would prevent the executive from remaining in that position. Where this intent is clear up front, interim managers are given the authority to circumvent protocol and other barriers that may have prevented successful implementation of these initiatives in the past.

Some exceptionally talented people have made careers functioning as interim managers, which requires keeping one or two potential next assignments in the wings because of the relatively short turnover of these positions. Interim managers also need a thick skin, as the decisions that are required are not likely to make you popular. Compensation for such talent is rather like combat pay; these are not easy jobs. There is a reason the previous occupant did not make these decisions.

People with executive experience but no appreciable consulting background may find these interim positions rather competitive. Interim posts are for people who are action-oriented and decisive, and who relish the risks of taking on such assignments. There may also be considerable down time between assignments. A few firms specialize in interim postings, and an active network is essential to securing such work.

ADVANCING YOUR EDUCATION

COVID-19 has fostered widespread familiarity with remote learning, including for advanced degrees. Some people have taken advantage of new technologies to advance their training. If consulting does not work out, then an additional degree or certification may be a reasonable exit strategy.

Try to determine in advance whether you intend to train for a new level of functioning or merely learn some additional skills. Your goals may determine how much time you are willing to spend on this. Top MBA programs, for example, are under some pressure to reduce the time commitment from two years to 12 or 18 months.

If you are merely trying to enhance your skills in the executive position you previously held, this might indicate an executive MBA or part-time approach. If you intend to qualify for new positions with a new degree, then consider how the additional education would change your compensation, or how more job opportunities may open as a result.

DEFINING SUCCESS

Consulting is personal. And while you get to define your own success, at least to some extent, the market does as well. So, let's cover both dimensions.

From a personal perspective, success is defined by meeting your unique needs and being satisfied with how you spend your time. People are attracted to wines because they enjoy the taste, not because someone else enjoys the taste. Likewise, success in your work life is intensely personal. Is it fulfilling? Does it help address the career goals that you have set? If consulting is not fully satisfying certain needs, does it at least hold the legitimate promise of doing so? Starting out, it may take some time to get to breakeven, however you define that. But a reasonable business plan will typically have at least an 18-month start-up period, if not a 36-month timeline.

Ultimately, though, the market will determine your success. Whereas satisfying your personal needs may involve subtle judgments, there is nothing subtle about the market. Either you are achieving the goal of brand recognition and client acquisition, or you are not. There is no gray here. Your phone, text, and email are active, or they are not. Your client list is growing, or it isn't. Very importantly, you have repeat clients, or you do not. While some consulting practices specialize in one-offs where the likelihood of repeat business is zero, most practices thrive on repeat business. McKinsey, at one point at least, bragged that 85 percent of their annual client work was for existing clients. Nothing makes a consultant practice more sustainable than clients who trust you with future work after that first assignment.

I am often asked how long it takes to determine whether you are successful. I was always told that the magic number is three years, and this worked for me. After three years, if you do not have consistent work, it is probably time to consider a different path. But after three successful years in a new business, absent a major change in the economy, you can be more certain that you have a "going concern," as the accountants say.

RECOMMENDATIONS

1. You will know when it is not working.

2. Once you have given it enough time and effort, make a clean break and move forward; you have benefited from the attempt.

3. Relying on your growing network becomes even more critical if things don't work out. This is true whether you are changing firms or moving away from consulting altogether.

4. Several options are more likely to yield opportunities under these circumstances, but familiarize yourself with the tricks to the trade.

5. Success, while personally defined at some level, is largely dictated by the market and individual feelings. Your definition of success is not necessarily mine, but be clear in your own mind when it is time to move on, and be decisive about it.

REFERENCE

Cohen, L. D. 2013. "Moving Forward: How to Overcome a Career Failure." The Muse. Published August 18. www.themuse.com/advice/moving-forward-how-to-overcome-a-career-failure.

Let the Journey Begin

But nobody wins afraid of losing
And the hard roads are the ones worth choosing
Someday we'll look back and smile
And know it was worth every mile
—Chris Stapleton, "Starting Over"

YEARS AGO, A favorite client of mine and I adopted a phrase that seems to capture the times: "No straight lines." When something did not appear to follow any logical trail, we would look at each other and recite the mantra. The individual profiles reviewed in chapter 5 (and expanded in the appendixes) are a further testament to this adage. Much of what these leaders experienced in their careers was not planned. Expect the unexpected.

Things happen for a reason. Granted, I did not always feel comfortable with everything that happened, nor was I always able to find that elusive "reason," but I stood by the belief that every event could teach me something. At times, the refrain became "I'm learning lessons I don't need to know." In some cases, like the child who touches the hot stove, the only thing I learned was "Don't do it again!"

Like most careers, mine took some twists and turns. There is no solitude for an adventurous spirit. We don't all live for an adrenaline rush, however. Those who are susceptible to this will, I hope, harness their energy at some point and do well, regardless of the circumstances. For those of us who feel less adventurous and are risk averse—requiring a rationale with some guardrails to justify our pursuits—any career change can work. But I hope this book has shown you that a successful career change takes time and some dispassionate analysis.

TAKE A LEAP OF FAITH

When I used to facilitate merger discussions, I would always begin with a brief speech. It went something like this:

We will spend the next few months analyzing important data, sharing visions for the future, and otherwise getting to know each other. This will be time well spent, regardless of the outcome. An informed decision is far superior to an uninformed one and is much easier to live with when all is said and done. But there is a simple reality to such discussions when you get to the end of the process. If you want it to happen, it will. If you don't, it won't. Sometimes things happen that are clearly out of your control. What is in your control is how you feel about the situation, how you manage your expectations. After all the discussion and analyses, you are left with a simple proposition: a leap of faith.

No amount of prework or analysis can prepare you for every possibility. There will always be some uncertainty as we enter the future. Our work here can begin to eliminate some doubts but may pose new ones. Solving today's problems is one thing, and we can forge a granular view of the past based on existing data. But we cannot fully anticipate the future. And while we will be better informed at the end of this process, nothing can eliminate the reality that, in the end, we must trust that this decision to get together now can also enable us to better address future challenges. This involves a leap of faith.

In the end, any decision of consequence involves a leap of faith. Not everything is knowable.

AVOID NEGATIVE FANTASIES

The second thing that I point out in these pre-merger discussions is our tendency to have "negative fantasies." The half-full or half-empty mindset applies here. Attitude is key during a career launch, which is what a career change is. If you tend to approach things from the perspective of what can go wrong (being cautious or even pessimistic), I ask you to resist.

Negative fantasies involve visualizing everything that could go wrong. Granted, in the days of COVID-19, there is a tendency to be more open to "black swan events." But we have enough stress already without coming up with countless scenarios, some of which are clearly implausible.

If you find yourself trapped in this netherworld, then perhaps a career change is not in the cards. Your vision will tend to be skewed toward the negative, and any setback, no matter how minor, will fall into the category of "I told you so." Do not listen to Mr. Negative. He is not being invited on this journey with you. Mr. Negative not only will keep score on everything that goes wrong but is also likely to pull the plug too soon. Rather than shrugging off the occasional setback, Mr. Negative thinks of these events as cumulative, and in short order the burden becomes too much to bear.

I have long admired the ability of professional golfers to put that last bad shot behind them. Likewise, the professional consultant can compartmentalize setbacks for later redress and remain in the moment. Consulting is a stage, and the show must go on. Consultants cannot afford to let their guard down when the going gets tough. Your client is counting on you, especially in times of high stress.

To protect against a negative mindset, set benchmarks along the way as part of your monitoring plan and commit to allowing your new direction enough time to succeed. Benchmarks could be spread out monthly or quarterly, and each may have a different focus. Barring any major setbacks, I think a transition to consulting should be given at least a year. And, if keeping score tends to be your thing, then make sure you are scoring the right things. For example, at the end of each month, ask what three things you learned, recall the best thing that happened, and identify anything you would be careful not to do again. This kind of scorecard is more in keeping with the learning curve you will face and with the attitude required to make it a positive, energizing experience rather than a negative, draining one that locks you into a declining cycle.

As a consultant, I have found that time passes more quickly than in the typical executive job. I felt busier. If anything, I have found it harder to relax and get off stage. I have enjoyed always having something to do. However, sheer stress has compelled me to take time off and learn to intentionally manage my on-stage time.

USE COACHES AND MENTORS

Executive coaches did not really exist when I first entered consulting—only career counselors. Mentors were certainly present at the executive management level, usually coming out of administrative residencies and fellowships. One thing that hasn't changed much is the apprenticeship model in consulting, at least when it comes to the basics. This has stood the test of time.

When I first started in consulting, I had to rely on my manager to provide feedback. The person responsible for this would vary from project to project, but then there was the practice manager responsible for a particular office. I spent more than 30 years trying to overcome the advice this practice manager gave me in my first annual review as a consultant: "Scott should consider whether consulting is in his future." I had occasion to interact with this person many years later. I'm not sure if he remembered giving me this feedback, but I confess to being pleased when, unsolicited, he told me he was proud that I had been so successful in establishing my own consulting firm. The apprenticeship model, while still important, does have its limitations.

Today, extensive resources are available to help you in your journey, including executive coaching. "Coaches are in the transformation business," according to B. Joseph Pine II, coauthor of *The Experience Economy* (Harvard Business Review Press, 2019). They try to get their client to a new level of performance—of results. You may infer that executive coaching is more focused on leadership than management, but it clearly can apply to both.

Executive coaching can be expensive when not provided as a benefit by an employer. As noted previously, such coaches were initially made available to executives as part of outplacement—not an entirely endearing task. They have since been able to apply their skills to a much broader range of pursuits. If you can secure this help, executive coaches can be very valuable.

Some executives seek the limelight. Setting the tone (having the ball, in basketball terms) may be important to them. Their interest is more in a leadership role that focuses on the why and the what. There are only so many corporate jobs in the healthcare industry, especially as hospitals and other healthcare organizations consolidate into larger regional health systems. Given that the likelihood of ascending into one of these few leadership roles may be slim, a more likely way to work with such people is as a consultant.

For other executives, being part of a large regional health system where you manage one of multiple units, focusing on the how can be plenty challenging. Clearly, the executive must be comfortable with the why and the what that comes from corporate. Again, an executive coach can help sort out these thoughts.

Like athletics, much of executive coaching deals with the roles that executives are asked to play and how they gain comfort and skill in doing so. The new consultant will have much to learn about how to be integrated into a consulting team and work with a client. This is made even more challenging by working with multiple consulting teams. Imagine if a college athlete had to work every other month with a new team, taking on varying roles in each. That is both part of the fun and the challenge of consulting. While not for everyone, it can be quite stimulating. There is little to no chance of becoming bored, given such varied experiences.

Coaches see things others miss. When you are in the moment, whether as an elite athlete or a proven professional, muscle memory kicks in. You know what to do next because you are in total sync with the group. Even though it may not be true, it feels as though you have been there before. This muscle memory comes from practice (repetition), coaching, and open interaction within the group.

General Stanley McChrystal and other enlightened leaders have found that their job is creating a culture wherein the players are receptive to the quest. The team gets comfortable, even though they cannot predict everything that will happen. This describes a culture of complexity, which simply cannot be ignored as we address the future of healthcare. Under such an approach, the values that drive actions are understood and provide guardrails between which the players respond. The result, while creative, fits into a group response that is both constant and adaptive.

For those who are receptive to coaching (i.e., coachable), it can help us rise above what we might have been capable of on our own. This is the gift and the challenge of coaching. If you are coachable, you should consider using an executive coach in your career change. It will be challenging enough to sort out the options and determine if consulting is the right path. Not everyone has a high tolerance for risk. A good executive coach can help moderate this risk through understanding. The earlier an executive coach is involved with your decision to make a career change, the better position they are in to monitor progress and help you process the feedback you are getting once you have begun the transition. A coach can help you focus the lens used to process this feedback, making it supportive and not deflating. An executive coach can also help you dissipate the stress.

SUPPORT DIVERSITY IN HEALTHCARE LEADERSHIP

Key information for this book came from interviews with full-time executives who made the change to full-time consulting, providing the profiles of *early pioneers* and *contemporaries*. Notably, I could not find many full-time early pioneers from minority backgrounds, despite efforts to do so. I was able to talk with a few leaders from under-represented demographics who met the qualifications, but too few.

In previous chapters, I mentioned Diane L. Dixon's 2020 book *Diversity on the Executive Path*, in which racially and ethnically diverse healthcare leaders share their experiences and the lessons that helped them advance to CEO. Many of the insights from Dr. Dixon's research apply to making a career change as well.

A 2015 survey by the American Hospital Association's Institute for Diversity in Health Management (now the Institute for Diversity and Health Equity) found that only 9 percent of hospital CEOs belonged to racial or ethnic minority groups. A 2021 report by the Chartis Group and the National Association of Health Services Executives found that only 6 percent of US hospital CEOs are Black. In the Chartis report, Black healthcare leaders stressed three key factors contributing to their success in these roles:

- Bringing their authentic self to the workplace.
- "Boldness and bravery" in confronting implicit biases and advocating for the health needs of Black communities.
- The presence of a support system to help them navigate difficulties.

Projections from US Census Bureau models suggest that minorities will compose more than 50 percent of the US population by 2044. The deficiency in minority representation among healthcare executives is something we all need to care about. As healthcare strategic planning accounts for disparities in the health system—social determinants of health[1]—everyone will benefit from people in leadership positions who have lived experience with these disparities. It will remain difficult to close this gap until more minority

---

1   See chapter 15 of *The Healthcare Consultant's Handbook* for a more complete exploration of this topic.

role models occupy leadership positions—whether in C-suites or consulting firms.

In time we will have more examples of successful consultants from minority communities, but it is time we had them. Many C-suites are making gains in diversity, including several prominent US healthcare systems that have promoted minority executives to the CEO level in recent years. Just as women have made significant gains, notably at the CEO level, it seems clear that there will be many more examples of racial and ethnic minority executives, as this network expands to include consulting.

All indications from my interactions while writing these books are that most major healthcare consulting firms are eager to shift the scales in this regard. I remember interacting with young consultants of color in years past, but I do not remember any that reached the level of practice leader or officer. As of this writing, minority groups are much better represented in the starting ranks of many consulting firms; however, it will take time for these younger consultants to rise through the ranks.

A key factor in reducing these disparities is growing the funnel of minority undergraduates who are eligible to enter graduate programs. The number of minority executives who turn to consulting obviously depends on the number of minority healthcare executives. Prominent groups such as the American College of Healthcare Executives are aware of the shortage of minorities serving in an executive capacity in healthcare organizations, and their long-standing focus on diversity and inclusion is beginning to pay off. Virtually every graduate program in health administration with which I am familiar has a strong, successful recruiting program for minority students.

Knowledge and experience are the at the core of the Consultant Value Chain reviewed in chapter 8. While there are exceptions, my experience has been that the most successful consulting firms are the ones that function as meritocracies. As documented by Dr. Dixon's research on the perspectives of minority CEOs, performance counts. Successful consulting firms are eager to promote successful role models from minority communities, as doing so will open the profession further to a wealth of talent that is currently underrepresented. This will accelerate our understanding of healthcare disparities and help us create better ways to extend the reach of healthy living and the delivery of essential healthcare services.

I hope the absence of racial and ethnic minority representation among those interviewed for this book will be viewed not as a lack of sensitivity to this opportunity, but as a recognition that work has yet to be done and the door is wide open to make a difference in this regard.

LEAN ON FAITH AND FAMILY

Until now, my references to networking have focused on the professional component. However, most networks include family and other people of influence. Faith and family have become controversial in popular culture. I was fortunate to function during a time that honored such connections and I strongly argue for continued reliance on these tried-and-true pillars of support.

One of the many effects of the COVID-19 pandemic has been to shine a bright light on mental health and our fragile nature. We all need to acknowledge that none of us were born with an "S" on our chest, able to jump tall buildings or run faster than a bullet. In this spirit, I offer this section for your consideration. I acknowledge up front that this may not resonate with everyone, in which case you are welcome to skip ahead. But any profile of my career would be incomplete or inauthentic without reference to faith and family.

While national statistics may imply a waning influence of personal faith, my experiences reflect the importance of being able to periodically retreat to some safe spaces. For me, there have been times during a stressful transition when such a retreat was essential. In a similar fashion, millennials refer to "the third space," where they can get away from their hectic schedule (and judgmental social media feeds) to collaborate with others or merely reflect in silence when something has become overwhelming. Starbucks is an example of a company responding to this demand for a third space. While distancing may have been recommended to combat the coronavirus, it should never have been called "social" distancing. We are social animals after all—never more so than during times of extreme stress. No doubt, part of the mental anguish of the pandemic has been the isolation and absence of normal social discourse.

I have been graced with faith during much of my life, which becomes most evident during times of utter exhaustion or when trying to address particularly challenging issues. I have often felt guided by a higher power and have tried to remain receptive to such influence. I recognize faith is not for everyone, but it has worked time and again for me. Just when all seemed lost and clients were not responding, a new opportunity would come along. At other times, a message might be delivered as part of a sermon or a speech, or in something I read (as a practicing Christian, this obviously includes the Bible). These connections have helped me reconcile things when I was struggling.

In one instance, I traveled to a national meeting on governance in Florida feeling sorry for myself about a difficult client situation that was draining my energy. Fortunately, I was not presenting, so I was able to pace myself and catch a few presentations. I was among several hundred peers from hospitals and health systems who were also looking for some answers. My confidence was low, and I felt unappreciated and ineffective, consumed by this challenging client issue. My fuel gauge was on empty.

By chance, I ran into someone from a client I had worked with years before. My work with this client had involved helping the CEO who hired us realize they were the problem, and it was time to move on. To say the engagement was uncomfortable is an understatement. The assignment had haunted me for some time, and I was unable to reach closure—until I ran into this executive. She approached me, identified herself, and caught me up on her organization. Not only had the organization improved after the CEO left after our assignment was over; it had also flourished. Further, the CEO who left was now in a position that was more personally rewarding for them.

The executive seemed somewhat taken aback by my outward reaction to her kind words. She was under no obligation to bring this to my attention, yet she opened her heart and extended herself to share this feedback. Her comments brought tears to my eyes, and I thanked her for taking the time to share this with me. My battery was instantly recharged by this exchange, and I was grateful to have run into this messenger who, by sharing this story, helped deliver me from my personal struggle. Consultants rarely get this kind of feedback several years after completing a client engagement, but it can surely have an impact on those rare occasions when it happens.

At times, we might question our value in a particular situation. For example, it is not always comfortable to be right. I have often found myself commenting, "I would prefer to be wrong on this observation, but it seems to us . . ." I always struggle with decisions that cause people to uproot their families and seek employment elsewhere. I will own up to a bias: I attempt to exhaust other organizational solutions before bringing up personnel changes, because of my hesitancy to cause anyone personal pain. But all too often, a personnel change is part of the solution to an intransigent problem. My hope in such situations is that the organization has gone out of its way to give everyone the best opportunity to succeed. Only after expending such efforts and being disappointed is such dramatic action warranted. Often, I have been proud of my clients in this regard. When companies call in consultants, they have usually exhausted internal efforts to deal with a pernicious situation. Healthcare may be more sensitive in this regard because dealing with pain and suffering is so core to patient care (though not everyone will agree with this observation).

I also remember limping home on many a Friday evening, exhausted after a typical full week of travel (often Tuesday through Friday). A consultant can easily get lost in their work. Plane rides seem shorter because you are consumed by a recent exchange with a key executive or a task force meeting, or the challenge of trying to represent a situation in terms that can spur a client to action where they are struggling with a difficult decision. A friend calls this "unbillable time."[2] Yet, I have often found this time necessary and effective when dealing with complicated client issues.

But when I got home, I could look forward to spending the weekend on my kids' activities and quiet time with my wife. Road warriors learn to deal with frequent absences, and we gain a stronger appreciation for our time with family and friends. It becomes sacred. I should add that I did not always feel comfortable talking things out with my family. They had their own concerns and, while I desperately needed to recharge my battery with quality time at home, I did not feel the need to draw them into professional details. I simply needed to spend time with them and get away from client concerns. For professional issues, I usually approached other members of my team or fellow consultants I respect. Obviously, it did not hurt that my wife, Melanie, is also a hospital administrator and a member of my professional guild of healthcare executives. She was among the few who understood when I shared a client interaction that might fly under the radar for people less familiar with the vagaries of healthcare. It is hard to place value on the ability to have these occasional exchanges.

PAY IT FORWARD

The acknowledgments for this book allowed me to recognize some of the many people who have made my journey as a professional consultant both possible and fulfilling. I believe most successful people recognize they had help; we all require help along the way. Some of that help will come from expected sources; some may come from surprising sources. As you look back, if you are like me, you will come to realize just how important this help was.

Now it is your turn. Pass it on.

---

2   A lawyer friend counted this "thought time" as billable time, but then they tended to keep time in 15-minute increments versus by the hour. I always limited charges for travel time to 1.5 hours max.

My experience reinforces the adage, "The more you give, the more you receive." As you grow in consulting, you will probably begin to recognize that while there were things you would change if you could, you can usually learn from these lessons—or at least use them to avoid such situations in the future. A lot of learning goes into a successful consulting career. Just when you think you have seen it all, you realize the learning never stops. And this learning often comes from asking questions. Talk less, listen more.

A corresponding opportunity is teaching. It is said that one does not really know something until they can teach it. While not all of us are drawn to teaching, it can be therapeutic. As a strategist, I found teaching an integral part of the practice. We may teach a client to embrace other points of view, to look at problems through different lenses. One of the true joys of my consulting career has been to work with younger, less experienced consultants as they started their journey. I am often amazed at their energy, insights, and willingness to innovate. Seeing someone grow in such a demanding professional is genuinely fulfilling. Physicians in teaching hospitals say the questions medical students and residents ask during rounds keep them sharp. I believe this with all my heart. Cultures that do not include a strong component of learning get stagnant.

Despite some legitimate criticisms, the apprentice model is alive and well. This work involves tradecraft, as one of my children is finding out as a newly minted consultant. I encourage you to embrace the opportunities to pay it forward; seek opportunities to pass on what has worked for you as part of this process.

Previous chapters discussed sponsorship. I am convinced that most young consultants just starting out are blessed by being sponsored by a key person early in their careers. Yet sponsorship is no less important later in one's career. The profiles in this book speak of sponsors and partners who helped executives make the transition to consulting. I can think of no more personal way to pass on lessons. Further, with regard to diversity and inclusion, there can be no better way to contribute to reducing disparities than by committing to a sponsorship that crosses racial or ethnic lines.

Performance evaluations are another way to pay it forward. As you progress in your practice, you will likely be involved in evaluating the performance of others, just as others evaluated you along the way. Keep in mind that there is a proper way to provide meaningful feedback, while recognizing that reviews are not a one-size-fits-all undertaking. Learning to apply different approaches, different words, to such exchanges and to adjust as necessary to connect with each person is part of the exciting challenge. Becoming fully engaged in teams and with individuals on these teams is one of the great privileges of the profession. Nothing can compete with the joy of seeing someone you are invested in thrive in this demanding role.

On a related note, Rice and Perry (2012, 134) found, "It is not an accident that many retired healthcare professionals pursue writing, teaching, consulting, and government board service, areas in which they have valuable lessons to share and the motivation to give back to the profession." The number one interest expressed by people they interviewed on retirement was teaching—hardly surprising. You entered consulting thinking you had knowledge and experiences that could benefit others; teaching and writing are among the best ways to codify them.

MAY YOU BE SO BLESSED

Among professional golfers, scoring averages differ by fractions of strokes. Virtually all winners on the PGA Tour pay reverence to "luck" when they win a tournament. Even when they are playing their best, there always seems to be some luck involved. The Hollywood translation might be "May the Force be with you."

Clearly, consulting is no different. Prepare as we might, some luck is involved. As mentioned earlier, *The Healthcare Consultant's Handbook* compared two college graduates who were starting out together in consulting. One had the luck of some positive client experiences right out of the gate while the other started with a few duds. This was clearly beyond their control. Yet, as that case pointed out, success is probably far less about what cards you are dealt and more about how you handle the results.

You celebrate the success of working with great clients. But do you allow negative experiences to accumulate, or do you use them as learning opportunities to gain some insights that will benefit future clients? So often, what counts is what you make of your experiences, not the experiences themselves. Only so much of any experience is under your control; however, you can control what you do with the experience. Does it bring you down or build you up? The right attitude probably influences most of the outcome.

Avoid the common mistakes reviewed in this book and take a more calculated approach to this career change, mindful of both the opportunities and the risks. This can make the experience everything you hope for and more, regardless of the outcome. If things work out and you have a successful consulting experience, then great. If you find that consulting is not your calling, you have still pursued something you believe in. You have earned the right to not spend a minute regretting that you never tried. Take pride in that.

I leave you with this thought. If consulting were easy, anyone could do it. It is not. Whether you were pushed toward consulting because you were dissatisfied in your current position or you were simply attracted to the promise of consulting with your eyes wide open, you tried it and you are at peace. If consulting ends up being your calling, then you, your clients, and your loved ones will benefit, and you will have many fulfilling experiences ahead. May you be so blessed.

RECOMMENDATIONS

1. View a career change as a launch, and stay sharp and receptive.

2. Recognize that an optimistic attitude is important, and "negative fantasies" can work against an effective launch.

3. While the apprenticeship system is alive and well, also consider employing an executive coach during this transition. You do not have to do this without help.

4. Diversity is a gift; it must be expanded to meet shifting demographics in the United States and to improve the value of insights offered through the consulting process. Teaching and becoming a sponsor are integral parts of most consulting and can allow you to pay it forward as a rewarding part of your new journey.

5. There is no failure if you have given consulting a fair chance. You have accepted the challenge and the results will become apparent. Regardless of how it turns out, you are a success. Be at peace.

REFERENCES

American Hospital Association and Institute for Diversity in Health Management. 2015. *Diversity and Disparities: A Benchmarking Study of U.S. Hospitals in 2015.* https://ifdhe. aha.org/benchmarking-study-us-hospitals-surveys.

Chartis Group and National Association of Health Services Executives. 2021. *Leading While Black: Addressing Social Justice and Health Disparities.* https://info.chartis.com/healthequity.

Dixon, D. L. 2020. *Diversity on the Executive Path: Wisdom and Insights for Navigating to the Highest Levels of Healthcare Leadership.* Chicago: Health Administration Press.

Rice, J. A., and F. Perry. 2012. *Healthcare Leadership Excellence: Creating a Career of Impact.* Chicago: Health Administration Press.

Appendix page begins

Early Pioneers

F. KENNETH ACKERMAN JR., FACHE

For over 30 years, Ken served in several capacities for Geisinger Health System, retiring as president emeritus of the Geisinger Medical Center, the health system's flagship hospital, in 1995. He changed careers in the later stages of his career as a consultant and business leader.

Ken and his wife, Pat, both grew up in Mansfield, Ohio. His father was in sales and sold into hospitals. One day, he suggested to Ken that he should consider managing hospitals for a living. Ken acted on his father's advice, completing his graduate studies at the University of Michigan. Walter McNearney, chairman of the graduate program in hospital administration at the time, played a large role in Ken's start. In mid-December in his senior year at Denison University, Ken met with Walter following a long day of interviews with other members of the Michigan faculty. Ken was awestruck by Walter's larger-than-life personality, keen intellect, and knowledge of the healthcare industry. Following a lengthy interview, Walter asked Ken about his plans for the holidays. Ken replied that he and Pat were getting married that Saturday and would be taking their honeymoon in New York City until the day before Christmas. Walter paused briefly, then casually informed Ken that he should consider himself admitted to the Michigan program.

Ken never seriously considered attending any of the other graduate programs that had accepted him, and enrolled in Michigan in the fall of 1961. While attending Michigan, Ken was selected to do his administrative residency with the legendary Dr. Robin C. Buerki at the Henry Ford Hospital in Detroit. Henry Ford Hospital's unique culture was greatly influenced by the Henry Ford Medical Group, where the group model included a full-time, salaried, hospital-based multispecialty group practice that was actively engaged in teaching and research in addition to their primary patient care responsibilities. This unique model of healthcare delivery was in contrast to the independent medical staff model that dominated the healthcare landscape at that time.

Ken enjoyed the renown of Henry Ford, where seemingly weekly there were domestic and international delegations visiting to see how the group practice model worked in an integrated system. The multispecialty medical group model, he said, "blew me away," and he embraced the same model when he took his next job as assistant administrator at Geisinger Medical Center in 1964. Ken became convinced that this unique model of healthcare delivery seemed like a wonderful way to practice quality medical care, giving salaried physicians the opportunity to teach residents and medical students and be involved in medical research.

Ken was hired into Geisinger by Dr. Ellsworth R. Browneller, who had worked with Dr. Buerki at Henry Ford ten years previously. Geisinger, like Henry Ford, is a culture-driven organization where the staff and employees have a common sense of purpose and are laser-focused on serving the needs of the patient and the consumer. While the delivery model was similar, adjusting to the rural community of Danville, Pennsylvania (population 6,000), was a significant challenge after life in Detroit. Soon after moving to Danville, the Ackermans began to raise a family; their three sons were all born at Geisinger Medical Center. As their family grew, Ken and Pat grew to better understand the advantages of rural living; small town living fit with their changing family values.

Joining the Geisinger organization early in his career afforded Ken the opportunity to be on the ground floor with this rural health system as it grew into a regional delivery system. The system launched

Geisinger Health Plan in 1972, which would become the largest rural health plan in the United States. Two years later, Ken was elevated to chief operating officer, reporting to Dr. Browneller. Three years after that, Dr. Browneller was appointed Pennsylvania Secretary of Health.

Ken, then aged 29, was appointed to succeed Dr. Browneller. His ascendency to this position opened many doors, and Ken became actively engaged with several state and national healthcare associations. He was invited to join the Healthcare Research and Development Institute, an important affinity group for senior executives, becoming its youngest member. When Ken was elected chairman of the Medical Group Management Association, he was the youngest person to hold that office in the 95-year history of the association.

Like Henry Ford Hospital, Geisinger often hosted CEO site visits from across the country, as it had long been held out as one of the best examples of a rural-based integrated regional health system, supporting a dyad leadership model.[1] Like Kaiser Health, Geisinger combined the three elements of an integrated health system, with the hospital, physician, and insurance components all part of one organization. The insurance model was originally a closed health maintenance organization (HMO) exclusive to the Geisinger Medical Group, but evolved over time to a more open model. By the time Ken left the organization, the system had grown to four hospitals and nearly 1,000 physicians.

Transition to Consulting

Ken's transition to consulting began in 1995, when he joined prominent healthcare leaders Jim Block, MD, former president of Johns Hopkins Hospital, and Don Arnwine, former head of Voluntary Hospitals of America, in shifting to McManis Associates, a nationally

---

[1] This model, which has since grown in popularity, pairs a clinical leader with an administrative leader. It has become a dominant approach to clinical service line management. See chapter 3 for more information.

recognized healthcare consulting practice in Washington, DC. McManis was assisting some of the nation's leading healthcare organizations with their strategic direction. The McManis organization was in the process of being acquired by MMI Companies at the time of Ken's move. Ken brought with him his extensive professional network and an in-depth knowledge and understanding of the healthcare industry, and of how to build and lead integrated healthcare systems. After serving as vice president at McManis for five years, Ken was recruited by a longtime colleague and friend, Don Wegmiller,[2] who was leading the Clarke Consulting group in Minneapolis.

Don asked Ken to consider joining Clarke with the understanding that Ken would succeed Don as CEO of the company. Don and Ken worked closely together over the next year to ensure an orderly transition of leadership for the company. Clarke was about ten times larger than the McManis organization, and as its president Ken could better use his leadership skills in addition to working as a consultant. Eventually, the Clarke organization was sold, the name was changed to Integrated Healthcare Strategies, and the company was listed on the New York Stock Exchange. Years later Clarke was sold to Gallagher Human Resources and Compensation Consulting, where Ken continued in a full-time senior advisor role till January 2020.

Ken's consulting practice included board governance, executive and physician compensation, and issues involving governance of integrated delivery systems and medical group practices. It also included improving governance performance using governance best practices.

Observations

The impetus for considering the move from executive to consultant was clear to Ken at the time: He had a passion for healthcare, a strong

---

2 Don was another early pioneer who left a successful leadership position with a health system to enter consulting.

work ethic, and a desire to continue working as long as he was able—but not at the same thing that he had been doing for over 30 years. He was ready for a change. He was impressed with the consultants he had worked with as a client, including Anthony J. J. O'Rourke, MD, who had completed a long-term facilities master plan for Geisinger. Ken had thoroughly enjoyed serving in advisory consulting roles with state and federal government, the Joint Commission for Accreditation of Healthcare Organizations (now Joint Commission), and the Healthcare Research and Development Institute while he was still at Geisinger, and he wanted to try something new.

"Leaving Geisinger was the toughest decision of my career," Ken told me. "I knew relatively little about consulting when I joined Jerry [McManis]. Transitions are exciting but sometimes scary. They can also prove to be personally and professionally rewarding." Early in the transition period, Ken told Jerry, "I am here to learn." In the beginning, "every day was an exciting new experience."

The senior leadership team at McManis helped Ken make a smooth transition. He had a wonderful experience with the firm, though he admits that he missed the people at Geisinger and being in a position of leadership. The client work was stimulating and included a host of challenging engagements working with CEOs of some of the nation's best hospitals and healthcare systems, as well as state and national trade associations including the American Hospital Association (AHA), American Medical Group Association, American College of Healthcare Executives (ACHE), The Joint Commission, and the National Association of Children's Hospitals and Related Institutions.

Before joining McManis, Ken briefly considered going out on his own, but concluded that he would do better to join a firm with a well-established reputation and a prestigious client base, so he could learn and best use his skills and be excited by the challenge. Confidence was critical. Moving to McManis was a calculated risk, with no guarantee that it was going to work. Ken figured that if it did not work out he could always "return to what I had been doing all of my career."

Ken is quick to point out that he would never have made the move to consulting earlier in his career. It was important that his three sons were grown and out of the house (working or in college), and his wife was very supportive ("I had an angel on my shoulder"). Without his family's support, he would never have considered a change. "Making this move earlier in my career would have required sacrifices involving my family that I was simply unwilling to make."

When he was actively considering a career change, Ken spoke with Don Arnwine, who had shifted from CEO roles—including at the University of Colorado Medical Center, Camcare in West Virginia, and Voluntary Hospitals of America—to build his own consulting firm, Arnwine Associates. Don told Ken that he was surprised at how challenging it was to build a robust consulting practice from scratch. Don had as broad a professional network as anyone in the business and expected his phone to ring off the hook. This did not happen.

The shift to Clarke Consulting presented a different challenge, involving leadership skills in addition to consulting. Ken came in as a new leader from outside the firm—never an easy process—and his friend Don Wegmiller was making a transition at the same time. Ken had to act decisively on several occasions to reposition the firm for future growth. This was not easy, and he relied heavily on his leadership experience and the rock-solid relationship he enjoyed with the board of directors, always mindful of the consulting company his friend had built and led for many years. In the end, it all worked out and he is grateful for this experience, which permitted him to work into his eighties. "It proved to be the perfect capstone for my career. I am so fortunate."

Ken believes some of the most important things he brought from his prior career were his understanding of governance and leadership in highly complex healthcare organizations, a robust national network of contacts, a deep passion for healthcare, a belief in the product, and a love of people. Being visible and having a strong presence in the marketplace is also important.

"When presented with opportunities to present or participate on programs at state or national meetings, seize them. Often such opportunities will prove to be productive marketing venues for your firm." Ken became a better listener over the years. Being intimately familiar with the relatively slow pace of consensus decision-making in healthcare systems, he had developed a natural patience that helped him work with resistant clients. One challenge that took some time to get used to was that consultants did not have the authority to make change, but rather had to cajole and persuade clients of the need for change. This could be frustrating, especially when working with dysfunctional community hospital boards.

Ken managed his roles at McManis and Clarke while maintaining his primary residence in Danville, Pennsylvania, which was important for him to minimize any disruption to his family. In the end, given the chance, he would not change a thing. "The totality of the experience has been personally fulfilling and greatly exceeded my expectations. I was most fortunate to have had the opportunity. It has been a privilege!"

Advice to Others

Be certain your career change fits with your values and family life at this stage of your career. Family and friends are key. Do not underestimate the impact of travel. Ken had traveled a lot during his Geisinger days when he was actively involved in several professional associations, participating on programs, and serving as a guest lecturer from time to time. He cautions that consulting is "all consuming," and says, "It is important to love what you do . . . otherwise, it becomes too much like work. I honestly feel that I never worked a day in my life. It has been a blessing!" Ken strongly recommends seeking the counsel of trusted colleagues and friends beforehand. "Be careful with this kind of move," he warns. "This is not for everyone."

JAMES A. RICE, PHD, FACHE

Jim Rice's career began during a softball game in Minnesota involving several young healthcare executives from Fairview Health. Jim had held many different jobs at a few area hospitals, starting as an orderly, and was taking all the required science classes at the University of Minnesota as an undergraduate intending to pursue a medical career. Then, softball teammates Don Wegmiller and John King introduced him to the concept of hospital administration, and displaced his previous interests. He migrated from entry-level clinical jobs at the hospital to more administrative roles, moved between different areas of the hospital such as the lab and purchasing, and started attending administrative meetings.

Once he graduated, these same young executives talked Jim into graduate school at Minnesota's School of Public Health. He had eloped with his wife between his junior and senior years and was starting to think more seriously about a career and making money. The graduate program had just entered an experimental phase where they were extending graduate study to a two-year classroom program—a change from the previous program of a year of didactic work followed by a year of administrative residency in a healthcare organization. Jim was one of only six students tapped for the new program. They were effectively allowed to design their own class structure, opening the doors for him to pursue interests in urban planning, organizational behavior, psychology, and sociology.

Jim did not have to complete a residency, as he had been working part-time, including time with Carl Platou at Fairview Hospital, one of the early pioneers of regional health system development. As Fairview blossomed, Jim attended administrative meetings and was fascinated by the different management styles of Carl and Jim's friends Don and John. Carl, who was a generation ahead of Don and John, let them manage things at the two hospitals while he focused on big picture items. Both young executives welcomed and took advantage of the opportunity. The culture was collaborative and team based. Jim was able to see how different management styles worked and consider which attributes were more comfortable to him as he later forged his own style.

The projects that came up during his time at Fairview, in retrospect, were effectively on-the-job training. In one situation that Jim remembers vividly, there was an infection outbreak in one of the clinics. Through the process of elimination, they determined that some old sheets had been torn up for cleaning rags but had not been sanitized adequately. Thus began Jim's exposure to formal problem-solving techniques.

In another key situation, a donor from a suburban Lutheran church had contributed 30 acres of land to Fairview in a prime area, ripe for future expansion. Not much was there at the time. Remarkably, this project was given to Jim. Not sure what was expected, he set about trying to determine what they should do with this property, developing strong project management skills in the process. He interviewed a nearby commercial real estate developer, who showed him how iso-chronal timelines were used in retail shopping center development planning. If a mall and connected residential housing were developed, what health facilities would they need? Eventually, this project developed from a unique community health center into the Fairview Ridges Hospital as Fairview evolved into one of the first documented multihospital systems in the United States. (As of 2021, Fairview consists of seven hospitals, 90 clinics, more than 34,000 employees and a network of over 5,000 providers.)

This event also had implications for Fairview's management structure. The chairman of the board at the time was also the CEO for a bank holding company. Fairview felt that this might be a good model to apply to its young health system, so Jim was tapped to talk to executives from banks, hotel chains, and local public utilities to explore concepts and techniques for corporate strategic planning and marketing. His research resulted in the adaptation of the bank holding company model for Fairview and the publication of a landmark article that he wrote with Carl Platou for *Harvard Business Review*.[3]

While Jim was in graduate school, during one summer break, he joined a consulting project with the Albuquerque, New Mexico, Job Corps Residential Training Center to set up a clinic for 300 adolescent girls and young women. Later, after finishing his master's program during the Vietnam War, he was given a US Public Health Service Commission that allowed him to enter into the doctoral program at the University of Minnesota. Jim continued his work with the Job Corps in Washington, DC, the following summer, during which he was technically a contractor to a consulting firm, Medserco. The firm was actually located in St. Louis, where he subsequently moved his growing family. This company had secured financing to build similar community health clinics as entrepreneurial ventures involving physician owners, and Jim was hired to lead this effort.

Jim was subsequently called back to the Twin Cities to grow the new Health Central system, a new multihospital system in the region and a competitor to Fairview. Comprised initially of three hospitals (two suburban hospitals and an urban acute care and behavioral health center) and a few doctor groups, the Health Central system exposed Jim to competitive strategy and the challenges of growth. The AHA began referring international health executives to Jim to see a privately owned, nonprofit multihospital system in action. A for-profit subsidiary corporation was formed at Health Central to allow Jim to participate in this international work. One group ended up hiring him to develop an HMO with Life of Jamaica. Then, a large bank employee union from Chile decided that they needed an HMO to provide services for their 35,000 employees. Jim introduced them to Kaiser's integrated health system model, and they asked him to build a similar system. The project became the largest HMO in Chile, Banmédica (now owned by UnitedHealthcare).

---

3   Platou, C. N., and J. A. Rice. 1972. "Multihospital Holding Companies." *Harvard Business Review* (May-June): 14–18.

One of the more unique consulting projects in Jim's career was to live in Russia for two years while developing a distributed health system under a US government grant. The project involved establishing offices in four cities, including Moscow, and managing 35 people with a budget of $26 million per year. As Jim was finishing up this project, he got a call from a well-known consultant named Charlie Ewell, formerly of Arthur Young. Charlie and Jim had become acquainted through Associated Health Systems (AHS), of which Health Central was a member. Jim had been an active member of the health planning affinity group formed by the ten founding organizational members of AHS, and Charlie had started a joint purchasing group for AHS. Charlie was starting a governance group called Governance 100, and invited Jim to partner with him. Jim flew nonstop from Moscow to California, leaving the dreadful Russian climate to be greeted by a limo in sunny San Diego. The offices were located on a bluff in La Jolla. Jim thought he had died and gone to heaven.

Governance 100 took the networking group model from AHS and built the same subscription model around a focus on the "black box" of the industry—governance. No systems at the time were doing governance very well, and there was a genuine desire to raise the bar by shared learnings. Combining this focus on governance improvement with the draw of going to nice resorts for seminars and a nice round of golf or tennis, with meals at swanky restaurants, proved to be a winning formula.

Transition to Consulting

Jim's career path is unique and defies common role transitions. He was exposed early in his career to the rigors of consulting, not through a particular firm, but through his graduate school and the teachings of its founder, James A. Hamilton, who also maintained a consulting firm under his name. Hamilton made sure that all graduates from the Minnesota program had some experience with project management and related case studies (such as consulting engagements). The best and brightest students were hired into his consulting firm to sell business to his other graduates, who ran hospitals all over the country.[4]

Thanks to this exposure, Jim was immersed in consulting while in graduate school and working part-time in the administrative suite of Fairview Health System. In his subsequent government work, he participated in early interdisciplinary teams. His engagement into both private and government-funded projects required significant project management skills, not to mention a familiarity with government contracting, and he had to make multimedia presentations. While these projects involved significant consulting initiatives, he was rarely required to sell; the projects were assigned. Only in the later stages of his career, when he was connected to the Governance Institute, was he engaged in direct sales.

The model for the new joint venture facilities while in St. Louis was a bit more complicated than previous projects, involving investment models, strategy development, and recruiting. Having money readily available eliminated one of the challenges that most entrepreneurs face right from the start. This effort even involved some of the first ambulatory surgery centers.

At Health Central, which subsequently became Health One (and later became part of Allina Health), Jim was tasked with growing the system organically and through mergers and acquisitions. Consolidation was sweeping the nation, and Minneapolis was the tip of the spear in the late 1960s. A unique aspect of this transition in Minneapolis–St. Paul was also the relatively new HMO phenomenon; consolidations at the time involved mostly hospitals and managed care plans (not physician groups). Small plans were rolling up into bigger plans. UnitedHealthcare, the largest managed care plan in the United States, had its origins in the Minneapolis

---

4 See chapter 16 and appendix B in *The Healthcare Consultant's Handbook* for a more detailed explanation of some of the early years of healthcare consulting, much of which centers around Hamilton and the University of Minnesota.

area. Accordingly, Jim was once again in start-up mode, formulating strategies and innovations destined to sweep the country. The Chilean HMO was also a unique experience and taught valuable lessons that would last the rest of his career.

Observations

Rather than listing Jim's projects, let us examine what they have in common. Jim built programs from scratch. He took new ideas, notably in ambulatory care and managed care, and developed them locally and internationally. He was exposed to entrepreneurial models before they became the rage, including with physician investors. He was there at the early development of regional health systems, even publishing the seminal article on applying the bank holding company model to healthcare.

Incredibly, Jim survived his first 20 years in consulting without formal training in consulting skills or any exposure to direct sales. Both attributes are considered essential components of any consulting career, yet Jim managed to thrive without them. How is this possible?

Let's start with sales. Before joining the Governance Institute, Jim was involved only in marketing strategy. He was presented with consulting projects, or people came to him with things they wanted to achieve (e.g., the HMO in Chile). Only after he joined with Charlie Ewell at the Governance Institute was Jim exposed to direct sales. And Charlie was a sales wizard. When he first introduced Jim to the new venture, Charlie called it "dialing for dollars." The concept was as remarkable as it was simple. Jim and Charlie would go through the AHA Guide and find the CEOs of bigger hospitals. They would put in cold calls with the central message, "You should be part of the club of CEOs supporting the effectiveness of their boards." Charlie and Jim originally had a goal of 100 hospital subscription members; they soon exceeded 700 members, with year-to-year renewals of almost 100 percent. A key selling point in their calls was asking each CEO to give them five other names to contact.

Jim is impressed by the consultation training programs developed by the large global firms. He was pushed into projects where he had no choice but to develop these skills at an early age. He succeeded because he is a model professional with lifelong learning at his core (he finished his doctoral degree years into his career). It is a testament to his superior education that he has been able to seamlessly shift in and out of executive positions and consulting engagements.

Jim's career does not represent a typical progression into consulting. To know Jim is to know an accomplished advisor with a remarkably eclectic career. Perhaps he was destined to be an advisor from the start. Rather than an example of a path to success, his path might be more accurately portrayed as aspirational—an extraordinary example of what is possible. His many faculty appointments and awards bear witness to an exceptional career: He has held faculty positions at the Strathmore University Business School, Nairobi, Kenya; the Advance Healthcare Management Institute in Prague; the Cambridge Judge Business School; and the healthcare administration program at the University of Minnesota School of Public Health. His awards include the Distinguished Alumni Leadership Award from the University of Minnesota School of Public Health, a doctoral fellowship from the National Institutes of Health, a US Public Health Service Traineeship in hospital management, a Bush Leadership Fellowship at the National University of Singapore, and the AHA's Corning Award for excellence in hospital planning. Jim is also a Fellow of ACHE.

Advice to Others

Completing a training program through a major consulting firm is a great way to accumulate the required skills for consulting. Jim was able to experience this more directly when his son went through training at Ernst & Young early in his career.

REGINALD M. BALLANTYNE III, FACHE

Reg Ballantyne began his career as one of the youngest hospital CEOs in the United States. From the initial base of Phoenix Memorial Hospital he established PMH Health Resources Inc., a multiunit healthcare system. PMH was acquired by Vanguard Health Systems, headquartered in Nashville, Tennessee, where Reg then served for 12 years as senior corporate officer. Vanguard was subsequently acquired by Tenet Healthcare Corporation, headquartered in Dallas, where he then served as senior strategic advisor. When he left Tenet several years later, Reg launched his consulting firm, offering strategic collaborative services to businesses, healthcare enterprises, and government entities.

Reg served in leadership capacities for state and national entities and associations. He was AHA chairman in 1997 and Speaker of the AHA House of Delegates in 1998. He served on the board of commissioners for The Joint Commission and was chairman of the AHA Committee of Commissioners. He was also on the board of advisors for Clarke Consulting, the Bayer Diagnostics Economic Advisory Board, the Health Care Advisory Council of The St. Paul Companies Inc., and the board of directors of several organizations. Reg has been a senior consultant to both Centerre Healthcare Corporation and Symbion, and currently serves as strategic advisor to VisionGate. He also serves as a chairman or officer of numerous regional and national professional, community, and civic organizations.

Transition to Consulting

Reg is a unique example of an internal or corporate consultant functioning as an ambassador and expert for two prominent hospital management companies. Rather than selling consulting services and growing consulting revenues, as an independent consultant would, Reg was responsible for improving the performance of the hospitals owned and managed by these two companies. He also developed a wide network of hospital executives, identifying prospective groups that were considering selling their facilities. His career in this role was propelled by his adaptability and by four crucial skills: collaboration, negotiation, communication, and creativity.

Reg learned the importance of collaboration in his twenties. For him, collaboration is about *connections* and *networks*. He was challenged to make connections with payers, government officials, and others, and with connections came the power to effect change. He quickly learned that his passion for change could be used as a calling card, allowing him to develop a vast network of contacts. Reg likes to say that he became "skillful at breaking ice and opening doors." He effectively became an ambassador for Vanguard.

His skill with negotiation may have begun with the sale of his hospital to Vanguard. Before opening discussions with Vanguard he spoke with several other in-state health systems who clearly did not see the future the same way he did. Reg determined that the lack of shared vision among these systems made the Vanguard option more attractive and comfortable. Importantly, the PMH board came to the same conclusion—Vanguard understood PMH's mission and had a proven track record of investing in similar missions with other hospitals that were now a part of its national network.

Reg gained the respect of the Vanguard principals during his initial merger negotiations, which included securing difficult government approval for the transaction; as part of the final deal, Vanguard insisted Reg join the company as a senior corporate officer. His initial role in joining the Vanguard executive team was to shore up relations with governmental entities and payers, just as he had done for PMH. He also managed to negotiate not having to relocate as part of the deal—a feat he repeated when Vanguard was later acquired by Tenet, which was headquartered in Dallas. Unsurprisingly, Reg was among the few Vanguard executives to join the post-merger Tenet organization, where he facilitated integration of the combined Vanguard/Tenet team.

Reg faced dramatically different cultures in each of these organizations and learned how to function as a remote worker before it was common, underscoring his communication skills. His remote work is remarkable for two reasons: First, Reg was more of a traditionalist, relying on his larger-than-life personality and the in-person relationships he had worked hard to establish. Few people who have met Reg forget the encounter. He is no fan of videoconferencing and takes being on camera seriously, thanks to his time on the *PM Magazine* newscast as a healthcare correspondent. When contemplating a video call, Reg says he felt like he needed to be "either in a tux or a bathing suit" to pull it off. Second, Reg convinced his Vanguard colleagues that because his position required frequent travel it did not matter where he lived. (His frequent travel masked another aspect of this arrangement that few people knew about— Reg was not particularly comfortable flying, as he had experienced a harrowing in-flight event early in his career.)

After these merger-based transitions, Reg says his easiest change was his shift to independent consulting. His creativity is evident in the way he has adapted his skills to a variety of different environments and cultures. He moved his uptown Phoenix office into his home (pre-pandemic), hired a chief of staff who manages contracted parties, and launched his firm. The transition was relatively seamless, as many of his Vanguard and Tenet colleagues had expressed interest in continuing to work with him if he ever left the company. Reg also had a national reputation that translated easily into securing new business. His unique linkages with a variety of communities, government officials, nonprofit and investor-owned health organizations, and business coalitions across the country remain valuable in his consulting work.

Observations

Reg exudes a certain confidence and has always been open to trying new things. Early in his career he was already an accomplished and in-demand keynote speaker. In one slight detour, he became a minor celebrity thanks to his appearances on the local *PM Magazine* newscast in Phoenix. People started noticing him in airports and at public meetings and would approach him to say that he looked familiar. Reg's joking response was, "Yes, I'm on *General Hospital.*"

The remark is typical of Reg's wicked sense of humor. People enjoy his talks, and his banter keeps people on their toes. He has a way of making people feel at ease. In one fun interaction, he was leading a board meeting as chairman of the Arizona Chamber of Commerce and Industry. Near the beginning of the meeting, participants looked over at him and started to chuckle. Finally, he caught on and looked at the tent card they had placed in front of him. Instead of his name, someone had written "The Godfather." The nickname stuck.

Reg brings the same energy to everything he does, as well as a flair for politics. His vibrant personality and political prowess led him to several influential chairmanships and the boards of a number of associations and commercial enterprises. He notes with pride that his first CEO position, while still in his twenties, was at a hospital that served an underprivileged population in South Central Phoenix. Arizona was the last state to adopt a Medicaid program, and Reg was instrumental in securing legislation and gubernatorial approval for the Arizona Health Care Cost Containment System, which supplied funds to support the ongoing mission of his organization and many others. His ability to position his organization for a successful sale to a for-profit firm (somewhat rare and controversial at the time) was a testament to his skill at operating on at least a breakeven basis in areas with challenging socioeconomic conditions.

While the acquisition by Vanguard adjusted PMH's structure, Reg likes to point out that Vanguard enhanced the hospital's ability to continue serving its core mission through ambitious ambulatory health center initiatives. The leadership positions he assumed raised his exposure through speaking engagements in front of healthcare leaders across the country. These executives would often approach him with questions, and in sharing his experiences with the Vanguard leadership team he created interest among these executives in considering a similar strategy. He made connections when onboarding new hospitals into the Vanguard network, or when advising on complicated negotiations with governments at all levels (given the need for approval of such transactions). He developed a number of approaches that created win–win situations for the acquired entities, payers, employers, the state and Vanguard—not an easy proposition.

Among Reg's great attributes are loyalty and adherence to tradition. He has only had three executive assistants in his extensive career. He likes to say the first one, Doris, trained him for success. During the hiring process, she informed him that she was about to go on vacation for two weeks, making Reg wonder if perhaps he had not selected the best candidate. Doris was there for the first two weeks, took vacation for the second two weeks, and when she returned on the first day of the fifth week, said, "Well, you've had the benefit of my services for two weeks and been without me for two weeks; which do you prefer?" Clearly, she knew how to manage Reg. She stayed with him for many years and trained her successor when she retired.

Reg never forgot his commitment to the citizens of South Central Phoenix. During his tenure with Tenet, he fostered a collaborative venture involving several prominent healthcare systems to support expansion of Medicaid under the Affordable Care Act, which some members of the Arizona Hospital Association had successfully resisted. Believing that Medicaid expansion was vital to continuing Tenet's mission in Arizona, in a courageous move, he pulled Tenet out of the association to advocate this position; a move that was followed by other major systems in the state (Dignity Health, HonorHealth, and Banner Health). Together, they then formed the Health System Alliance of Arizona. In a stroke of brilliance, Reg enlisted the support of the business community to push legislation across the finish line. This unusual arrangement, which survives to this day, qualifies as *disruptive collaboration*[5] under any definition and is further testament to his collaborative skills.

---

5   A term I coined in an article that I wrote while employed by ECG Management Consultants.

Another example of his natural leadership instincts involves something very personal—his cancer diagnosis—specifically a type of seminoma with a high mortality rate. Reg relied on his network to get him to the most experienced providers, including the physician in Indiana who eventually cured his cancer. People react differently when confronted with such a challenging event. For Reg, skirting death was just another learning experience. He immediately became a national advocate for early diagnosis of seminoma, imploring men in his wide circle of friends and colleagues to monitor themselves, just as women have been advised to do self-checks for breast cancer. Anything he has done, he has done with gusto. His dynamism and ability to captivate an audience probably ended up saving many lives in this case.

Advice to Others

Reg is quick to point out the need to conduct an honest self-assessment of your skill set—stressing the *honest* part. Consulting came naturally to Reg, and adaptability allowed him to accomplish several outcomes similar to the PMH–Vanguard solution. He believes that enduring partnerships across the healthcare spectrum are required to secure true success.

Reg underscores his belief that executives need to develop strong communication skills early in their career to grow their network and create career options such as establishing a consultancy. Before making a career change, he suggests asking these questions: "Are you going to be comfortable in the new environment? Will you enjoy what you do as a consultant?"

Reg says his journey has been "joyful." He plans to stay with it for the foreseeable future even if he decides to reduce his consultancy activities to two to three days a week. He notes with enthusiasm that his work fits in between tennis matches and power walks. "I believe that I am providing a valuable resource to many. For me, it has made life more robust and enjoyable."

FRED HOBBY, CDM

Fred Hobby is a true pioneer in many ways. He may be the first full-time chief diversity officer in a healthcare setting. Often the first African American to serve in a position, he played a big role in the development and training of chief diversity officers in healthcare organizations.

Fred started out in government, serving four years as the executive director of the Affirmative Action Department for the City of Louisville, Kentucky, during which he was also on the faculty of the University of Louisville. He began his hospital administration career with Humana Inc. in Louisville, as administrative resident. While he held a graduate degree, it was not in health administration. (Fred has a bachelor's degree in history and political science from Kentucky State University and a master of arts degree in sociology from Washington University in St. Louis.)

Fred picked up operating skills over many years while serving in a variety of assignments with Humana. He held positions in Virginia hospitals in Newport News, Norfolk, and Virginia Beach, and served as CEO of one traditionally Black hospital. Ultimately, his 43-year career included executive positions across three states and six hospital systems. This included ten important years with the Greenville Hospital System (GHS) in South Carolina, where he was first encouraged to expand more into his area of expertise. His work at GHS included clinical services and establishing a diversity and inclusion program aimed primarily at an influx of Latino patients in the region. This work led to development of a training program that was picked up by the South Carolina Hospital Association.

His work at GHS gained the attention of the AHA, which at that time was recruiting for the third leader of the new Institute for Diversity in Health Management. He was hired as president and CEO of the Institute, where he stayed for ten years, becoming the organization's longest serving chief executive. Among his many accomplishments at the AHA was the development of the

Certification in Diversity Management (CDM) program for chief diversity officers.

While leading the Institute, Fred served as an internal consultant to many fledgling programs that began springing up among member hospitals. In 2015, he left the AHA to become an independent consultant with CulturaLink LLC, a full-service language assistance and health equity consulting company in Atlanta.

Fred also serves on the advisory board of InveniasPartners, served two terms on the national board of the Certification Commission for Healthcare Interpreters, and was founding president of the South Carolina chapter of the National Association of Health Services Executives (NAHSE). Fred frequently appears at national conferences as a featured speaker, and has received several awards, including "Senior Executive of the Year" from NAHSE. He was one of *Modern Healthcare* magazine's "100 Most Powerful People in Healthcare" in 2006 and 2007 and a *Chicago Defender* Man of Excellence in 2010, and he was featured in *HR Pulse* magazine in Winter 2006. In 2010, he served on the Office of Minority Health committee that updated the National Standards for Culturally and Linguistically Appropriate Services in Health and Health Care. In 2015, Fred received the ACHE President's Award for his work on equity and a Lifetime Achievement Award from the Chicago chapter of NAHSE.

Transition to Consulting

Fred is recognized as "the Godfather of diversity in healthcare" due to his pivotal role. It was a natural transition to put his skills to work with hospitals attempting to develop such programs, but it did not happen by chance.

While Fred was vice president of clinical services at GHS he approached Frank Pinckney, the system CEO, and pointed out a serious deficiency related to an influx of Latino patients who did not speak English and could not navigate the health system. Pinckney acknowledged the issue and noted that these patients were becoming prevalent primarily in departments under Fred's control (e.g., imaging, lab, intensive care, the therapies). Fred was sent to a rigorous training program at the American Institute for Managing Diversity (AIMD) founded by Dr. Roosevelt Thomas, who became widely known for his pioneering work in diversity management. At the time, Fortune 500 companies were sending people to AIMD to train for this growing need. Fred spent a week there as the only person from a healthcare organization.

As important as this training was, what set him apart from others was what came next. Fred returned to GHS and wrote a white paper on "Managing Diversity for Organizational Performance" that he took through the management chain and eventually presented to the full board of trustees for approval. He then spent the next few years offering training and assistance at all four GHS hospitals in addition to his ongoing management responsibilities as vice president of clinical services. The CEO at the South Carolina Hospital Association noticed his efforts, and things took off from there.

Observations

Fred's lived experiences allowed him to empathize with the plight of other minorities trying to access the health system. He developed an extensive Language Assistance and Interpretation Center at GHS to improve services for patients who spoke limited English or were hard of hearing. One of the first of its kind in a hospital setting, the center is one of only two programs in the country to receive a recognition letter from the US Department of Health and Human Services Office for Civil Rights acknowledging the hospital's compliance with the federal limited English proficiency guidelines.

Fred's initial efforts were focused on Latino patients and their need for translation and related services. For these patients, the hospital "was not a welcoming environment," according to Fred. The local demographics were changing, and GHS was ill-prepared to deal with those changes. Over time, the program expanded to include staffing, recognizing the acute need to add people of color to management teams.

When he first started with the AHA in 2005, the Institute's focus was mostly on leadership and governance. This quickly evolved to include cultural sensitivity training with a focus on care of the workforce. Fred recalls that the mantra at the time was "the browning of America." The Institute aimed to assist hospitals in developing programs for diversity and inclusion. Fred took the program from 280 dues-paying participating hospitals to over 1,200 during his ten years as CEO of the Institute. The ten-month online CDM certificate program, created under his guidance in collaboration with the American Leadership Council, is still active.

Fred became convinced that the C-suite of a community institution such as a hospital should reflect the community served, but no one knew how many minorities there were in hospital C-suites. This led to the development of a benchmark survey among AHA member organizations. The results of the first effort in 2009 were considered invalid because of a low participation rate, so AHA began repeating this survey every other year. In 2015, the benchmark survey finally gained national notice, indicating the low rate of minority hiring among hospital C-suites. The 2015 survey had a significant impact and prompted follow-on research; Diane Dixon built on this research as part of her 2019 book *Diversity on the Executive Path*.

Fred's success in bringing visibility to the issue got him invited to speak and work with many groups, and the AHA Institute held a national conference every other year that attracted people from member organizations. Fred is quick to point out that his work involved a lot of politics and some controversy. He worked hard to expand his network to include key people throughout the industry and was heavily involved with NAHSE.[6] Fred was approached by the National Association of Latino Health Executives and the Asian

---

6 The National Association of Health Services Executives has been around since 1930s or so under different names, and its membership comprises mostly health administrators of color. It now boasts some 800 members.

Health Care Leaders Association to form similar affinity groups for their members, and he helped them do so.

By 2010, Fred felt the Institute had made significant progress but that something was lacking. He spent some time consulting with Richard Umbdenstock at the AHA, advocating for some level of personal support from the top. At the annual Health Forum meeting in 2011 the executive leaders of ACHE, the Catholic Health Association of the United States, America's Essential Hospitals, and the Association of American Medical Colleges took the stage with Rich and issued a call to action to eliminate healthcare disparities. This statement created significant momentum and culminated in 2015 with the #123forEquity Pledge to Act, which includes four key initiatives (from https://ifdhe.aha.org/123forequity):

1. *Increasing the collection and use of race, ethnicity, language preference and other socio-demographic data*
2. *Increasing cultural competency training*
3. *Increasing diversity in leadership and governance*
4. *Improve and strengthen community partnerships*

The first two items were obvious, but the third proved controversial, as it was interpreted as somewhat threatening by some, and merely another variation of affirmative action. Around this time, Fred felt he had accomplished all he could with the Institute and decided to become a consultant.

Advice to Others

Fred describes his work using the metaphor of a man in the park feeding pigeons: He has something that is of value to the pigeons, core to their sustenance, but it is ultimately up to the pigeons whether they choose to eat the grain. Likewise, Fred has knowledge to share with his clients, but the clients remain free to use what he gives them or not.

Fred spends a lot of time keeping his network vibrant. He reflects this in his advice to others: Keep your network close. "As minorities we are just now making it into inner circles. Classmates become executives; everyone you meet coming up is a potential client. Become a trusted ally with everyone you meet."

Contemporaries

CHRISTOPHER L. MORGAN, FACHE

Chris views himself as a transformational leader, having held literally dozens of administrative positions in seven states and abroad before he became a consultant. He is the founder and CEO of Health Strategies, a consulting firm that provides population health services to providers seeking to transition to value-based services, including direct contracting with employers. Using mostly a virtual firm model, he has assembled a pool of some 35 independent contractors—consultants who have experience developing clinically integrated networks and accountable care organizations.

Before founding his consulting firm in 2017, Chris served in variety of hospital administrative positions, in both military (US Air Force) and civilian health systems. Starting out as a trained emergency medical technician, Chris followed an eclectic career path bridging operations, planning, and collaborative ventures. His operations experience covered three deployments abroad (in Chile, Trinidad and Tobago, and Southeast Asia) and two domestically (with the US Veterans Health Administration and the US Department of Defense TRICARE contractor network).

After finishing his 20 years in the military, Chris transitioned to civilian healthcare with a focus on clinically integrated networks and managed care. He had already held a wide variety of executive positions throughout the United States and the field of population health was receiving greater attention. He served in executive positions in Danville Regional Health System in Virginia and WellStar Health System in Georgia before launching his own firm.

Chris has a bachelor's degree in business administration and business management from Troy University and a master's degree in business administration with an emphasis in healthcare planning and marketing from William Carey University. He is a Fellow of the American College of Healthcare Executives (ACHE) and served as the ACHE Regent for Mississippi. He has won several awards for his commitment to improving the careers of other healthcare leaders.

Transition to Consulting

Chris's consulting transition was extraordinarily easy, but he had a 20-year military career under his belt and had set up several clinically integrated networks by the time he hung out his own shingle. Money was not his motivation; in fact, he earned a meager $35,000 in his first year in business when he was only able to work part-time. Business quickly picked up from there.

A pivotal moment in Chris's career happened at the 2011 ACHE Congress. Among the seminars he attended was one on Transitioning from the Military to Civilian Healthcare. After the session, he asked Chris Anderson, CEO of Singing River Health System in southern Mississippi, to review his resume. A few days later, Chris was invited to a one-hour interview with the CEO. During the discussion, Anderson asked if Chris could help with a population health initiative. Chris replied that he was not familiar with the term, and the CEO pointed out that according to his resume Chris had been doing this work for several years. The one-hour meeting lasted more than three hours, and Chris was hired on the spot.

Chris soon realized that the work he did for the military was in great demand in the civilian sector. He went on to set up similar systems for Danville and WellStar, and then accepted an invitation from Vanderbilt Health Affiliated Network—a new consulting subsidiary of the health system. They agreed to hire Chris while he continued to reside in Mississippi to offer population health services. This arrangement allowed him to set up other programs for a few new clients. The firm took care of the infrastructure and taught him about other elements of consulting, which involved a lot more travel than his previous position.

Then, life intervened; Chris needed to stay home to assist his wife, who was dealing with a chronic disease, and shifted to a part-time work schedule. He adapted to more remote work and realized that he could complete much of his work without traveling. He finally decided to go into business for himself and has never looked back.

Chris had seen the positive impact that a clinically integrated network and other population health programs can have on patient care. Everyone benefited—including the providers, who had a far more manageable case load. The payers and employers were pleased because they saved money. Accountable care organizations have become more popular as Medicare Advantage expands. Chris easily secured future business as the industry rushed toward value-based care. The key to his success with his unique consultancy is a clear exit strategy for his contracts: Do the work the client needs, train their staff, and move on.

Observations

Chris had a knack for consulting, in part because he had spent so much time as a customer. He had prepared many requests for proposals and learned over the years what he liked and disliked about the many responses he received. He learned to dislike consultants who, after completing one assignment, would aggressively upsell two other engagements the client did not need.

When Chris started consulting, he had already developed several clinically integrated networks and accountable care organizations, and the work had become second nature. He developed a unique baseline program: Rather than trying to upsell additional work, he structured his approach to maximize client benefit. He strictly limits his contracts, writing himself out after the first four months of work and requiring the client to hire a full-time operator who will take the program forward. The last thing Chris does on the engagement is train the new operator. It is essentially a "plug and play" model. "Why pay me consulting rates to operate the business part-time," he asks, "when you can hire someone full-time to be the operator at far less cost?"

This attitude obviously resonates with clients, especially where competitive bids are involved. His firm competes actively with Premier, Dixon Hughes Goodman, Advisory Board, and others and is often hired in part because he charges less and makes a point of being there only as long as necessary before making a clean handoff to the client. As a result, many clients ask him to develop add-on programs such as referral management systems, coordinated care, direct contracting, relevant payer contracts, and vendor selection for population health information system support.

Chris's consulting model is so compelling that a few years ago one of the executives at a client organization called to see if he could buy part of the firm; he believed these services were in high demand and things would take off. Chris was not looking to add employees, but he recognized that a one-man shop had its limitations and he could use some help. So Chris sold part of the firm and developed a 35-member stringer pool of independent contractors with his new partner. The Health Strategies network now includes physicians, nurses, contracting experts, accountants, attorneys, and more, making it relatively easy to scale their business and compete against larger firms with much bigger payrolls.

Advice to Others

Chris says his biggest surprise was his lack of experience in starting a new consulting business. If he had it to do over again, he would hire an accountant and an attorney on day one to set up the business and the books. To explain why, he tells a story about his start-up years, when he was picking up new clients. His wife, who managed the household accounts, would ask him when he got paid next. Chris would write a check for $10,000 or $15,000 and not think twice about it. After a few times through this cycle, she finally suggested that maybe he should work out a regular pay period.

Chris emphasizes the need for a routine and an office in which to conduct business. Because he works out of his house, he believes in the importance of dedicated office space that is separate from the rest of the house. (He operates his firm out of the spare bedroom suite in their home.)

By far the toughest part of his transition was to "curate the business." When Chris brought on a partner, he needed to ensure they would have a similar approach to client work. They had to standardize contracts, proposals, and so on. Chris came to appreciate the efficiency of this approach, and realizes that this difficult work played a big part in their ability to scale.

Chris's final point is that he fell into the approach that he uses to this day, which is to use independent contractors for much of the work and have a small skeleton staff of full-time employees. Using a virtual firm model (see chapter 8 in *The Healthcare Consultant's Handbook*) allowed him to avoid the pressure of carrying a big payroll and to let existing business push the growth of his consultant network instead.

NICOLE DENHAM, RN

Nicole is an excellent example of an entrepreneur who began as a clinical practitioner. Her story illustrates what can happen when clinical experts reach the pinnacle in terms of promotions and recognition within an organization and choose to reach out in the interest of expanding their influence.

Nicole's 16-year nursing career began at a hospital in metropolitan Atlanta that she helped grow into one of the largest heart centers in

Georgia. She accumulated experience in cardiac services, critical care services, and learning resources. She spent several years managing teams and overseeing cardiac processes within the healthcare system and was able to inject herself into teams at other organizations that were dealing with similar issues.

Nicole eventually decided to pursue her longtime goal of earning her master's degree, which helped her with business relationships and catapulted her into the next level of consulting. These experiences, combined with her passion for change and process improvement, led her into the world of full-time consulting.

Since cofounding COR Consultants, Nicole has worked alongside healthcare leaders throughout the country in a variety of public, private, and government healthcare organizations. She teams up with her clients through strategic planning, clinical optimization, and training solutions. Nicole has a bachelor of science degree in nursing from Georgia State University and a master's degree in health administration from Pennsylvania State University, and is a certified John Maxwell coach. She is also an active member of the Georgia Association of Healthcare Executives, a chapter of ACHE.

Transition to Consulting

Gregarious and curious, Nicole loved nursing from the start, and migrated quickly to critical care and the development of system-level programming. Over time, her expertise in these key clinical areas expanded to include the full continuum of care in the context of a clinical service line. In her last clinical position, she effectively wrote her own job description focused on connecting high-risk patients with key technologies. While in this position she was approached by a start-up company that was testing a new technology but could not afford a full-time clinical resource. The founders asked Nicole to help them position their applications in the cardiac market that she knew so well.

Coincidentally, Nicole's friend and colleague Bonnie had a similar role at the health system where she was employed, so they began to collaborate on these opportunities. People began coming to them with questions related to processes and strategies for improvement. Nicole and Bonnie formed a limited liability company and quickly realized that they had something of value, as the business began expanding into healthcare more broadly.

As these requests grew, the new business began to pull them away from their day jobs. What started off as an avocation became Nicole's vocation. She developed a strong interest in doing more with the business, but lacked any real understanding of the business side of healthcare. In fact, her work in nursing had exposed her to a rather strong cultural bias against the business side of healthcare. Nicole, however, was "intrigued," and she sought out opportunities to understand more about the business aspects of healthcare, which exposed her to fascinating people representing diverse areas of the industry. As a "lifetime learner," Nicole decided she wanted to know more.

Instead of seeing their lack of business experience as a barrier, Nicole and Bonnie quickly turned it into an exciting challenge. Their interests and their considerable skills were complementary, which also helped. Nursing is built around the acquisition of knowledge about procedures and techniques—commonly referred to as *competencies*. Nicole and Bonnie took some time to do some visioning for the firm, focusing on gaps in the competencies that would be required to be successful in the consulting business. Then, reflecting their ambition and energy, they each went to graduate school. Nicole pursued a master's degree in health administration through a remote learning program offered by the World Campus of Pennsylvania State University (which required ten years of previous experience), while Bonnie focused on adult education and leadership training through a master's degree in nursing education offered by Duke University. After completing their graduate studies, they quit their hospital jobs within a month of each other and went full-time at-risk in their firm—COR Consultants.

Going from a large healthcare organization to a small company was a challenge, particularly in terms of outlets to build their professional networks. Through the local ACHE chapter, they met other interesting people with vast knowledge and energy. They challenged each other to volunteer and get involved in related activities, in part to market their services. They have fun with this, too. Once, Nicole nominated Bonnie for "employee of the month," which Bonnie proudly posted on LinkedIn. (COR is still a two-person company.)

Nicole and Bonnie also maintain a rapport with a growing network of long-term clients. Nicole points out that virtually none of their clients hire them for just one engagement. For them, consulting is about a relationship, not an engagement. In clinical services, trust is involved from the outset and clinicians are eager to use their expertise. Nicole notes with interest that one of the impacts of the pandemic has been an increase in networking, albeit using remote technologies in many cases.

Observations

"There is only so much time in life," Nicole says. This realization motivated her to look for more out of her career. She enjoyed nursing, but as people came to her for advice she realized she was capable of broader pursuits. Ever confident, and proud of being a "relationship person," she came to feel that nursing was confining her. She loved patient care, but her curiosity carried her into other areas.

All along this journey, Nicole and Bonnie confronted boundaries and barriers. Just as management can have silos and blinders, so do nursing and academia. Through consulting, they found they were able to better connect the dots involving a broader set of issues related to improving processes and systems of care. One shared outcome from a midcareer graduate degree was an emerging focus on "leadership training." Becoming trained leaders cemented their desire to facilitate greater dialogue between the health professions. Their mission as professionals had grown.

Not many nurses move into the business world. There has long been a chronic shortage of clinical nurses, and this kind of move is openly discouraged in the profession. COR Consultants initially sold strictly through word of mouth because of this. Incredibly, their firm did no marketing and did not give it much thought until they had been in business for five years and the pandemic struck. Nicole never worried much about having clients, as she was convinced that there were a lot of opportunities with both start-up companies and hospital organizations. When they set out full-time, they committed certain goals to writing, including income expectations; these were met in their first year. When they finally worked with a marketing firm—something Nicole particularly enjoyed—describing their intentions and being more disciplined about the development of their elevator pitch was an eye-opener. They established specific plans to get out and expand their network to include prospective clients.

Pre-pandemic, as much as 75 percent of COR Consultants' work was focused on healthcare information technology—more specifically, addressing work processes and information flow tailored to an organization's cultural nuances. Clinical care, despite representations to the contrary, is not a one-size-fits-all world. The pandemic had a big impact on their practice. Existing clients cut way back on consulting, and Nicole and Bonnie were left to find a whole new group of clients. Their previous marketing work had helped them better define the scope of their services and confirmed they were making a niche play, so they actively worked to narrow their focus. They reverted to their clinical training and recommitted to service delivery—specifically, emergency preparedness. It was a tough year, but they managed to adapt to this major disruption.

Advice to Others

Nicole suggests that understanding your competencies is critical to making this career change. Where gaps exist, you need to seek help; have a mentor. Nicole still works with a mentor and has taken the time to mentor others. She has become a disciple of leadership, and true believer in the potential to improve healthcare. While healthcare has been characterized as having numerous silos and isolated interests, developing future leaders becomes an integrating force. Nicole and Bonnie now consider themselves healthcare leaders as well as clinical nurses. They recognize that more leaders are needed to accelerate quality improvement as part of the healthcare transformation.

Nicole says starting a business is exciting but hard, and maintaining one is even more difficult. In addition to the business concepts learned in graduate school, many of which she uses daily, there is still so much more that you need to know.

Nicole worries that people tend to stay in a place just because they get comfortable. There is a risk of becoming complacent; beware of the "comfort zone," she warns. If she has any regret, it is simply that it took her so long to make the commitment to consulting. She has become so comfortable with this new role that she is surprised that she did not do it sooner. She also mentioned the great comfort of having a business partner that is so committed to the company, the industry, and serving the patient population.

Her strong drive for lifelong learning propelled her to make this career change, and that drive has not subsided. As a healthcare leader, she still believes she can learn something from everybody. Nicole recognizes that although switching careers to consulting was never easy, it was clearly the right choice for her and for Bonnie. She feels fortunate to have had a business partner with whom to share this journey.

KIM ATHMANN KING, FACHE

Kim is founder and president of Strategy Advantage. She not only made the transition from executive to consultant, she also changed firms and boomeranged back to her own firm some years later.

Before launching Strategy Advantage in 2002, Kim held executive positions in marketing and business development at both Saint Agnes

Medical Center in Fresno, California, and Cedars-Sinai Health System in Los Angeles. She began consulting as a subcontractor and then joined one of the well-known specialty healthcare consulting firms, Kaufman Hall, where she served as Senior Vice President, Strategy Services for three years. She then decided to relaunch Strategy Advantage, Inc. under a new virtual firm model with a range of expert advisors as part of a contracted network.

In 2014, she created a new service to help healthcare leaders and organizations practice "zigzag thinking" and stay on top of the many disruptive innovations in healthcare. In 2015, Kim launched "Outside the Lines," a biweekly point-of-view email newsletter that offers a perspective on the lesser known, nontraditional trends and events occurring in and around the industry.

Kim attended St. Cloud State University as an undergraduate and received her master of business administration from California State University, Fresno. She resides in Los Angeles, and maintains a second residence in her home state of Minnesota. Kim has been involved locally and nationally in numerous professional societies, including ACHE, the Society for Healthcare Strategy & Market Development, and the Healthcare Financial Management Association. She is a Fellow of ACHE and a member of her local chapters, as well as a member of the Healthcare Consultants Forum committee.

Transition to Consulting

Kim's transition to consulting is a story of skills developed on the job as a healthcare executive and put into practice as she became an independent consultant. This journey took her down several paths, culminating in her relaunch of the firm she now leads.

Kim was clear about her new vision to become a strategy consultant. Once she completed her graduate degree, she left Fresno in search of a larger platform. Her transition to Cedars-Sinai was motivated by recognition that her brand was limited and a desire to grow professionally. To be more credible as a senior executive, Kim perceived that she had some barriers to overcome. One of these was being typecast as a "marketing person." She was encouraged to "get into operations," but this did not appeal to her.

Cedars-Sinai offered a bigger stage and an opportunity to generate a platform, thanks to its significant name recognition and long-standing brand tied to the celebrity patients in the Los Angeles market. She was hired to develop marketing and communications for clinical service lines, but transitioned into a business development role, working to set up this new function and develop business plans for dozens of new Cedars-Sinai specialty centers.

When Cedars-Sinai started a strategy office, they hired a director from outside the organization and began pulling together a vibrant division. People flocked to the new director's meetings, and Kim saw how engaging these conversations were. Reports from outside experts were often reviewed as part of executive briefings, and Kim decided she would enjoy this kind of work. The experience reinforced her realization that strategy was her true love, and she recognized that healthcare needed more structured strategy.

Although she had a good experience working at Cedars-Sinai, Kim decided she was ready to branch out. Cedars-Sinai made some effort to accommodate her interests, but she ultimately decided to strike out on her own as an independent consultant. She was interested in working across a broader spectrum of health systems, ideas, and challenges.

Kim opted to launch her firm, Strategy Advantage, via a strategic affiliation with the Strategy Group in Norfolk, Virginia. She became The Strategy Group Los Angeles, fulfilling the firm's need for a presence on the West Coast. This kept her busy but never quite reached the required level of sustainability. After several years, she paused her company and joined Kaufman Hall. Experiencing life in a larger branded specialty firm was a major transition for her and opened her eyes to the rigors of running a consulting business that depended on sales for growth. After a few years, she began to miss being on her own and returned to independent practice by relaunching her firm.

Observations

Kim did not set out to be a healthcare consultant or to start a consulting firm; she started out in public relations. Looking back, though, it seemed like a logical path even early in her career. As a junior executive in the 1990s, she was blessed with full immersion by becoming a member of a state-of-the-art strategy division within Saint Agnes Medical Center. A dynamic team of six people had been given carte blanche to explore trends and develop scenarios that forged new strategies for the organization. The strategy division was an integral part of the culture, occupying a prominent position in the C-suite—which was still unusual at the time. It helped that the Holy Cross Health System, the parent health system for Saint Agnes, required their hospitals to use a scenario development process as part of their mandated strategic planning. Market surveys, focus groups, facilitated white board sessions, executive briefings, and a war room were also embraced by this group. This investment made Saint Agnes a market maker: first to embrace a consumer-friendly "greeter model" (think Walmart), first to foster new programs (e.g., men's health), and first to apply sophisticated tools to its strategy and marketing communications departments. The Saint Agnes system became an incubator for Kim to expand her skills.

With the help of "great mentors," her executive responsibilities progressed from the original marketing and communications position to business development and, ultimately, strategy. The integration of these three functions became critical to her outlook as a professional and motivated her to continue her education. Kim, a single parent at the time, completed her masters degree part-time over five years. She quickly became enamored with the process of tracking and interpreting critical market trends and focused on strategic intelligence—using industry research and analytics to derive critical factors required to implement key strategies. Eventually she decided that she needed more room to grow her career and more credibility than she could find in Fresno.

After starting her career at a regional medical center that was part of a nationally distributed health system, Kim experienced something quite different in Los Angeles. It is a huge market with lots of competition. Cedars-Sinai was just beginning to embrace the concept of being a system and extending its resources beyond the traditional hospital scope. She witnessed the process of setting up corporate functions and shared services and became involved in business development efforts to develop and expand the health system's service lines, medical delivery network, and niche programs. While this was an exciting learning experience, she also was exposed to the raw elements of the politics of healthcare as things changed quickly. She kept her head down and essentially became an internal consultant, focusing on the development of some 40 new specialty center business plans. It was difficult to get the organization to see her in a broader role, though. She wanted more. Her business development skills were well honed, and she began to feel constrained in this role.

In 2002, Kim took the plunge and launched Strategy Advantage, only to discover the challenge of winning clients. She quickly realized that she could start out more comfortably without taking on full risk by allying herself with another established consulting team. The Strategy Group provided that opportunity, and connected Kim to Karen Corrigan, founder of the Strategy Group and former vice president of strategy for Sentara Healthcare. In Karen and her team—based in Norfolk, Virginia—Kim found a true mentor and great partners, who had conquered the market and forged significant business with key clients, notably through a formal relationship with Voluntary Hospitals of America.

Kim became the West Coast division of the Strategy Group. Not yet having the name recognition or network needed to foster sufficient clients to maintain her business, Kim made a name for herself in the consulting world through this affiliate relationship while limiting her risk. She worked hard to develop West Coast business, running the local team and even hiring an employee or two. But she remained mostly dependent on the Strategy Group network to generate her leads and keep her busy. While this approach worked for a while and was a great transition path, the West Coast versus East Coast distances proved, over time, to be difficult to maintain. She enjoyed the work and the network, but again she felt the call to do more. She wanted to focus more in the strategy realm, she felt ready to build more of her own business core and culture, and she wanted to build toward "the next price point." Accordingly, she began to consider other alternatives.

Kim joined Kaufman Hall as Senior Vice President, Strategy Services. Her Los Angeles office was designated Kaufman Hall's West Coast office. This experience exposed Kim to the rigors of a larger firm and the inner workings of a broadly recognized healthcare consulting company. The firm was adding a strategic service practice, building from its solid financial services reputation. She learned a great deal from the partners and team members there, including the advanced business development tools for selling to generate new business. This move also provided the financial security she sought at the time. The work was interesting and there was a learning curve that held her attention, at least at first. Over time, however, she found that she still wanted more. Like any firm, Kaufman Hall had its own way of doing things, and Kim was somewhat of a free spirit.

Finally, she resurrected Strategy Advantage and relaunched her firm. She characterizes this as a "freeing experience." She found it satisfying to build a strategy practice and provide services in her own way—and still does. She thrived in this environment and began to find her voice, including as a writer. She was able to pursue new clients and strategy engagements that sparked her interest, and she had opportunities to introduce new directions and innovative ideas with her clients. Her entrepreneurial DNA is evident in the way she has built her company; there are now 16 people on the Strategy Advantage team. Her entrepreneurial spirit also shows in her writing, which includes a biweekly newsletter that she has maintained since 2015. "Outside the Lines" helps her reconnect with tracking strategic intelligence trends and preparing executives for future changes. She enjoys helping clients grow and compete successfully, ultimately benefiting patients and communities. She enjoys being a thought partner with clients to help them develop new approaches, ideas, and programs. And she has never looked back, until forced to do so by this interview.

On reflection, several things stand out for Kim as she reviews her career change to consulting. She finds it satisfying "to be a partner with healthcare leaders, especially those with big and bold visions for their health systems." This, she believes, provides an opportunity "to make a difference," with no boundaries when considering possibilities. Personally, she says, "my life, family, husband, and daughter are very important to me." Kim has found a way to coordinate her family's life events (e.g., her daughter entering high school and college) with decisions about her evolving consulting career. That her California-raised husband was willing to have a second home in Minnesota is a testament to her persuasive personality. She feels blessed by the freedoms and fulfillment that have come with her career change to consulting, but she adds that no one should think it was an easy transition. She learned a lot along the way.

Advice to Others

Kim stresses the unique skills required in consulting. You are no longer the decider. Consulting requires a "push the envelope perspective"; the ability to motivate is important. Perhaps most important is the understanding that past experiences cannot necessarily be replicated today. Consulting places a premium on growing, learning, and evolving. As consultants, "we have a responsibility to constantly be discovering and developing new thinking." Especially as a strategist, fully embracing change and always working to stay on trend—in fact, in front of the trends—has been key to her success.

A colleague once told Kim, "There is nothing beige about you." To Kim, this meant that she owns her opinions and retains independence while working collaboratively to add value to her clients. At that same time, she says that as a consultant you must always focus on your network and recognize the value of deeply trusted relationships and the nurturing they require, year in and year out.

Selective Consultant Story

J. LARRY TYLER

Larry is a self-made entrepreneur with a strong work ethic. He never set out to become a consultant, but his strong penchant for sales propelled him into a highly successful career as founder of Tyler & Company.

Larry started out as an accountant doing audits, which he despised. The day he qualified as a certified public accountant, he quit PricewaterhouseCoopers and went to work as chief financial officer for one of their clients. After a series of positions, he was introduced to search, where he quickly excelled. He started Tyler & Company in Atlanta in 1983 and grew his firm to over $5 million in annual revenues and five offices (three main offices and two satellites). He became so well known that his consulting peers elected him chairman of the American Association of Healthcare Consultants—the first search consultant to hold this post. He eventually sold Tyler & Company to Jackson Healthcare in 2013 and is now more focused on governance.

Larry set ambitious goals for himself from the beginning. He worked his way through Georgia Institute of Technology and always was focused on the need for qualifications. He felt from the start that he would need a master's degree and to be a certified public accountant to succeed in consulting. These credentials provided instant credibility with prospects. He is also a Fellow of the American College of Healthcare Executives and the Healthcare Financial Management Association and has a Certified Medical Practice Executive credential from the Medical Group Management Association.

Observations

Larry did both physician and executive search during different phases of his business, although his real love was executive search. He is constantly looking to fill other needs in the industry—further proof that he is really an entrepreneur at heart. This drive propelled him to write his first book on the search process—*Tyler's Guide: The Healthcare Executive's Job Search*, now in its fourth edition (Chicago: Health Administration Press, 2011)—which addresses what he felt were the unrealistic expectations many executives had about the search process.

As Larry interacted with volunteer board members at hospitals and health systems where he conducted searches, he became increasingly convinced that many of these boards needed to better understand governance and develop related skills. He approached his friend Errol Biggs, then leader of the health administration program at the University of Colorado Denver, and they coauthored *Practical Governance* (Chicago: Health Administration Press, 2000). Within five years of publishing the book, he had ramped up the firm to provide a more comprehensive response to inquiries and requests related to hospital governance.

Larry's entrepreneurial spirit also shows in the "Transitioning from the Military to Civilian Healthcare" seminar, which is the longest running seminar at the annual American College of Healthcare Executives Congress. Larry saw a need almost 30 years ago and developed this seminar to help people who are leaving the military prepare to enter the civilian healthcare industry. Many people who have made this transition successfully would credit Larry with helping them.

Larry understands the transition to consulting well, even though he never really made the transition himself. He is a born salesperson with boundless energy, a strong work ethic, and an effusive personality. His mantra is "go an inch deep about everything but a mile deep in a few things." One of his important attributes is the ability to observe others, ask questions, and learn what made them and their business successful by picking up details in their stories. When asked about his success in sales and as a consultant, he credits emulating what he saw in several key people during his early years—paying attention to the small things. He notes that his sales ability could have grown his search firm to be much larger than it was, but that he enjoyed the work too. "Some firms do sales well but fail to execute. My mother constantly referred to a common biblical phrase, 'Having a good reputation is better than riches.'"

In his wide-reaching CEO network, Larry has been close to a few people who have made the transition from executive to consultant, though he believes the shift is difficult for most executives, primarily because of sales. "CEOs seem to think that because they know a lot of people, this will translate into sales. But it does not." He feels strongly that to succeed in consulting, you must be an extrovert. "Introverts are only comfortable around people they know," he says.

Advice to Others

Options are important, Larry says. If your current effort does not work, what will you do? Always have an alternative ready. At the same time, he believes one thing that helped him was having no fear of failure and a strong will to work hard.

Larry also advises aspiring consultants not to sell something they can't produce. He believes this is why cross-selling does not work in most firms. People tend to think that because they can convince friends of something, they can sell anything. "This is just wrong," Larry says. The real question is, "Can you sell something to a stranger? You can't count on friends to buy from you." He believes consultants should understand that most firms structure incentives around the performance of a consulting unit and not individual consultants.

Larry has two great concerns for consultants. The first is "getting stale." Do not let this happen, he warns. You must remain relevant. The other relates to travel. "They underestimate travel," he says. "They think it is like traveling on vacation." The demands of consulting travel affect those around you, too; talk to your family about travel requirements. If your family circumstances rely on having you nearby, Larry believes you are setting yourself up for failure. Also, traveling out of a hub is different than traveling to secondary markets. Travel takes a lot of energy, and sometimes you might fly for a few hours and then drive for a few more to get to a rural client. You are often out of town a lot, and "some towns don't have nice hotels."

Case Study of a Failed Engagement

A client brought in a consulting team, led by a charismatic CEO turned consultant, to help them sort through a problem. The consulting team conducted interviews to determine the nature of the problem and to better understand the organizational culture and the skills possessed by key members of the leadership team. The consulting group carefully and precisely defined the problem, and everyone on the client team signed off.

Next, the consulting team led a brainstorming session to identify alternatives for solving the problem. True to the brainstorming approach, the alternatives were submitted without judgment during the session. Once this exercise had identified possible options, the alternatives were compared in subsequent white board sessions, including a comparison to the status quo option (i.e., do nothing). Following some clarification of the different approaches, the lead consultant presented one approach as preferred, and the client quickly confirmed the approach for implementation. With the engagement complete, the consultants moved on to the next client. As is the case with most consulting engagements, the recommended solution was left to the client to implement.

It failed.

The failure became clear when the lead consultant visited the client about six months later. During this visit, the client shared their frustration with the results and expressed a lack of confidence in the decision that was made and the process that was used. The client also raised some personnel issues that may have affected the organization's ability to successfully implement the recommended solution.

What happened?

We will call the CEO turned consultant Rocky, and the CEO client Jane. Here's how their conversation went:

Rocky: *So how did things go after we left?*

Jane: *Rocky, the truth is, not so well.*

Rocky: *Wow, I'm surprised. What happened?*

Jane: *Well, to oversimplify, I'm not sure every member of the team was really committed to the approach. People kept asking questions about the why of our decision. Somehow, these questions didn't come out while we were brainstorming. A few people seemed to feel that other options weren't fully developed.*

I had designated Joe as the lead on this initiative and he was as frustrated as anyone. He said key people either didn't understand the approach or didn't agree with it, or both. I thought about changing the lead but determined that we needed to pause and let some time pass before revisiting the situation.

An important tenet of consulting is that failure to execute makes any consulting engagement a failure, even if the solution was otherwise correct. Clearly, this engagement was a failure, and it was likely to affect the client's willingness to hire the consultant again. Two possible interpretations of this situation are offered, to illustrate what can happen with a CEO turned consultant who finds it difficult to separate themselves from their past experiences.

ROCKY'S INTERPRETATION

Rocky met with the consulting team to share Jane's feedback. He went into detail on what had happened, including a review of the key metrics that the client was attempting to achieve. While a few had been met, most had not, and the management team quickly became frustrated. The client CEO was clearly frustrated. That was when things became revealing. Rocky continued the conversation with his team:

I felt from day one like this team was really underperforming. One or two key members of the team tended to be rather negative in their comments and raised concerns about virtually every story that I told. If I had been the CEO at this organization, I might have taken these people aside and discussed how their negativity was affecting the discussion. In fact, [Person X] should probably have been counseled out of the organization, as they never got engaged in the process at all.

Clearly, Joe was a poor choice to lead this initiative. I have no idea why Jane chose him, although there were rumors. My team at my previous organization would not have tolerated the dissension within the team and would have made sure that key targets had been met each step of the way. This client was clearly not ready to embrace what was required to make this work.

I don't know what we could have done differently. The recommendation was exactly how we had fixed the problem before at my place. I was totally honest with the team about the resistance I had experienced and how we overcame these obstacles before. I am not sure why the client was unable to achieve similar results, but I put the responsibility with the CEO, who seemed reticent and should be held accountable by the board. I note that Jane has been CEO for less than two years and clearly lacks experience.

Ouch!

THE CLIENT'S INTERPRETATION (THE REAL STORY)

The problem wasn't the client. Jane, invoking a more collaborative style of leadership, had solid reasons for not wanting to be more directive, and had empowered the team to fully participate in this process, as virtually every member of the team would share some responsibility for implementation. She had determined at the outset that "buy-in" was the most crucial thing.

A postmortem by the executive team came to a vastly different conclusion than Rocky did: *Rocky was the problem.* They all liked Rocky and admired the experience that he brought to the conversation, but they quickly became concerned that Rocky was dominating the conversation and that his experience was the only experience that was being discussed; he became an advocate for his approach and lost credibility as an objective source. The forcefulness of his arguments (hubris) turned off some team members, who felt like they were competing with Rocky for airtime, so the conversation shut down. The executive team members came to resent how sure Rocky was of himself and quickly determined that this was someone who did not want his views challenged.

Several members of the team had a sidebar conversation once or twice during the four-month process, attempting to determine what had been different about Rocky's organization versus their own. One member of this group had a conversation with someone they knew who had been part of Rocky's team where he had last been CEO. That executive's characterization of the process and results were different than the picture Rocky painted. Another team member had a friend at a similar-sized organization where they had experienced the same problem. They took a different approach and felt that it had worked well for them. While this other approach had been identified as one of the alternatives, it had not been fully considered by the group, because Rocky had no experience with that approach.

It turned out that one of the critical differences between the two organizations was that Rocky's organization was in a market with a radically different patient profile. At Rocky's previous organization, fewer than 40 percent of the patients were government beneficiaries (covered by Medicare or Medicaid), while for the client this segment was closer to 80 percent of their patients. It was pointed out later that location was a far more prevalent variable for the client than for Rocky's organization. In other words, it was important for the client that key delivery sites would be accessible via public transportation routes. As the team continued the postmortem discussion, additional points of comparison arose, and it became clearer that the solution Rocky had implemented at his prior organization was never likely to work for this client. The process had simply failed to identify these key contextual differences or to make the necessary accommodations in the recommended actions.

Index

Note: Italicized page locators refer to exhibits.

Specialists: scope and, 137, *137*
Specialized consulting, 152, 155–56
Spencer Stuart, 72, 158
Sponsors: finding, 220–21, 231
Sponsorship, 277, 280
Staff development: coaching and, 158
Staffing function: matched to consulting
    categories, *138*; within POSDCORB
    conceptual framework, 135, *136*
Standardization in performance: drive
    for, 59
Stanley, Natasha, 35
Stapleton, Chris, 265
Starbucks, 273–74
Start-up firms, 76, 79–80
Status quo: comfort with, 37, 38;
    disrupting, 38; having clear
    understanding of, 29, 30
Steele, Marshall, 153n2
Stories: connection to purpose and, 92;
    returning to operations and, 258–59
St. Paul Companies Inc., The: Health
    Care Advisory Council of, 295
Strategic Building Blocks approach: to
    career change, 3, 4, 5, *5*; how? in,
    3, 4, *5*, 125; key questions in, 4, *5*;
    sequential process in, 3, 5, 6; what?
    in, 3, 4, *5*, 69–70; when? in, 3, *5*, 193;
    who? in, 3, *5*, 249–50; why? in, 3, 4,
    5, 11–12
Strategic consulting, 153
Strategy Advantage, Inc., 101, 102, 316,
    317, 318, 320, 321
Strategy Group, Los Angeles, 318, 320
Strategy Group, Norfolk, Virginia, 318,
    320
Strathmore University Business School,
    Nairobi, Kenya, 294
Stress: healthcare executives and, 49
Studer, Quint, 16, 44, 182
Sturt, D., 45
Subcontractors, 121, 235
Success: defining, 31, 262–63
Succession planning, 77, 158
Suicide rate: among dentists, 26n2
Supervisory interference: as key dissatis-
    fier for healthcare executives, *42*

Supply chain management: consulting in,
    112, 155
Support group/support system: relying on
    your network and, 253; strong, doing
    your homework and, 257. *See also*
    Networks and networking
Surprises, 30
Swedish Medical Center (Seattle), 63
Symbion, 295
Systemness, 178
Systems theory, 169

Talent people, 86; insights from, on
    executives turned consultant, *106–7*;
    summary of observations about,
    105–6
Tangible output: consulting and, 116
Taylor, Frederick, 135
Teachable moments: executive coaches
    and, 44
Teaching, 277, 280
Team building, 137; evaluating teams
    and, 221–22; successful CEOs and,
    168–69
Team of Teams (McChrystal, et al.), 222
Teams: cross-functional, 160; evaluating,
    221–22; highly educated, autonomous,
    185–86; high-performing, 183–84, 206;
    interdisciplinary and intercultural,
    114–15; multifunctional, 156; success-
    ful, five attributes of, 183–84
Technical expertise: demand for, 156
Technical schools, 26
Technology: women consultants and, 110
Technology disruptions, 25
Temporary staffing firms, 76, 77
Tenet Healthcare Corporation, 95, 295,
    296, 299
Terminations, 15, 19–20
Testimonials, 203
Thinking organizations: mechanistic
    organizations *vs.*, 143
Third space: demand for, 273–74
Thomas, Roosevelt, 303
Thought leadership, 219
Time: compressing, 188–89; managing,
    197; scheduling time off, 225–26

About the Author

Scott A. Mason, DPA, FACHE, is a speaker, entrepreneur, author, and trusted advisor to hospitals and health systems. His career has spanned diverse strategy assignments with more than 400 organizations in 40 states. In addition to joining Booz Allen Hamilton and founding his own firm early in his career, he has held senior executive positions with a number of well-known consulting and commercial real estate firms. Mason has also served in a variety of interim management positions when asked to by several existing clients, including as a hospital executive and president of a regional health system. After selling his consulting firm to a health technology company in 1997 (after 17 years), he helped start two other technology firms related to electronic health records.

Mason is a recognized thought leader in healthcare strategy. A trusted advisor to executive teams and boards, he has written extensively and established himself as one of the industry's prominent voices in dealing with key trends and their implications. His consulting practice was always focused on the strategic success of his clients.

The focus of Mason's strategy engagements has evolved over the years from aggregating regional hospital systems (more than $20 billion in hospital mergers and almost 40 regional health systems formed) to conducting post-merger integration following these initial mergers. He was an early advocate for clinical service lines as an essential component of a growth strategy. Recently, his focus has shifted more toward improved management through "systemness" related to what he calls *disruptive collaboration*, including shared clinical service lines. He emphasizes improving the customer experience by adopting retail strategies and embedding them into modern ambulatory care facilities that extend into strategic community-based locations.

As a Fellow and faculty member of the American College of Healthcare Executives (ACHE), he has taught an evolving two-day seminar to senior healthcare executives titled "Growth in the Reform Era" for almost a decade. He is proud of previously being elected chairman of the American Association of Healthcare Consultants and, more recently, being appointed chairman of the ACHE Healthcare Consultants Forum Committee.

A popular speaker at regional meetings and board retreats, Mason has published extensively. In 2016, he received the coveted Dean Conley Award for best article of the year for his article "Retail and Real Estate: The Changing Landscape of Care Delivery," published in *Frontiers of Health Services Management*. In 2021, he published the acclaimed *Healthcare Consultant's Handbook: Career Opportunities and Best Practices*.

Mason is a graduate of Duke University, where he majored in neuroscience and was a walk-on basketball player. He completed a master's degree at Pennsylvania State University (and residency at Milton S. Hershey Medical Center) and a doctoral degree in healthcare management at George Washington University. Mason is also a volunteer in the acclaimed Executive Partners Program in the Mason Business School at the College of William and Mary.